ISBN **1449565700**
EAN13 **9781449565701**

Printed in the United States of America

Author's Note

Some of the names of characters in C Trick have been changed, and several characters are composites of two or more people. Because this book is intended to convey a mood and a sense of the times, artistic license was taken in the telling.

This book is dedicated to all former members of the U.S. Army Security Agency who served in Berlin and the people of Berlin.

To Annette, my lover, best friend and mentor

"In God we trust -- all others we monitor."
— **Unofficial U.S. Army Security Agency motto**

C TRICK

By

Donald M. Cooper

Prologue

When I arrived in Berlin, the hottest spot of the Cold War, it was a cold, gray winter day (which I soon learned was a typical winter day in Berlin); I was 19 years old, ready to take on the big city and I was absent without leave (AWOL) from Fort Dix, a sprawling Army base near Trenton, New Jersey, where I ended up by mistake.

About three weeks earlier, I had completed training at the National Security Agency and hitched a ride back to Arkansas for the Christmas holiday. I was told to stay there and my overseas orders would be mailed to me.

A few days after getting back to my folks' in Texarkana, I received the orders, which also instructed me to take a copy and go to Red River Army Depot and get the shots that I needed before going to Germany.

According to the orders I was assigned to the 78th Army Security Agency's special operations unit in Berlin. I was to report to Fort Dix, N.J., and ship out from nearby McGuire Air Force Base.

My father worked for the trucking subsidiary of Missouri-Pacific Railroad, so he gave me his rail pass and I rode for free from Texarkana to St. Louis.

I wore my uniform because when I got to St. Louis and switched trains, I could ride half-fare. It was going to be longest train ride that I had ever taken, going from St. Louis across Illinois, Indiana, Ohio, Pennsylvania and northern New Jersey on my way to Trenton.

Until leaving that January day, the longest train ride I had taken was from Salinas to Los Angeles when I had finished my German course at the Defense Language Institute in Monterey, Calif.

The trip across the Midwest was fun; I got to see many places I had only read about – and I got free meals, drinks and smokes from other passengers, all of whom said they just wanted to do something for "one of our boys wearing the uniform."

Everything was going smooth when I got off the train in Trenton and caught a shuttle bus that took me to Fort Dix.

I checked in, was assigned a bunk in the transit barracks, issued blankets, bed linen and towels, and drew a meal card for the mess hall.

I had my first hint that all was not going to be well in my world when I was sitting in the barracks, which looked as if they were pre-World War I, relaxing from the long train ride.

A staff sergeant came in the barracks and bellowed:

"Fall out!"

Everyone in the barracks went outside and got in formation. A corporal, holding a clipboard, started calling off names on a list.

"What's going on?" I asked a sleepy-eyed PFC next to me.

"They're getting their orders," he said. "I just got him. They told me it's going to be a few days before I know where I'm going."

I already have my orders, I thought. There must be a mistake.

When the last name was called, I sidled up to the corporal and said, "There must be a mistake. I already have my orders."

"You don't have orders now," he said. "They were canceled when you checked in here."

It was cold, but I know that I broke out in a sweat.

"Canceled?"

I shuddered. No Berlin, maybe not even Germany. All of a sudden, images of dense jungles in Southeast Asia flashed through my mind. A miserably hot, wretched, mosquito-filled place where people would be shooting at me.

Vietnam. The very place that I had enlisted to avoid.

I rushed back to the barracks, wadded up the blankets and linen, grabbed my orders and went to the supply room. No one was there, so I dumped the bedding on the front steps and ran to the taxi stand near the PX.

"Maguire," I said as I jumped into the taxi.

A few minutes later, I was checking into Maguire Air Force Base. A few hours later, I was on a chartered Pan Am jetliner winging across the Atlantic Ocean on my way to Germany — and AWOL from Fort Dix.

Arrival

1 A sudden jolt almost threw me out of the top berth of the sleeping car, jarring me from the sound sleep I had been in since the U.S. military train pulled out of the train station in Frankfurt am Main.

It was January 16, 1966, and I had arrived in Berlin, the former capital of Germany, or as some of the television commentators liked to say, the island of freedom in the communist sea. A city of nearly four million inhabitants, divided into east and west by a concrete block wall that cut through its heart.

I stretched and swung down from the top berth, nearly dropping onto the Pope.

"Goddammit, watch what you're doing, jerkoff!" the Pope said.

"Jesus, Pope," I said. "You hung over or something? I didn't mean to bump you."

"Sorry," he said. "But my goddam head's pounding. Why's the train stopping?"

"We're in Berlin."

Sliding open the compartment door, I peered out of the window and saw that the train had stopped beside a platform leading up a ramp into a red brick station. Three soldiers, wearing the Army's olive-green fatigues and field jackets, scarves and pile caps with the fur-lined ear flaps laced together atop the caps, carried duffel bags and boxes toward a big truck with the Quartermaster Corps insignia painted on its doors.

"Move it, soldier," a man behind me said.

Turning, I saw an artillery captain carrying a duffel bag and holding a big manila envelope probably filled with his military records — an entire life told on a few pieces of papers.

"Sorry, sir," I said as I stepped back from the window.

He didn't say anything as he shoved past me and headed for the exit at the front of the car.

"We in Berlin?" the Pope asked.

"Sure looks like it. Everyone's getting off, so I guess we're not in Leipzig."

I reached up on the top berth and grabbed my uniform coat and cap. I pulled on the coat and jammed on the hat. Then I tightened my tie, which I had loosened as soon I had gotten on the train the night before, and got my duffel bag and a small carrying case into which I had put my folder of military records for the unit personnel office, a couple of paperback books, a change of civilian clothes, and a carton of cigarettes that I had bought in the PX before leaving Frankfurt.

"Let's go, Pope," I said to my companion, a stoop-shouldered young man who gave the impression that he was carrying the weight of the world.

The Pope was a Russian linguist and had been in my class at the National Security Agency's headquarters on Fort Meade, an Army base about midway between Baltimore and Washington, D.C. He grew up in Boston, the second son of a proudly Irish and devoutly Catholic family that expected him to become a priest. He attended Jesuit schools and had been in the seminary for a few months when he had what the clergy called a "crisis of faith." In fact, there had been no crisis of faith, there just was no faith.

"Hell, I didn't become an atheist or anything like that," the Pope said one night while we were drinking beer in one of the bars conveniently located directly across the road from the front gate of Fort Meade. "I just woke up one morning and realized I just didn't give a shit about religion. I'm not anti-religion, it just doesn't have a place in my life anymore. So I quit the seminary. Hell, the Church doesn't need a priest who doesn't give a shit."

"I don't know about that, Pope," I said. "I grew up Baptist, and I think it'd be a hell of lot better if more Baptist preachers didn't give a shit."

"Well, maybe so. But I didn't want to be one of those priests that don't give a shit, so I joined the Army. At least this is one outfit where not giving a shit's a good thing."

After basic training, he was shipped to the Defense Department's language school at Monterey, California, where he studied Russian and picked up a new name. When his classmates learned he had been a seminarian, he became "The Pope."

We were the last two to get off the train, much to the annoyance of the 78th ASA's bus driver, a Cajun from the swamps of southern Louisiana who called himself Mr. Greyhound and complained because his bus didn't have a dog on the side.

"Come on, newks, I'm Mr. Greyhound, and I'll be taking you to your new home," he said as the Pope and I straggled across the cobblestone parking lot in front of the train station. Newk, I found out later, is short for newcomer.

It had snowed overnight and there were huge mounds of it scattered around the area from the snowplows that the Berlin work crews had fired up as soon as the first flakes hit the ground. It also was a typical winter's day in Berlin — cold and gray, without a hint the sun ever existed.

"The sun ever come out here?" the Pope asked Mr. Greyhound as we climbed on board.

"July the second. We all have a goddam picnic," he said sharply as he slammed the door closed and, with a clashing of gears, hit the accelerator. The bus lurched into the traffic and headed down the broad avenue toward Andrews Barracks, home of the 78th Army Security Agency's Special Operations Unit. For the next three years, it would be my home.

The bus rolled through the iron gates and crossed a broad cobblestone parking lot, and pulled to a stop behind a massive, three-story red brick building a few hundred yards from the main gate.

Andrews Barracks opened in 1873 as the cadet school for Kaiser Wilhelm I's Imperial German Army. In 1933, the compound became the S.S. Kaserne Lichterfelde, the home of Adolf Hitler's personal bodyguards, the S.S. (Schutzstaffel) Leibstandarte Adolf Hitler. After the occupation of

Berlin, the U.S. Army took control of the compound and named it Andrews Barracks, honoring Frank Maxwell Andrews, an Army Air Corps lieutenant general during World War II.

"Here you are, weeds," Mr. Greyhound said.

The Pope and I wrestled our duffel bags down the bus' narrow aisle, but I stopped just before stepping off the bus.

"What's a weed?" I said.

"When did you get here?" Mr. Greyhound said.

"Today."

"That's what makes you a weed," he said. "Personnel's at the end of the hall," he said, pointing toward the doorway at the top of a series of concrete steps leading into the building. A sign mounted on the wall beside the door read Company A, 78th Army Security Agency Special Operations Unit.

The Pope and I heaved our duffel bags onto our shoulders, climbed the steps and entered the building.

"This is like walking into a museum, Pope," I said.

"Jesus, you could play basketball in this hallway," he said. "Damn ceiling must be fifteen feet high."

In the personnel office, we were greeted unenthusiastically by the company clerk, an obese specialist fourth-class named Adams. He was short, no more than 5' 5" inches tall and almost as broad as he was tall. His uniform had been let out at least twice to accommodate his growing girth because there were two broad strips in the seat of his pants that were a darker green than the rest of the material. He had beady little eyes that almost seemed to come together over his upturned nose. He sighed when he saw us.

"You must be the new Marys," he said.

"Marys?" the Pope and I asked in unison.

"What's your MOS?" Adams said, referring to our military job titles.

"We're 98Gs. I'm German; he's Russian," I said, gesturing toward the Pope.

The 98G code identified us as voice-intercept operators, which meant after getting our duty assignments we'd spend our shifts eavesdropping on East German or Russian radio and telephone conversations. I guess it made us some sort of high-tech spies.

"Then you're Marys," Adams said. "All you guys from Monterey are called Marys. The other guys are the Devens Dollies," he said, referring to the soldiers who were trained in Morse code and electronics at Fort Devens, Massachusetts.

"Give me your orders and your records, and we'll get you signed in. You'll be put in the transient quarters until after you get your security briefing," the fat clerk said.

"When do we go to work?"

"I don't know. Most weeds spend a couple of weeks picking up cigarette butts in the parking lot, or painting, or whatever the first sergeant needs done around here. You have to get your security badges, and go through some briefing before you can do anything else."

After completing our processing, Adams handed us some papers and told us to go to the supply room to pick up our gear.

"What gear?" the Pope said.

"An extra field jacket, a pile cap, trench tool, sleeping bag, gas mask and some other crap you'll never use. Oh, yeah, you'll have to go by the arms room and sign up for an M-14. You'll never use it either, just go down and clean it now and then."

The Pope and I looked at each other, wondering what kind of unit issued equipment we weren't ever going to us. We shrugged and went to the supply room, which was in the basement of the barracks, and drew our sheets, pillowcases and blankets. The supply clerk, who was annoyed because two weeds had interrupted his nap, tossed a faded field jacket at me and then rummaged through a box until he found a small bundle of private first-class stripes and some Berlin Brigade patches for my uniforms.

"Oh, you gotta lose that," he said, pointing to the ASA patch on the upper right sleeve of my uniform.

"How come?" I said. "I am in the ASA."

"'Cos we ain't here," he said. "Some bullshit about the ASA not supposed to operating in Berlin. Whatever reason, the 78th's the only unit in Berlin that can't wear its patch. Now, you come back back in a couple of days and we'll have you some name tags," he said brusquely.

I looked at the field jacket, which had sergeant first-class insignia on the sleeves and the name tag "Eckford."

"Who was Eckford?" I said.

"Eckford?" the clerk said and looked at the jacket. "Oh, he was a platoon sergeant who retired a month or so ago. Real asshole."

A few minutes later, the Pope and I were hanging our uniforms in lockers in the huge squad room that housed the 78th's weeds. The room had several double bunks, but because the Pope and I were the only two new arrivals, we didn't have to beat out anyone else for a lower bunk.

Just as Adams said, the Pope and I, joined by Alex Garza, who had been in the German class behind me at Monterey, and Tommy Anderson, a red-haired Morse code transcriber shipped in from the ASA detachment at Shemya, Alaska, spent the next two weeks picking up cigarette butts in the parking log, folding sheets in the supply room, and painting the company commander's office. When we finished the paint job, the company clerk told us to get into our dress uniforms, it was time for our security briefing at the unit headquarters.

Like the Pope, I had been shipped to the NSA headquarters when I completed my language course at Monterey. Combining the security consciousness from that NSA training with the identification badges, security clearances and constant thundering in the press about this or that Berlin crisis, it was easy for a new arrival to be serious about the security briefing required before a duty assignment.

The company clerk marched us to the 78th's security offices on the second floor of the Headquarters Company barracks, which also housed the unit mess hall and post office. He verified that we weren't Russian spies in deep cover, and an MP ushered us into the headquarters' suite of offices.

Our security briefing really consisted of filling out a bunch of forms, none of which any of us bothered to read.

"Sign here, here and here and initial here, here and here," the bored intelligence clerk said.

We did, and the security briefing was over, except for the intelligence officer's speech.

Major Frederick Minor was a puffy, pompous little man who looked like an overstuffed pigeon. He was one of those people who enjoyed having a little bit of power and overused it. When he entered the room and we all had to snap to, he'd pause and look to make sure that everyone was properly at attention before releasing us and going about the business at hand. It wasn't that he let it go on and on, it just seemed like it was just a few seconds longer than was really necessary.

During the talk, we were given a list of all the bars and clubs that were off limits to U.S. military personnel. There were as many reasons for bars being off-limits as there were bars.

"There have been reports of pro-Soviet activity at the KBS Bar," he said.

Exactly what pro-Soviet activity there might have been wasn't said. We just were supposed to be satisfied to know there had been activity and we shouldn't go there. Another bar was off-limits because of reported homosexual activity; another for reported incidences of anti-American behavior; and another for reported ties to organized criminal activity.

"These establishments are off-limits to all military personnel — and you can be assured that there will be penalties if you should enter one of these bars," he said.

They're probably off-limits because that's where the officers all go to drink, I thought.

"You must remember that you are members of one of the most important units in Berlin," the major said. "As members of the 78th Army Security Agency Special Operations Unit, you are entrusted with the gathering of vital information that the Soviets would love to have. The Soviets will make every effort to find out who you are. Whatever you do, don't tell anyone what unit you're with. If anyone asks you for your unit, tell them you're a clerk in Berlin Brigade."

"A what?" I asked.

"Who're you, private? What's your name?"

"Cooper, sir. Don Cooper."

"Well, Cooper, you're a clerk in Berlin Brigade. You got that? You're not with ASA. You've never even heard of the ASA. You're a goddam clerk in Berlin Brigade. You got that, soldier?"

"Sir?" I asked, knowing I'd run the risk of spending the next several weeks painting or picking up cigarette butts.

"Yes, Cooper, what is it?"

"What do we do if they already know we're ASA?" I tried to ask the question as innocently as possible, something made difficult because I could sense the Pope struggling to keep a straight face.

The major glowered, his face turning a fiery red. He took a step toward me, then shouted, "You trying to be funny, boy?"

"No, sir."

"You're a goddam wiseass, Cooper. Just keep it up and you'll live to regret it."

I believe I already have, I thought.

"Jesus, what an asshole," the Pope said a few minutes later as we were leaving the headquarters building and heading back to Company A for our trick assignments. "I thought he was going to have you taken out and shot."

Because the 78th worked around the clock, seven days a week, 365 days a year, the company was split into four shifts, or "tricks." One trick, on days, worked from seven o'clock in the morning until four o'clock in the afternoon, when it was relieved by the swing, or "eves," trick that would work until midnight, when the graveyard trick, or "mids," took over. The fourth trick was on break. The tricks rotated, so that everyone worked all shifts.

Each trick was designated by a letter, and I was assigned to C Trick, which was mid-way through eves. I didn't have much time to get ready for my first night on the job — just enough to stow my gear in my new room on the third floor of the barracks, introduce myself to my roommate, a lanky New Yorker known as Doc, and catch the bus that would carry C Trick to work at the spy post on the Hill, the name given to Teufelsberg.

Teufelsberg (Devil's Mountain) hadn't been in the vast Berlin forest before the end of World War II. Berlin was bombed day and night by the Americans and British for most of the last two years of the war, and then there were artillery barrages and fierce house-to-house fighting when

PHOTO/Jeff Gammon

Teufelsberg ("The Hill") in 1968

the Russians captured the city. At the end of the war, Berlin was destroyed and left a vast ruin. The rubble was hauled out into the forests that surrounded Berlin and piled up. The piles grew steadily until there were several mountains of rubble. Because Teufelsberg was the tallest of these rubble mountains, British and American intelligence officers decided it would be the ideal place to build a site for intercepting Russian and East German communications. The Hill became festooned with several buildings housing a variety of antennas and radio receivers tuned to the frequencies used by the Russians and East Germans.

It was a typical January evening in Berlin — cold, with a mixture of snow and rain falling. It was a miserable night out, so I decided to wear the old field jacket that I was issued when I checked into the 78th. In my rush to join C Trick, I hadn't removed my regular field jacket from my duffel bag. While on transient duty, I wore the Eckford field jacket. I'd sewn my private first-class stripe on the sleeves, but I didn't bother to replace the name tag , so when I showed up at the Hill, Roadrunner, the trick sergeant, just assumed that was my name.

"Eckford, you've got the low-level scene tonight," Roadrunner told me, motioning me across the Pit to an empty chair in front of a radio receiver and reel-to-reel tape recorder.

"Right, Sarge," I said. I plopped down in the chair and

put on the headsets, adjusted the volume and waited to hear my first East German military transmission.

Doc leaned over. "I thought your name was Cooper."

"It is."

"What's with the `Eckford' name tag?"

"I didn't get around to getting mine put on and my other jacket's in the bottom of my duffel bag," I said.

"Roadrunner'll shit. That stupid asshole probably will think you're an East German spy," Doc said.

Sure enough, a few minutes later Roadrunner darted up, looked sharply at me and rubbed his chin.

"Eckford? I don't have an Eckford on this roster. You know why?" he said.

"That's because my name's not Eckford. I just didn't have time to get the name tag changed. My name's Cooper. See, there it is," I said, pointing out my name on his duty roster.

"You didn't have time? You had time to get those stripes on that jacket, didn't you?"

"I sewed them on myself."

"Oh, you did the sewing scene? Hmm," Roadrunner said, rubbing his chin and tapping his foot. "Then why did you try to pass yourself off as Eckford?"

"I didn't try to pass myself off as anyone. I just put on the jacket and came to work. It's no big deal. I'll get the name tag fixed as soon as we get off the Hill."

"You do that. But I'm keeping my eye on you, private," Roadrunner said.

Fang, a diminutive New Yorker with two missing front teeth who had been watching my exchange with Roadrunner from the Pit's main console, took off his headsets, hung them on a hook beside the small desk used to log in messages, and sidled up to me.

"Congratulations, Cooper. It took you less time to piss off Roadrunner than any newk ever on C Trick," he said, grinning broadly.

"Well, I didn't intend to piss him off quite so fast."

"Don't worry about it, just try to stay out of his way."

"How the hell do I do that? He's the trick sergeant, for Christ's sake."

"I can get you assigned to Violet."

"What's Violet?"

"Violet's where we monitor the SED"

"SED?"

"Oh, yeah, it's your first night. SED's the Sozialistische Einheitspartei Deutschland, you know, the ones who run the East German government. Anyway, Violet's in that wing over there," he said, pointing toward a dimly lit room across the hall from the Pit. I could make out banks of tape recorders and radio receivers with flickering lights.

"What's the deal with Violet?"

"I'm not sure, but Roadrunner doesn't like to go in that room. It's like he's afraid something'll happen to him if he does. He sticks his head in to see if everyone's there, and then he hauls ass. If you want, I can get you assigned there. Hell, he thinks everyone in there's weird anyway."

"Violet sounds fine to me," I said and shrugged.

"But don't worry too much about Roadrunner. You should have seen what happened to me when I got here in '64."

"What happened?"

"Oh, Jesus, not the 'poor Fang' story," Doc said and groaned loudly. "Hey, Fang's telling his arrival story again."

I heard a chorus of moans.

"Hey, screw you all, you're goddam newks and you know it," Fang shouted, then he pulled up a chair and sat down next to me.

"When I got here, it was like no one knew I was coming. I got off the duty train early in the morning and there wasn't no one there to pick me up. I didn't have a goddam clue as to where I was or nothing. Anyway, I caught a ride to Andrews, and ended up in the MP mess hall because nobody knew where I was supposed to be."

He paused to shake a cigarette out of a pack of Marlboros, then extended it to me. I took one, lit it and held the match for him to light his cigarette before he resumed his story.

"Anyway, I finally got someone to catch on that I belonged somewhere else, like with that 'secret unit' as the MP guy said. When I finally made connections and got to the 78th, I was stuck in the transient room for nearly three weeks. I lived out of my duffel bag the whole damn time. I was in a total state of military disrepair, and I really liked it."

"What were you doing?"

"Nothing, not a goddam thing. I got up about seven o'clock and wandered over to the mess hall for breakfast, then I went back to the room and hung out. Nobody seemed to even know I was there."

"Beat the hell out of painting rocks," I interrupted.

"Yeah. Well, one night the Toad — he was a little short fucker who was the first sergeant at the time — showed up and told me I was on C Trick now and to get over there for an inspection. No goddam warning, nothing, just show my ass up.

"So, I got my stuff and the Toad and I went over to the C Trick area and I met up with Eckford — he's the one who had your field jacket — he was the platoon sergeant and a real Class A asshole. He asked me, with the Toad standing right there, what was wrong. I said I just got assigned to C Trick, and he said I had to be ready for a full inspection," he paused to take a deep drag from his cigarette.

"What then?" I asked.

"Well, I said I'd try, but I couldn't guarantee the results. Man, you should have seen them. Eckford and the Toad both started screaming and ranting about how I'd better damn well be ready for the inspection. I guess they finally just lost their energy yelling at me because the Toad muttered something about how I'd better shape up, and Eckford gave me the 'I'm going to keep my eye on you, soldier' crap."

"Did they?"

"Did they what?"

"Did they keep an eye on you?"

"Shit, no. The Toad was shipped out to Korea, up near the DMZ. I keep hoping I'll hear someday the bastard's stepped on a mine or something like that. Eckford's retired and gone back to the States. Hell, he's probably pumping gas in Shithole, Georgia, or someplace like that. So, just don't worry about Roadrunner. I'll get you in Violet, and you'll hardly ever see him."

"Hey, Doc," I said. "How can Fang get me shifted to Violet? I thought Roadrunner was the trick chief."

"He's a legend and Roadrunner knows it," Doc said.

"A legend? What d'ya mean?"

"Well, it was about a year ago," Doc said, leaning back in his chair and letting his earphones hang around his neck like a pair of stethoscopes. "Fang had been on a raunch ..."

"What's a raunch?" I asked.

"Well, it's when you go out and spend the whole night out just getting drunk. Anyway, Fang had hit his rack about an hour before the German garbage collectors made their stop near the barracks.

"They were banging the cans around, just slamming the cans into the truck and everything and it really pissed Fang off. He had this pellet gun in his locker and he leaned out the window and dinged one of the cans.

"The Herms thought it was a sniper or something and they took off. They reported it to the Mps, and the next thing we knew the CO and first shirt and the platoon sergeants pulled a surprise barracks inspection," he said.

"What happened next?" I said.

"Well," Doc said, "it was during Fasching and just about everybody had bottles of that cheap champagne that they won at the festival ..."

"Don't forget the porn collections," Big Ed interrupted. There was enough to open a dirty book store -- and most of it was Doc's."

"Bullshit," Doc said with a grin. "But there were guns, Bowie knives, all kinds of booze. I know there was some hash, but the treads didn't know what it was. Couple of guys on D Trick even got a couple of women out of the barracks just before the treads got there."

"Then what happened?" I asked.

"There was a couple of meetings with all the treads," Doc said. "Our trick sergeant -- not Roadrunner, the guy before him -- tried to put in a good word for us, but the CO just pointed at all the contraband ..."

"Filled the whole goddamn day room," Big Ed interrupted, drawing a glare from Doc, who continued.

"As I was saying, our trick sergeant went down to plead

the case for the C Trick offenders, and the CO pointed to the pile of evidence and said, 'I have bigger problems than you, sergeant. How do I go about court martialing the whole fucking unit?

"They just ended up giving Fang an Article 15 and dumping all the stuff they'd collected," Doc said. "Well, not everything. All of the booze somehow ended up in the NCO Club."

I was shifted to Violet, just like Fang said, and I didn't have any more run-ins with Roadrunner during the next two nights before C Trick went on break, so I was relaxed on my first night off duty since arriving in Berlin.

That night, I claimed my pass and wandered around the neighborhood close to the barracks. I strolled into the Whitehorse Bar, which was about four or five blocks away from the barracks, drank a couple of beers, and tried out my Monterey-trained German on some of the Berliners, who laughed at my mispronunciations. They spoke very slowly and distinctly because I had trouble following the conversation when they were speaking in the Berlin dialect, something the German instructors at Monterey hadn't prepared me for. They'd given the impression that all Germans, except for the Bavarians, spoke German just like they did.

"What unit are you with, my friend?" one of the Berliners said.

"I'm a clerk in Berlin Brigade," I said, remembering my security briefing.

"Oh, you're ASA," they said together.

Big Clyde

2 It was about two weeks after I joined C Trick that I met Big Clyde.

It was my second set of mids with C Trick, and I still was trying to get adjusted to the graveyard shift, something I never really managed to do. I had gone to bed immediately after finishing the shift, and it was mid-afternoon when I got up. I knew it would be nearly eight hours before starting mids, so I caught the A-18 bus to the Europa Center and wandered around the center of West Berlin for several hours before catching the bus back to the barracks.

By the time C Trick was ready to board the trick bus for the Hill, I already had begun yawning, even though I still had an eight-hour shift ahead of me. The first bus was nearly full when I climbed aboard. Moving carefully through the darkness, I found an empty seat next to a massive man, who sprawled with his head resting against the window and one foot on the seat. He was snoring loudly.

I eased onto the seat carefully, trying — unsuccessfully — to keep from bumping him, but the bus suddenly lurched forward and I lost my balance. I put out my hand to catch myself and clapped him on the shoulder.

"You goddam newk!" he said, bellowing like a grizzly aroused from hibernation.

I had met Big Clyde. He had just returned, hung over and sunburned, from a two-week leave in Majorca, and the cold, grayness of Berlin in February didn't do anything to improve his bear-like disposition.

Big Clyde deserved his name. He was physically imposing, a great hulking man who should have been playing middle linebacker for the Chicago Bears, not sitting at a console at an ASA listening post on top of a mountain of rubble in Berlin.

His appetite for life was as big as he. He ate mountains of food, swigged gallons of beer, and laughed louder than thunder. Everything he did was done as if he were about to take his last breath and he wanted to get as much out of life in those last few moments as most people do in a life-time.

When I joined C Trick on the Hill, Big Clyde was almost a short-timer. He had a little more than three months left before he would be rotating back to the States and getting his discharge.

Big Clyde was not a perfect soldier: he lacked military courtesy, failed to spitshine his boots, let his hair get too long and paid little attention to the condition of his uniform. Combining that general disrespect for the military with the dwindling number of days he had to serve, Big Clyde was contemptuous of the "treads." Treads, who were known as lifers in other units, were those guys who had re-enlisted, or re-upped.

Big Clyde may not have been a model soldier, but he was extremely good at his job. He would sit at his radio console in the Pit, the name given to the racks of receivers and tape recorders that encircled the airlock and ladder that led from the first floor of the building to the three levels of antennas that were inside the huge bubble atop the building, and scan through the frequency bands and quickly distinguish which sounds were static and which were Russian or East German communications. He was the best there was in the unit at detecting the signals and quickly identifying if they were German or Russian. Because he was so good, the treads generally left him alone when he was at work.

Once in a while some new tread on the Hill would spot Big Clyde and be stunned by the length of the big soldier's hair.

"Soldier, you need a haircut," the tread would say.

"Fine? Just fucking fine," Big Clyde would reply. "Make up your mind. You want me to go get a haircut or do you want me to do my goddam job? What's it going to be?"

Shocked, the tread would rush to the site commander to

report the gross insubordination, only to find out that Captain Weldon preferred to have the East German and Russian signals monitored properly — even if the job was being done by a big guy whose hair was a bit too long and whose uniform was rumpled.

Big Clyde had just six weeks left before rotating back to the States when one of those days that GIs dread more than anything occurred — some high-level VIP from the Pentagon decided to check out things on the Hill.

Even though I still chafed under the term newk, I already had become used to the comings and goings of the important and self-important gaggles of majors, colonels and brigadiers. But it was different this time. This visitor was the Air Force Chief of Staff, a full general with four stars on his shoulders and probably hundreds of assorted medals and ribbons. His visit also meant hours and hours of sweeping, mopping, and polishing, and then doing it all over again.

We had to get ladders so we could clamber up and scrub down the tops of the racks of radio receivers and tape recorders, because one of the trick sergeants had become convinced the general would put on white gloves and climb a ladder to sweep his hand across the top of the racks to see if there was any dust.

Grates covering the ducts through which the antenna and power cables ran were removed, polished and returned, but only after the ducts themselves were completely and thoroughly vacuumed.

"Goddamn, what next," Grumpy John said. "We going have to bend over and spread our cheeks for butthole checks?"

"Yeah, Grumpy, the general's coming here just to get a good look at your asshole," Hairy Ranger said.

"Well, if he wants to look at my ass, I'll cut a good wet one when he gets down there close," Grumpy John said.

"I can see the headline in the Overseas Weekly now," I said with a laugh. "General Dead of Fart!"

Finally, the day came for the general's visit. The treads were in a complete frenzy, rushing to the restroom frequently to make sure that no unwanted hair had popped

out on their heads in the last ten or fifteen minutes, and
inspecting themselves for any lint or dust that might have
worked its way onto their belt buckles or brass.

When the general arrived, he hung his overcoat on one of
the hooks in the foyer at the side of the building and began
his inspection tour. As inspections went, it was ordinary.
The general tried to look interested in what we were doing
— the officers who stayed at headquarters all the time, except when a Pentagon official was visiting, tried to impress
him with their intimate knowledge of what was going on
— and the enlisted men tried not to laugh at them.

After the inspection was over, the general and his entou-
rage went to gather up their overcoats and leave. When the
general reached for his overcoat, he noted the four stars on
one shoulder was missing.

"Well, for crying out loud," he said. "Someone's taken my
stars."

The colonels clustered around were thrown into a panic at the enormity of the crime. They couldn't decide what course of action to take.

"Shakedown! Let's have a shakedown inspection," the base commander said.

"Let's get all of the enlisted men out here and search every damn one of them," the general's aide said.

The general stood calmly, holding the overcoat and watching the other officers as they tried to deal with the situation. He shook his head and laughed.

Tugging on the overcoat, he said, "What the hell. If the son of a bitch has the balls to steal my stars, let him keep them."

Then he opened the door and went out to his waiting car, leaving the officers standing there, confused and not knowing what to do next.

Nothing was said about the general's missing stars, although the site commander decided that whenever high-ranking officials came to visit in the future, one of the trick non-commissioned officers would be assigned to guard the coats and hats.

There were no more important visitors to the Hill during the next few weeks. Everyone seemed to have forgotten about the general's stars until several weeks later at Tegel Airport.

Big Clyde, uncomfortable in the Class A greens which hung in his wall locker for most of his three years in Berlin, had his duffel bag packed and his orders in his hand while waiting to board the plane that would take him back to the States and civilian life. After shaking hands with several of us who were there to see him off, he headed for the boarding gate. Just before going through the gate, he turned and opened his uniform. There on his chest was a new tie clasp — four silver stars.

A New Name

3 It seemed like C Trick spent more time on mids than any of the other tricks. Now, I know it wasn't true because the tricks rotated shifts regularly, so each one spent the same amount time on mids. But I guess I hated the graveyard shift so much it just seemed like C Trick got stuck with mids more than it should.

I hated mids because I could never seem to develop the knack for that shift. I'd hit the bunk as soon as C Trick came down off the Hill, so I'd wake up about three or four o'clock in the afternoon, and still have to face another eight hours or so before it was time to go to work. The only comforting thing about mids was just about everybody felt the same way.

Mids were especially hard on those of us working in Violet because the East Germans closed up shop at five o'clock, so we just sat there looking at the racks of tape recorders and the motionless lines on the monitors. If this had been a hospital, East Germany would have been flatlining.

I learned a lot about my fellow C Trickers on mids because Violet became a gathering place where we would sit and talk about anything under the sun. You can learn a lot about what a person really thinks when he's so tired his mouth kicks into gear before his brain. We played word games, wrote letters home and held contests to see who could roll his chair the farthest.

And, we argued loudly and profanely about just about everything. The discussions were wide-ranging, from the Vietnam War to literature to sports. Nothing was off limits to our discussions, but anyone who offered an opinion had

Working mids

to be prepared to hear it ridiculed.

I loved those freewheeling discussions, whirling dervishes of conversation switching rapidly from one subject to another and carrying its participants along. The other guys must have felt the same way, because when Norman Thomas Aquinas Lebowski suggested we have a really formal structured discussion, he suddenly found himself the topic.

"I really think we ought to at least follow the etiquette of discourse," he said. Lebowski claimed to have been a philosophy major in some Midwestern university. He tried to give himself a nickname and even suggested he should be called Professor, but that was rejected out of hand. He never did get a nickname, unless "asshole," as in "Hey, asshole!" counted. He never stopped trying to be the Professor, choosing to wear a scarf even during the summer and affecting a pair of horn-rimmed glasses, which slipped down his long, thin nose. The sliding glasses annoyed him because he would push them back up and lean forward to make a point, only to have the glasses slide down again.

Hairy Ranger, a former University of Texas student, picked up his nickname because his body was covered with thick, dark hair, sat up straight on his chair and raised his hand, as if he were a student in class.

"See, even the Ranger agrees," Lebowski said with a smile. "What's your suggestion, Ranger?"

"I think our debate topic should be: 'Resolved, Norman Thomas Aquinas Lebowski is the biggest asshole on C Trick.' Who wants to argue that he isn't?"

Complete silence.

"Screw all of you," Lebowski said, spun around to face his monitor and clapped his headsets firmly atop his head.

It also was on mids that I picked up the nickname that would stick with me for the rest of my time in Berlin.

C Trick finished swings, which gave us 48 hours of break time before starting mids. I decided to enjoy my time off by wandering around the British sector. I liked the British sector of Berlin because I could visit a tobacco shop and indulge myself in a real Cuban cigar. Unlike the United States, the Brits didn't mind trading with Fidel Castro. I would take my time in the tobacco shop, examining the cigars until I found the one that seemed to suit my mood. Then I'd stroll around the streets, puffing away cheerfully.

The other reason I enjoyed the British sector was even more simple. There were no American MPs in the British sector, and the British MPs generally left Americans alone.

It was a typical early spring night in Berlin; a steady drizzle and cold wind soaked into the bones, and drove me into the warmth of pubs along the way. It had been raining when I left the barracks, so I had put on my black trench coat, which had been a Christmas gift from my father who remembered the cold and damp of England during World War II. I clapped an old snapbrim hat on my head before making the walk past the Scum and Linda's Lounge to the bus stop on Ringstrasse.

I got off the bus at the Europa Center and walked past the Kaiser Wilhelm Memorial Church, pausing to look up at the ghostly skeleton of the old church that had been destroyed during a British air raid. A couple of weeks earlier, I found myself outside the church during the day. A British soldier, holding a travel brochure, stood outside the ruins. An elderly German sidled up and said in heavily accented English, "There were children in that church."

The Brit's brows knitted in anger and he said in perfect German, "And, there were children at Coventry, asshole."

I smiled to myself when I remembered that exchange, then I walked down the Kurfürstendamm for a couple of blocks, then turned and made my way to Kantstrasse, stopping in a small pub for a shot of brandy and a beer chaser.

The pub, on a narrow side street, almost an alley, between the Kurfürstendamm and Kantstrasse was frequented by students at the Free University of Berlin. The university had been established in 1948 in the U.S. sector. When the university opened, the Berlin Airlift was under way, and it was seen as the replacement for Humboldt University, which was in the Soviet sector.

I sat quietly, listening to the students argue about the Vietnam War. I stayed in a corner so I wouldn't be drawn into the conversation. It wasn't that I supported the war — I didn't, and oddly enough had joined the Army to avoid ending up in Vietnam — but my Monterey German just wasn't good enough for me to get involved in a serious conversation.

After a few minutes, the chill had eased and I went back out into the night, walking along as close to the sidewalk as possible to avoid being completely drenched. When I reached Kantstrasse, I saw the Black Cat, a larger nightclub, across the street. Its name was scrawled in garish neon and I could see a group of young women, most holding umbrellas, standing near the streetlights in front of the club.

I crossed the street and stopped near the club entrance and looked at the posters inside a glass case. The posters announced the appearance of Tonga Lida, a stripper supposedly from some exotic country but who probably was a moonlighting college student. I could hear laughter, shouting in English and German and loud whistles inside the

club, as well as music, probably recorded, from The Stripper, so I knew one of the dancers was going through her
routine. I was about to open the door when I felt a tug at
my sleeve.

I turned and saw Karin, a streetwalker with flaming
red hair. I was surprised to see her because she generally
worked Savignyplatz, which was two or three bus stops
away. She had an infectious laugh and didn't have the
hard, mercenary look of so many streetwalkers.

I had met Karin not long after I got to Berlin. I was sitting at the bar on Savignyplatz when she came in, sat down
on the stool beside me and asked for a cigarette, pointing
toward the pack of Marlboros beside my elbow on the bar. I
slid the pack toward her and she took one out, then waited
until I fumbled in my pocket for my Zippo lighter. When I
flicked the light, I was stunned by the fiery red of her hair. I
guess it was obvious that I was staring because she grinned
at me.

"It's dyed," she said and chuckled.

I hung around the bar for a couple of hours, and Karin
would always slide onto the stool beside me when she came
in for a break. I didn't hang out at Savignyplatz much, but
when I did stop by the bar, I'd sit and talk with Karin for a
couple of hours. I wasn't so moral that I didn't become a cli-
ent, but mostly we just sat at the bar and talked.

So, when I stopped outside the nightclub on Kantstrasse,
I was surprised and oddly happy to see Karin. I also was
pleased when she slipped her arm through mine.

"Let's go in and get out of the cold. I'd like a cognac; what
about you?"

"Sounds good to me," I said.

Karin continued to hold my arm as we stopped for a moment in the foyer, letting our eyes adjust to the dim light.
The foyer opened up into a large room, which was much
longer than wide. A bar was to the right and a low stage,
now empty, was to the left. Three steps led down from the
stage to the floor and a well-worn carpet walkway led from
the stage to a doorway which had a heavy brocade curtain
instead of a door. That was the way to the strippers' dressing room.

We maneuvered our way to the bar, slid onto stools at the end and I motioned to the bartender who grinned at Karin, reached under the bar, pulled out two small brandy snifters and carefully poured the cognac.

"He's a friend of mine, so he gave us clean glasses and good cognac — not the cheap one most people get," she said.

I glanced toward the bartender, held up my glass as if I were making a toast and said, "Danke." Even though he grinned and waved, I knew if I hadn't been with Karin, I would be sitting at the bar drinking the rotgut house brand cognac.

"I think there's someone waving at you," Karin said and pointed toward a table near the stage. I squinted, peering through the dense clouds of cigarette smoke hanging in the air. Four young men sat at the table, a pile of beer bottles almost completely covering the top. They were members of D Trick, which was on days, and I knew two of them, Stashik, a blond, California surfer-type Mary who had been in my German class at Monterey, and Guiliano, a short, stocky Italian with thick, dark hair and an olive complexion, who spent a couple of days in the transient barracks with the Pope and me. I didn't know the other two, but I'd seen them around the barracks and on the Hill at shift change.

"They're from my unit," I said, leaning toward Karin. "I know the blond guy and the short dark-haired one next to him, but I don't know the other two."

She finished her cognac and patted my arm before sliding off the stool.

"I'm warm now," she said. "Are you going to visit with your friends?"

"Probably," I said with a shrug, and watched her as she glided through the crowd near the door and went back outside. I picked up my pack of cigarettes and shoved them in my coat pocket, downed the last few drops of cognac and carefully placed the snifter beside the change on the bar.

I eased my way through the crowd toward the D Trickers' table, which I could see had been chosen carefully because the curtain parted slightly and that table gave a view inside the dressing room. Obviously, one of the guys had been to this club before and knew where to sit to watch a naked woman put on the clothes she'd be taking off in a few minutes.

"Hey, Coop, whatcha' doing out by yourself," Stashik said loudly. "I thought C Trickers always traveled in packs."

"You ought to know, Stashik, 'cause I'm looking at a herd of D Trickers."

He looked around, saw an empty chair at the next table and pushed it toward me, spinning it around at the same time. I pulled it toward me and sat down.

"Coop, meet the Bear and Lurch," Stashik said. I could understand why they were called Bear and Lurch. Bear had thick, heavy muscles and coarse brown hair, much like his namesake, while Lurch bore a striking resemblance to the hulking butler in the Addams Family cartoons.

"Who was the redhead you came in with?" Louie said.

"Name's Karin."

"She's a whore," Louie said, "I seen her outside a hotel at Savignyplatz. I'd never forget that red hair."

"Shit, Louie, she's just trying to make a living," I said, and I guess he could sense my annoyance.

"I didn't mean nothing by it. I was just telling what she does for a living. I've been around hookers all my life. Let me buy you a beer, okay?"

I nodded.

I sipped on the bottle of Schultheiss that was slapped on the table in front of me.

"What's with all the bottles? You expected to clean up after yourself here?"

Stashik laughed.

"We been drinking them so goddam fast that they just decided to wait until we leave to clean up after us."

I grinned and shook my head, too vigorously because my hat fell on the floor. I picked it up, rolled it in a loose ball and shoved it in my left coat pocket. Then I saw Louie looking at me like I was someone from his past.

"You're not Italian, are you?" he said.

"No, Irish on both sides of my family."

"With that dark hair and tan, you'd pass for Italian. You sure you're not?"

"Positive," I said and took a sip of beer. I wiped my mouth and snapped my fingers. "Well, maybe I am by proxy. When I was a little kid — three, maybe four years old — Joe Connella, an old guy who owned a grocery store not far from my folks' house, always called me Tony. Said I looked a lot like his boy when he was about my age. Joe and his wife were both from Italy, so maybe I do look Italian."

"I know with that hat and trench coat, you look like a goddam gangster," Stashik said. "Don't he, guys?"

They all nodded and grinned broadly.

"Yeah, you look like a guy I used to see hanging out in the neighborhood. He never said anything about what he did, but everybody knew he was in the mob. What was his name? Blackie? Yeah, Blackie. That's what everybody called him. Blackie — and you look just like him. Well, you're a lot younger, but you still look like him."

"You sure you're not Italian, Coop? Or, should I say Blackie?" Stashik said.

"I'm not Italian, nor have I ever been Italian, and I've damn sure not ever been called Blackie," I said. "Jesus Christ, my Irish ancestors are probably spinning in their graves right now."

"Sure, sure," Louie said. "We know, you're traveling incognito, aren't you, Blackie?"

I shook my head. After hearing my parents talk of their Irish heritage for all of my life, in just a few minutes in a strip club in Berlin, I'd become Italian. My stomach growled, telling me it wanted something other than beer or cognac, so I stood, pushed the chair back to the other table and said, "I hate to break up your party, but I'm go to find something to eat."

"Ravioli?" Stashik said.

"Cannelloni?" Louie said.

"Maybe I'll go over to the NAAFI Club and have some Irish stew," I said. The NAAFI Club was the British equivalent of a U.S. post exchange. "But I'll probably grab a currywurst somewhere."

As I made my way toward the exit, I heard Stashik and Louie call, "Bye, bye, Blackie."

Good God, I hope they forget about this, I thought, but a sinking feeling in my stomach made me think I'd just been tagged for good.

When I got out of the club, I noticed the rain had stopped, but the street looked slick and shiny as the streetlights reflected off the wet surface. I took a deep breath of fresh air, hoping to clear my head from all of the cigarette smoke, and saw Karin, standing near the entranceway to a pharmacy. She gestured for me, and I walked slowly to where she stood under a canvas awning.

"Leaving already?" she said.

"Yeah, I'm calling it a night. I think I'll go get a bite to eat and catch a bus back to the barracks."

"Auf wiedersehen," she said with a smile.

I walked back along Kantstrasse toward the Europa Center, stopping only at a kiosk to buy a bockwurst and a hard roll, which I ate on the way. I didn't have to wait but two or three minutes before the A18 bus arrived; I climbed up to the second deck, slumped down into a seat, lit a cigarette and peered out the window at the sparkling lights that brought life to the city. I loved Berlin at night, with all of the restaurants, clubs and bars open and full of life, so unlike the deadness of the small town where I grew up, a town where everything but the bus station was shut up tightly at night.

About thirty minutes later, I stepped off the bus at the corner of Ringstrasse and Kadettenweg. I decided to stop in at the Goldene Sonne (Golden Sun). The bar, which was referred to derogatorily as the Golden Scum and later simply as the Scum, was directly across the street from the main gate of Andrews Barracks. Anyone walking down Kadettenweg to the bus stop on Ringstrasse about four blocks away would pass right by the Scum. The bar became the first place we'd stop on the way out for the night and the last place we'd stop on the way back to the barracks.

The Scum was in an old, poorly ventilated building that probably opened about the same time the Kaiser decided he needed a cadet school in Lichterfelde. It had seen its share of drunken soldiers, from the Kaiser's cadets in the 1890s, down through the Reichswehr's officer candidates during the brief life of the Weimar Republic, to Hitler's S.S. trainees and the American GIs who were there to let the Russians remember we were allies during World War II.

During the summer, the Scum's walls would be damp from the humidity, even with all the windows open and the ceiling fans cranked up high. During the winter, the Scum was still damp, but it would be cold and damp because the ancient coal-fired furnace in the basement could not generate enough heat to warm the old building with its high ceilings and air leaks around the windows.

The door creaked as I pushed it open, causing the bartender, Hans, to stop washing glasses in the sink behind the bar, wipe his hands on his apron and move back to the bar, where he waited for me to place my order.

I ordered a beer and had just started to take a sip from the bottle when I heard it.

"Hey, Blackie!"

Oh, good God, I thought, and I turned toward the main room, which was to my right. I saw Hairy Ranger and Fat Kenny in a booth near the big fireplace at the end of the room. They were waving at me, so I went to join them.

"What's this Blackie shit," I said, trying to sound stern.

"Why that's your new name, son," Hairy Ranger said. "A bunch of D Trickers were by here a few minutes ago and they said they'd run into you up in the Brit sector. Guiliano said you had a hooker on your arm and looked so much like a gangster he knew that you just had to be named Blackie."

"Shit, you guys keep that to yourselves, okay?" I said, knowing I was wasting my breath.

"Of course, if you don't want to be Blackie, then we won't breathe a word," Hairy Ranger said. "Is that true, Fat Kenny?"

"Oh, sure," said Fat Kenny as his grin spread. "Mum's the word."

Unfortunately, a nickname sticks like glue. Any doubts that I might have harbored were removed the next night when I climbed aboard the last trick bus as C Trick prepared to start mids. I nodded at Chief, who had drawn the bus driving detail.

"Hiya, Blackie, good you could make it," he said.

'Gators and Hookers

4 Winters in Berlin are damp and cold, with thick, dark clouds blocking out the sun so even the snow seems dingy gray, and you can't get away from the odor of sulfur from the low-grade coal burned in most of the residents' furnaces. From October until April, the city seems to be wrapped in a thick blanket of fog, leaving the city's residents fighting depression. I never checked it out, but I heard Berlin's suicide rate jumps during the winter. Maybe not, but it made sense to me.

The night was cold, and the March wind seemed to have fingers of ice flicking at you, reaching inside your clothes to penetrate your bones. The streets glistened from the rain that wasn't quite a rain. If it were a real rain, not a light drizzle giving the impression it would stop soon, Hairy Ranger, Shakey, a slightly balding little guy with an elaborate repertoire of nervous jerks, twitches and grimaces, and I probably would have stayed at the El Oso, the non-commissioned officers club at the Andrews Barracks.

As Spec Fours (specialist fourth class), neither Hairy Ranger nor I were supposed to be in the El Oso, but no one ever made anything of it unless you had gotten crossways with one of the treads. I couldn't go to the El Oso if Roadrunner were there, but on this night he apparently had stayed in his quarters, and Hairy Ranger, Shakey and I had a few beers at the club before we decided to venture out into the rain and hit a few bars. We wandered from one bar to the next, getting wet and chilled on the sidewalks and darting into the next available bar to dry a bit and have a beer or two before moving on to the next one.

We had started out that evening in Lichterfelde in the American sector and worked our way to Stuttgarter Platz in the British sector. Stuttgarter Platz was an ordinary Berlin shopping area during the day, with tobacco shops, bakeries, restaurants, pharmacies and fruit stands. But at night it underwent a transformation that never failed to astound me. After the shops closed, the bars exploded into light, and prostitutes and pimps took their places on the sidewalks. As if by magic, the bars and hookers' hotels, scarcely noticeable during the day, seemed to flow like lava across the plaza, changing its personality as surely as Dr. Jekyll became Mr. Hyde.

When we went in the bar, one of those dives that changed names and owners more frequently than most people change clothes, a group of four or five rowdy, drunken 'Gators were already seated at a table near the center of the room. Empty beer bottles teetered on the table amid the ash trays, change and packs of cigarettes. A cloud of blue smoke hung like fog over the table, a blue fog so thick even the chain-smoking waitresses appeared reluctant to approach it.

As members of the 78th ASA, Hairy Ranger, Shakey and I were part of an elite group in Berlin. We held 24-hour passes, which meant we could pretty much come and go as we pleased when we were off duty. Many of us had been through language school, so we spoke German and could avoid the military police by passing ourselves off as Berliners. Even the Army's chief of staff, General Harold Johnson, had come to Berlin and called us "technicians and linguists, not soldiers."

It was natural that we looked on ourselves as better than those simple 'Gators, the name we gave to the infantrymen who had to crawl through the mud and muck, the artillery men and tank drivers — all of those soldiers who actually had to do soldier things and who had to wear those military haircuts that left red stripes on their heads after a visit to the company barber.

'Gators didn't like the ASA, and the dislike was returned in spades. They had their bars; the 78th had its bars. They sneered at us contemptuously, calling us "goddam civilians," something we took as a compliment.

Hairy Ranger, Shakey and I eased into stools at the bar.

We ordered beer, but the bartender, an enormous former boxer with a flattened nose and cauliflower ear from about a dozen bouts too many, told us we had to order a cognac with the first beer.

"Fine with me," I said. "But make mine a Scotch. Okay?"

The bartender didn't say anything, but he pulled a bottle of Scotch down from the shelf and poured about three fingers of the amber liquid into a glass.

Hairy Ranger and Shakey shrugged and said, "Same thing."

We turned and looked around the room, trying not to look at the table of 'Gators.

Fang had warned me about looking at 'Gators, saying they enjoyed nothing more than fighting.

"They're like goddam Rottweilers," he said. "Don't ever look them directly in the eye because they can sense fear."

I took Fang's advice whenever I stopped in a GI bar; I tried to never look directly at a 'Gator, and I always sat close to the bar's entrance, in case I needed to make a quick exit.

So Hairy Ranger, Shakey and I kept close to the door as we sipped on the Scotch and let the warmth spread through our bodies. We felt a cold breeze as the door opened and two streetwalkers, one with flaming red hair, the other a platinum blonde (with dark roots), came in, closing the door quickly behind them. Both women wore extremely short and tight skirts that appeared to be molded to their bodies, low-cut blouses that gaped open to give everyone a good look at their breasts, and short fur jackets, their own concession to the night chill. The streetwalkers had come in to relax, enjoy a beer, and get out of the bone-chilling dampness for just a few minutes.

They paused and saw an empty table directly across from the 'Gators. The streetwalker with the red hair whispered to her friend, and they started moving toward the table, which took them past Hairy Ranger, Shakey and me.

When they neared us, the red-headed streetwalker smiled at me and patted me on the knee.

"Allo, Schatzi (Hello, Sweetie)," she said and leaned forward to brush her lips against my cheek, while whispering,

"Want to see me later?"

I know I blushed because she began to laugh heartily, then she and her blonde friend eased into the chairs at the table, all the while ignoring the noisy group at the neighboring table.

"You one of her clients?" Hairy Ranger said.

"Piss off, Ranger," I said.

"How come she knows you?" Shakey said. "You one of the regulars?"

"I've seen her over at Savignyplatz."

"Then how come she knows you?" Ranger said. "You've got to be one of her steadies."

"Ranger, I've never paid for it in my life. All I did was loan her forty marks on a couple of occasions, and she was so grateful that she gave me some."

"What's her name?" Shakey said.

"I think she said it was Karin."

"Don't they all?" Shakey said with a grin.

Ranger was about to say something, but suddenly one of the 'Gators began shouting at the two streetwalkers.

"Hey, ladies! You want to come and have a real party with us?" one of the 'Gators said. His extremely short-cropped hair indicated he was either a new arrival in Berlin or someone who had just re-enlisted.

As they swigged their beers, their taunting of the hookers became more raunchy until one of them, apparently the group's leader, stood up, swaying unsteadily on his feet. Finally getting his balance, the 'Gator, a hulking redneck with a bullet-shaped head, made his way, walking carefully as a drunk does when he's trying to look as if he hasn't been drinking, over to the table where the two prostitutes continued to talk in low tones, ignoring him.

He unzipped his fly and pulled his penis out of his pants. He laid the organ, which was prodigious, on the table directly before the blonde hooker.

"If you're real lucky, I'll let you suck on this," he said, looking back over his shoulder and grinning stupidly to his friends.

The two hookers continued their conversation as if there weren't a penis on the table between them. They never

glanced at it, but the blonde, without a pause in her conversation, picked up her beer bottle and slammed it down
as hard as she could on the penis, and casually returned
the bottle to its original location.

It took a few seconds for what had happened to sink in
to the 'Gator, a few seconds before the nerve endings in the
organ of which he was so proud relayed their message of
intense, excruciating pain to his fogged brain.

But when the message did reach his brain, the response
was immediate. His mouth popped open but no sound came

out, his eyes bugged out, and tears began to flow down his cheeks. Then he crashed to the floor and curled tightly into a fetal position with both hands clasped over his throbbing member.

Only then, did the two hookers turn and look in his direction. They said nothing, just looked at him and began laughing.

Their peals of laughter were contagious and soon the bar was filled by the hearty sounds of laughter that drowned out the moans coming from the 'Gator on the floor. Even his four buddies were laughing as they walked over to the table, picked him up, and carried him, still moaning and still in a fetal position, out of the bar and into the cold.

Walkabouts

5 "Walkabouts" are what the Australians call the Aborigines' wanderings about the vast outback. My first walkabout of Berlin happened by accident — I missed a bus.

It was a crisp Sunday in early April, one of the first days since I had arrived in Berlin that held some promise that the sun would break through the dark clouds enveloping the city. C Trick just started break, and my roommates, Doc and Hairy Ranger, took three-day passes somewhere in West Germany. I had the room to myself and time on my hands. I slept until nearly noon, then took my laundry bag and went to the laundromat in the basement of the PX. While the clothes were washing, I went upstairs to the snack bar and ate breakfast. After finishing breakfast, I bought a copy of the International Herald-Tribune and went back to the laundromat, where I sat and read the paper while my clothes were in the dryer. When the drying was complete, I shoved the clothes back in the laundry bag and walked across the cobblestone street to the barracks. I was putting the laundry away when I heard a knock on my door.

"Come on in," I said, opening the door for Grumpy John and the Pipe, a rotund, bespectacled native of Baltimore. The Pipe got his name because he was always cleaning, loading or puffing on one of his ten or fifteen pipes. Seated on his chair, which he always tilted back as far as he could. With his stubby legs and round belly, peering owlishly through thick lenses and blanketed by thick blue smoke from his pipe, the Pipe looked like a deranged Buddha.

"You doing anything?" Grumpy John said.

Grumpy John was a large, rumpled Arkansan who got his nickname shortly after he arrived in Berlin. He earned the nickname because of his personality, although he wasn't sullen or hostile. Grumpy John enjoyed a good laugh as much as the next person; but he was, for want of a better description, grumpy. It began soon after he enlisted.

Grumpy John had just finished high school and had already planned to enlist. The day after he had taken his final exams, he told his parents he was going to join the Army, but his mother begged him to wait until after the graduation ceremony, which would be on June 1 — about a week later — because seeing him receive his diploma would make her so proud of her baby boy. Grumpy John decided to please his mother and wait a few days longer before joining the ASA. On June 2, he went down to the recruiting station and signed up for a four-year stint in the ASA. Only later did he learn that

Grumpy John

had he joined in May, like he planned, his enlistment would have been only three years. The additional year for the ASA went into effect on June 1.

"No, I just finished my laundry. I was thinking about going to check out the zoo. I haven't been there yet," I said.

"Shit, Blackie, don't be a goddam tourist. Pipe and I are going to the Europa Center, why don't you come along?" Grumpy John said.

"What for?"

"We thought we'd check out the new waitress at the Hofbräuhaus. I heard she's got a set of knockers on her that won't quit, and she likes to lean over the table and let them hang out," Grumpy John said.

"Besides, there's a couple of cops we know who are going to be there, and they're always good for a couple of free beers," the Pipe said.

I thought a minute.

"Okay, just let me finish putting up my laundry and change clothes. I don't think the gate guards will let me out like this," I said, pointing out my clothes, a ragged Arkansas Razorbacks sweatshirt and my oldest and most faded jeans — attire that didn't meet the dress code of U.S. soldiers in Berlin. The U.S. commander had declared that all soldiers going out on pass had to wear a coat and tie. The guards at the barracks gates were ordered to make sure that anyone leaving the compound be dressed properly before being allowed to leave. Of course, most of us shed the ties as soon as we cleared the compound.

"I've got to get some smokes," Grumpy John said. "Why don't you meet us in the snack bar?"

"Okay. I'll just be a couple of minutes," I said, and quickly tossed all my clean socks and underwear in my footlocker, grabbed a towel and rushed to the shower room to clean up before joining my friends.

I put on a dark gray suit that I had bought a couple of weeks earlier at a men's store on the Kurfürstendamm, a broad thoroughfare that featured open-air restaurants, pubs, clubs and stores offering merchandise from around the world. I didn't want to wear a tie, but I knew I had to, so I rummaged through the bottom of my footlocker, and pulled out one that I had bought in a junk shop in Monterey. It was from the 1940s, wide and sporting a hand-painted, garish rooster, complete with feather tail.

"They want a tie, then they'll get a tie," I said to myself as I settled it into place. I looked in the mirror on the door of my wall locker. I grinned at the image of a slender young man with dark curly hair and dark complexion, and slammed the metal door shut.

"God, Guiliano was right. I do look like a goddam gangster," I said to myself, and rushed out to join my friends.

"Jesus Christ, where'd you get that piece of shit?" Grumpy John said when I joined him in the snack bar.

"I've had it since Monterey," I said. "Where's the Pipe?"

"Getting a milk shake," Grumpy John said, pointing toward the food line. "He thinks if he drinks a milk shake before going out drinking, he won't have a hangover."

"I think I'll have a cup of coffee before we go. Okay?" I said.

"Yeah, yeah. But hurry up. I want to have a few beers sometime today," Grumpy John said.

The Pipe, sipping contentedly on his milk shake, stared owlishly at my tie when I rejoined them at the table.

"I don't know if I want you with us if you're going to wear that piece of shit," he said, pointing at the tie.

"Don't worry, Pipe, it's coming off as soon as we clear the gate," I said.

"I hope to Christ it does. The goddam thing's obscene," Grumpy John said.

"Grumpy, I've always thought that if you have to wear a tie, you ought to wear one that makes people stand up and take notice," I said.

The Pipe chuckled.

"That one certainly will be noticed," he said. "Who knows? Maybe it'll make the General change his mind about us wearing ties."

At the front gate, the military policeman stared at the tie.

"What's that?" he said.

"What does it look like? It's a tie," I said.

"I don't know if it's regulation."

"Look," I said. "The General says we have to wear a tie to get off base, but he doesn't say what the tie has to look like. This is a goddam tie."

He shrugged and motioned us on through the gate.

Grumpy John, the Pipe and I started walking down Kadettenweg, a narrow street that ran about four blocks from the front gate to Ringstrasse. We hadn't gone a block before the ties, including mine, had been removed and stuffed into our pockets.

The A18 bus was pulling away as we arrived at the bus stop.

"Shit," Grumpy John said. "It'll be at least fifteen minutes before the next bus gets here."

"So? Are you in a hurry to get somewhere, Grumpy?" the Pipe said.

"I think I'll take a walk," I said.

"What for? The bus will be along in a few minutes," Grumpy John said.

"I know, but I don't want to just hang around here. I'll catch it at the next stop. Want to come along?" I said.

"Shit, no," Grumpy John said. "I did all the walking I wanted to do in basic training. I'll wait."

"Pipe?" I said.

"I'm with Grumpy. I'm staying right here like any sane person would do."

"Okay, stay here then. But I'm going on. I'll see you at the next stop," I said, and began walking off in the direction of the next bus stop.

In the two months since I arrived in Berlin, I had traveled throughout the city, but it was always by bus or subway. Now as I walked, I got a closer look at the neighborhoods that were just a flash as I had ridden by on a bus ride.

It was a beautiful spring day, and I could see the children playing and hear their shouts of joy. I saw couples working in flower beds, and neighbors engaged in conversation over fences. Often, someone would see me and wave.

I was still about three blocks away from the bus stop when the yellow, double-decker bus roared past. Grumpy John, in a window seat near the rear of the bus, saw me and grinned broadly and waved.

The bus was already gone when I reached the stop. I checked the schedule on the back wall of the shelter. The next bus wasn't due for twenty minutes, so I decided to keep walking.

As I continued my walk, the personality of the big city seemed to change. I could see that each neighborhood was distinct, with its own shops, offices, restaurants, clubs, and bars. I got the impression that Berlin wasn't just a huge sprawling city, it was a collection of several small towns.

But there was a big difference between these small towns and the small towns in southwest Arkansas where I was raised — these communities were full of life on a Sunday morning. I grew up hating Sundays at home, because except for the churches and the Greyhound station, everything was closed. Even the service stations and the movie theater were closed on Sundays. The only thing to do around town was sit on the front porch, waiting for Monday to arrive and bring life back to the town.

But here, in one of Berlin's small towns, was activity. Shoppers, many of them carrying fruit, vegetables, and loaves of bread, were entering and leaving the stores. There were people, engaged in animated conversations, sitting at tables at the sidewalk restaurants.

I noticed a small bar and decided to go in for a beer.

I had taken my seat at the end of the bar when I first noticed the bartender. I was surprised to see that it was Herbert Baugatz, a German construction worker on the Hill.

"Allo, Herbert," I said. "What are you doing here?"

He stared at me intently, then snapped his fingers, and laughed heartily.

"You're Cooper, aren't you? You were our keeper the other day, weren't you?" he said, referring to my stint on the Hill as guard of the German construction workers. Everywhere the German construction workers went on the Hill, the guard went with them, watching to make sure they didn't go where they weren't supposed to go, or see anything they weren't supposed to see.

When the German workers took a break, so did the guard. It wasn't bad duty because the workers all took a beer break in the morning and another in the afternoon. If no officers were around, the Germans often would slip a beer to the guard. Herbert, a short fireplug of a man with massive, work-roughened hands, came over to where I was sitting on a pile of lumber. He had a bottle of beer in one hand. His other hand was inside his brown corduroy jacket. He took a seat beside me, looked around, withdrew his hand from his jacket, and handed a bottle of beer to me. We sat on the pile of lumber, drinking our beer, until the break was over.

"Yeah, I'm Cooper. I almost didn't recognize you without your jackhammer. What are you doing here?" I said.

"This place belongs to my brother," Herbert said. "I help him out sometimes on Sunday. What are you doing here? You Americans never come here."

"I missed my bus, so I thought I'd just walk about. You know, get to know the city better," I said.

"That's good. You can get to know Berlin better if you don't just go to your PX and the GI bars."

"That's what I'm finding out," I said. "I didn't know every little neighborhood's just like a small town. You know, with its own stores and restaurants. You've got everything you need right here in your own neighborhood. You don't have to go all over the city to find what you're looking for."

Herbert had been wiping glasses with a washcloth. He looked up and said, "Oh, yes. Everything's right here, but if you want, you can get anywhere with the U-bahn (subway) in just a few minutes."

"I love that," I said. "At home, I have to drive everywhere. There's not even a bus system, and there's sure as hell no U-bahn. Even if we had a U-bahn, there's nothing open on Sunday except churches, so there's no place to go. God, I hate Sundays at home."

"You had no little bar you could go to?"

"Christ, no," I said. "There wasn't anything open on Sundays. I lived in a dry county."

"Dry?" Herbert said.

"It means you can't buy beer or whisky at all," I said.

"People enjoy drinking beer. Why would there be no beer?" he said.

"Too many preachers," I said. "The preachers don't want anyone to drink anything, so they make people think they'll die and go to hell if they drink a beer."

"That's foolish," Herbert said. "People are going to drink beer if they want to, even in your home town, I think. Where is your home town?"

"Nashville. It's in Arkansas," I said.

"Arkansas? I know Arkansas. It is a beautiful place," Herbert said.

"You're kidding," I said. "You've been to Arkansas? When were you there?"

"Oh, 1943, 1944, and 1945," Herbert said and grinned. "I was sent to a prisoner of war camp in Arkansas after I was captured in North Africa. For me, the war was not too bad. To me, your Arkansas was beautiful, but it was so terribly hot in the summers that I thought I would die. Oh, and the mosquitoes. My God, they were as big as Messerschmitts, I swear to you."

Our conversation was interrupted when several customers, all of whom seemed to be regulars, came in, and Herbert began filling mugs of beer. I finished my beer, waved goodbye to Herbert, and went back outside to resume my walk about the city.

For the rest of the day, and well into the night, I wandered the streets of Berlin, walking from Lichterfelde in the south to Wedding, near the sprawling Tegel International Airport in the north. Now and then, I would stop in a neighborhood bar, sipping my beer and watching the people as they enjoyed this beautiful spring Sunday.

As I walked about Berlin, I was aware of the aromas. Berlin was a city filled with a variety of aromas — exotic coffees brewing in the cafes, curried sausages sold by sidewalk vendors, beer when a keg was tapped in a bar, bread as it was removed from the baker's oven, and even the hay that fed or bed the animals at the Berlin Zoo.

In Wedding, my first walkabout came to an end. I was sitting in a small bar, listening to Frank and The Captains, a five-piece jazz band led by a GI saxophonist and which also had Germans playing guitar, bass, organ and drums. I was enjoying the music, but after several numbers, I decided to leave. When I got out to the sidewalk, I realized that I was completely exhausted. I saw the bus turning the corner on its way to the bus stop just outside the bar. I climbed aboard, paid for a transfer to the A18 bus that would take me back to Lichterfelde and the barracks, and collapsed into the first empty seat.

Forty-five minutes later, just before four o'clock in the

morning, I stepped off the bus in Lichterfelde, and began walking the final blocks to the barracks. But I turned just before the barracks gate and entered the Scum.

"Hey, Blackie," someone shouted as I approached the bar. I turned, and saw the Pipe sitting in one of the booths that lined the wall of the old bar. "Come on and join us."

"Just a sec, let me get a beer," I said, and motioned to the bartender. He slammed a bottle on the bar in front of me and snatched up the one-mark coin I slid across the bar toward him.

The Pipe moved to the inside of the booth, and I saw Grumpy John, his head cradled in his arms, sound asleep across the table from him. I sat down next to the Pipe.

"What's with Grumpy?" I said.

"He's catching some Zs, but he'll come to in a few minutes, and he'll want another beer. He always does," the Pipe said. "Now that you're here, will you keep an eye on him? He's really shitfaced, and I've got to get back to the barracks."

"Yeah, sure," I said. I got up and stood back, letting the Pipe slide out of the booth. Then I took his place across from Grumpy John.

"Where'd you go after you missed the bus?" the Pipe said.

"I took a walk."

"Hell of a walk. You've been gone about fourteen hours," he said.

"It was one hell of a walk, Pipe. I saw stuff that I'd never have seen on the bus. What'd you guys do?" I said.

"We stayed in the Hofbräuhaus, drinking beer with a bunch of Berlin cops until about midnight, then we came here. Grumpy went to sleep about thirty minutes ago, and I'm going to be asleep in about ten minutes myself, now that you're here."

I sipped slowly on my beer, and thought about my walkabout, which would be the first of many solitary walks around Berlin that I would take. I would take different routes, visiting different areas of the city, and, as I became more comfortable with my German, I would find myself drawn into conversation with the Berliners, whom I learned were wondrously talkative.

A few minutes after the Pipe had left, Grumpy John lifted his head. He shook his head and frowned until I came into focus. Then he grinned when he saw me sitting across the table from him.

"Blackie, we had a hell of a good time, didn't we?"

"We sure did, Grumpy," I said. "We sure the hell did."

The Green Weenie Award

6 Grumpy John liked to brag the Green Weenie Award was his idea; however, like so many other things Grumpy John liked to brag about, it just didn't happen that way. Grumpy John received the first Green Weenie Award, but Big Clyde came up with the idea a few weeks before he rotated back to the States.

Big Clyde said he got the idea because of all the dumb things the Army manages to do.

"Dumbness is contagious. Hell, I used to be reasonably bright before I joined the Army," Big Clyde said as he stood in the breakroom, sipping a cup of coffee and taking deep drags on a Pall Mall.

"You're still pretty bright, Big Clyde," I said as I flipped the lever and let the dark coffee run into my mug.

"Well, maybe I am, but I used to be a goddam Einstein. I could pick up anything and read it, like Dos Passos or Faulkner. Now about all I can read are comic books and Shell Scott. I've got to face it, I'm just getting dumber every goddam day I'm in the Army."

"Why worry? You're nearly short. In a few weeks, you'll be out of the Army and you can get smart again."

"I don't know if I know how. I'm afraid I'm going to be as dumb as a tread for the rest of my life. Now I know why those assholes stay in the Army; they've just gotten too goddam dumb. I bet even Roadrunner was smart at one time, but after a few years in the Army ..."

"He got dumb as a rock," I interrupted. "Shit, Big Clyde, if they gave out awards for stupidity, Roadrunner would be a Nobel Prize winner."

"You know, Newk, that's a damn fine idea."

"What is?"

"A prize for dumbness."

"If they're giving out prizes for dumbness, I think Dirty Joe ought to get one," Hairy Ranger said, startling Big Clyde and me. We didn't know Hairy Ranger had been standing in the doorway behind us.

"How long you been there, Ranger?" I said.

"Long enough to know a good idea when I hear one."

"Okay, we're going to have an award for dumbness, but what do we call it and who gets it?" Big Clyde said, his voice rising in excitement.

Ranger had opened the refrigerator and peered inside. He frowned when he looked at the Army C ration foodstuffs in the refrigerator.

"Goddam, look at this shit," he said, then rummaged through packages on the refrigerator shelves before finding a pack of C Ration wieners. He held up the package, turning it around several times in his hand. "The goddam things are green. Jesus Christ on a crutch, they're fucking green!"

He threw the package back in the refrigerator and slammed the door.

"Goddammit! Does even the goddam food have to be green! Green goddam clothes, green goddam buses and now we have to eat green goddam weenies," Hairy Ranger said angrily.

"That's it, by God!" Big Clyde shouted.

"What's it?" Hairy Ranger and I said in unison.

"The award, assholes. We'll present the Green Weenie Award to whoever does something really, really goddam dumb. Blackie, you said you used to draw cartoons, so you can draw up a green Weenie to go on a certificate and I'll get the Pipe to type up a certificate and we can give to the winner."

"When do we give the award?"

I had already grabbed a pencil and began to rough out a big, fat weenie on a piece of paper. All I needed to do is color it green, I thought.

"How about on the first mid after coming off eves' break?"

"Sounds good to me," I said.

"Me, too," Ranger said.

"Fine, now we can spread the word. Whoever does the

dumbest goddam thing on break after eves gets the Green Weenie Award. We'll all vote on it as soon as we start mids."

"What about the treads? They do dumb things all the time, and they might even want some recognition for it," Hairy Ranger said.

"No, hell no. No treads," Big Clyde said brusquely. "They're goddam professional dumbasses; the Green Weenie Award's just for amateurs."

It would be nearly three weeks before C Trick would be back on mids, and we gathered in Violet to decide who would earn the first-ever Green Weenie Award.

Big Clyde sat on top of a file cabinet, crossing his legs like a demented Buddha, and called the group to order.

"Okay, assholes, we're going to decide who's been the biggest dumbass of all us over break. Don't give me any piddling little stupid shit, only really Class A gross dumbass shit can be nominated. Who's got the first nominee?"

Hairy Ranger jumped up, waving his hand.

"Prince! Give the Green Weenie to Prince," he shouted.

"You sorry sack of shit," Prince said. "It wasn't dumb; it was just a goddam mistake."

"Some mistake, you asshole."

"Stow it, both of you. Ranger, what makes you think Prince deserves the Green Weenie?" Big Clyde said, then pulled a pencil out of his pocket and held it, poised, over the notepad.

"Well," Hairy Ranger said, pausing to look around for his chair. He made sure Prince, who had been standing behind him, didn't pull it away as he sat down. After settling safely into the chair, he put his feet up on the desk in front of the bank of receivers and tape recorders and resumed his story.

"I had been down to Randy's. God knows where Prince had been, but anyway, about two o'clock when I'm getting ready to go back to the barracks and cop some Zs, in walks Prince. I knew it was him without even looking because I heard the door slam and someone walk down the foyer. Then, all of a sudden, the footsteps stop, like someone's standing still, so I knew it was Prince because he always stops right under that light in the foyer so everybody can see that he's arrived."

"Hey, Prince, why do you stand under the light like that?" Shakey said.

"So you peasants can kiss my ass," Prince said and drew himself up regally.

"Knock off the bullshit, I still want to know why Prince deserves the Green Weenie," Big Clyde said.

"Well, like I was saying," Hairy Ranger resumed. "Prince came in and he was shitfaced. We drank a couple of beers and after Randy ran our asses out, we made it back to the barracks. I was sitting on my rack, trying to get my shit together when I looked up and there was Prince, his weenie out, starting to piss in my goddam locker."

Suddenly Ranger's feet slammed onto the floor as he straightened up in his chair, whirled around and pointed at Prince, whose face had turned beet red, and shouted, "Son of a bitch thought he was in the goddam latrine!"

"Fuck you! Fuck you all! I don't have to stay here and take this shit!" Prince shouted and stormed out of the room, nearly colliding with Roadrunner.

Roadrunner looked confused, then he saw the group gathered in the room. He sidled into the room, glaring at me as if I were somehow responsible for Prince's fit of temper. I tried to look back innocently at Roadrunner, although both he and I knew I'd just as soon go for his throat as look at him.

"Hmm, what's going on here? Playing pocket pool?" Roadrunner said, his Adam's apple darting up and down as he bounced on the balls of his feet.

"We're just deciding who gets the Green Weenie Award, Sarge," Big Clyde said. "We just got to finish voting, and then we'll be done."

"Green Weenie Award? What's that scene?"

"Just a morale-booster, Sarge. It's just something to get the guys going good on mids."

"Hmm, morale-booster? Hmm."

Roadrunner seemed to be turning this one over in his mind, afraid to ask anymore because it might have been something the 78th's commander came up with and if he didn't know about it, he didn't want us to know he'd been left in the dark, so he rubbed his chin, and then scurried out of the room.

"Jesus, what a dip," Hairy Ranger said.

"Enough of that, who's next?" Big Clyde wanted to get on with the business of selecting the first-ever Green Weenie Award winner.

"How about Grumpy John?" I said, then I kicked the bottom of his boot. Grumpy John had already gone to sleep, and even had begun to snore. I don't think Grumpy John had been awake a full mid since he arrived in Berlin.

Grumpy John shook his head and slowly opened his eyes.

"Wh-what? Time to get out of the Army yet?"

"Not yet, Grumpy. You've been nominated for the Green Weenie Award. You want to explain why you ought to get it, or do you want me to?" I asked.

"Well, why don't you just do it, asshole? You're going to anyway."

"Well, since Grumpy's so   modest, I guess I'll have to talk for him," I said, leaning forward in my chair.

"I guess most of us know about the El Dorado Bar ...," I started, but suddenly there was an explosion of laughter.

"Oh, my God! Not you, Grumpy!" Big Clyde said. "Son, you've been here long enough to have been down there."

The El Dorado Bar probably picked up half of its business from the 78th, with at least one group of old-timers rounding up a couple of newks and taking them out for their first real night out on the town in Berlin. After stops at the Scum, Linda's Lounge and a few other pubs, the group, with the newks feeling the first effects of all the beer, would arrive at the El Dorado Bar in the British sector.

The bar had an air of sophistication about it. It was most than just a bar. Inside, the music didn't blare from the junk box, the El Dorado featured a jazz combo with sultry female vocalists doing Ella Fitzgerald and Sarah Vaughn numbers. The bartender wore a cummerbund and a rakish bowtie, and leggy waitresses in evening gowns moved languidly throughout the bar filling drink orders. The place personified classiness.

One of the first things every newk noticed had to be the hostesses; it seemed as if all of the contestants in the Miss

World contest had taken jobs at the El Dorado Bar. The young women all exuded an air of seductiveness, of mystery.

But they weren't women.

All of the beautiful women — hostesses and singers — in the El Dorado Bar were men. The El Dorado Bar was the biggest transvestite establishment in Berlin, maybe even in Germany, and had been a permanent fixture on the ASA's off-limits list, although most of the newks had long since forgotten the off-limits bars by the time they arrived at the El Dorado.

After a few more drinks in the El Dorado, the newk would find a gorgeous creature in a long evening gown easing onto his lap, gently flicking a tongue in an ear, rubbing his hair and giving a long, passionate kiss, complete with heavy tongue action. If he weren't too drunk, the newk would quickly have an enormous erection.

The beautiful woman would suggest going to a more private place, pointing to the booths against the walls, all with heavy brocade curtains that could be closed. The newk gladly followed the gorgeous creature into one of the booths, all the while wondering why his buddies had shunned female companionship and were laughing so heartily.

Grumpy John, Chief, Buffalo Head and Tiny had been the old-timers who introduced me to the El Dorado Bar. If they had told me the beautiful women I saw around me weren't women at all, I wouldn't have believed them. In the small town where I grew up in Arkansas, a Baptist-dominated community, where homosexuals and transvestites stayed well back in their closets. Although I knew homosexuals were out there, I just couldn't believe that any man, no matter how effeminate, could pass himself off for a woman — even an actor as talented as Jack Lemmon couldn't make himself look like a woman in Some Like it Hot.

My buddies didn't tell me about the El Dorado's women, and they never intended to do so. As Grumpy John told me later, "Blackie, some things you just have to find out for yourself."

Like many ASA newks before me and many who would come later, I got my introduction to the Big Hummer, the nickname given to the tall, blonde transvestite who enjoyed fellatio and made odd humming sounds as she (or he) went about her business.

So, when Erika, a.k.a. Big Hummer, suggested we go into one of the curtained booths for a bit more privacy, I didn't protest, almost knocking down another hostesses in my rush to get behind the brocade curtains with this gorgeous creature who seemed to enjoy my company.

We shared several deep, passionate kisses and I felt a hand gently rubbing my erection. I slipped my hand under Erika's gown and slid it up her thigh, stopping suddenly when I encountered something that shouldn't have been there.

Erika had a cock that felt like a billy club. I didn't think I'd ever seen a cock so big in my life, and I certainly knew I hadn't felt one of that magnitude. My erection disappeared immediately; my eyes widened in stunned disbelief; I sat up rigidly in the booth.

"Oh, holy shit!"

Erika looked at me; he/she/it smiled crookedly.

"Bitte?"

"You're a man!"

"Do I look like a man?"

"No, goddammit, you're the most beautiful woman I've ever seen, but you sure as hell feel like a man, and I'm getting the hell out of here."

I stood up, straightened my clothes and, trying to be as casual as possible, tried to leave without being spotted. But I didn't get halfway to the front entrance before Grumpy John, Chief, Buffalo Head and Tiny saw me.

"There he is. Hey, Blackie!" Grumpy John called.

I ignored them and kept walking, not stopping until I was back on the sidewalk outside.

Moments later, my four chaperones, now laughing so hard they gasped for breath, joined me.

"Now, son, your life's complete; you've met the Big Hummer," Tiny said, throwing his arm around my shoulders.

"Is this some kind of goddam initiation?" I asked.

"As far as I know, just about every newk's been brought to El Dorado," Buffalo Head said. "Big Clyde brought me. I was so damn drunk it seemed like it took five minutes for my brain to figure out what my hand had found."

"Hell, we had one guy try to punch out the Big Hummer, and a goddam bouncer pulled a knife. I was afraid we weren't going to get him out of there alive," Tiny said, shaking his head at the memory.

"Dammit, it just doesn't seem fair for a guy to be such a good-looking woman," I said. "Jesus, what a waste."

When I started explaining why I thought Grumpy John deserved the Green Weenie Award, the group in Violet pulled their chairs closer together, like I had discovered the secret of life.

"Well, Grumpy John came by my room. He said Rock Weed needed to be initiated into the ways of the world, and he couldn't find anyone to go along with them. I didn't have anything better to do, so I decided I'd help Grumpy initiate the newk," I said, and paused to light a cigarette.

"Let's make a long story short. We went to the El Dorado Bar. Everything was going just like it's supposed to, Rock Weed was shitfaced and really making out with some new girl, guy, whatever. Anyway, they ease off to go to one of the booths, and I look around for Grumpy who was as shitfaced as the newk and then I see that son of a bitch disappearing into another booth with the Big Hummer."

"Grumpy, Grumpy, Grumpy. Son, what's the matter with you?" Big Clyde said and laughed. "I initiated you myself."

Grumpy John fidgeted, tried to light a cigarette, but his fingers seemed stiff and he couldn't hold the cigarette. Fang, who had just lit a cigarette, quietly passed it to the embarrassed Grumpy John.

"Anyhow, that's why I think Grumpy John deserves the Green Weenie. Hell, all of us have visited the Big Hummer, but Grumpy John's the only guy to get drunk enough to go back for seconds."

Everyone agreed, and Grumpy John became the first recipient of the Green Weenie Award — a C-ration wiener, painted green and placed on a bed of cotton in a watch box. The awards ceremony became a pleasant addition to our mids schedule for the next few months until Fang permanently retired it.

Halopowski's Wife

7After Big Clyde, proudly wearing his four-star tie clasp, rotated back to the States, the site commander decided to fill the vacancy on C Trick by shifting someone from one of the other tricks. He looked over the trick rosters and decided to take Halopowski away from D Trick, which was on break, and put him on C Trick, which was on eves.

I didn't know Halopowski. I only knew he did the same thing on D Trick that Big Clyde had done on C Trick. On the day Halopowski would join C Trick, Stashik bumped into me in line at the PX snack bar.

"Hear you're getting Halopowski," he said, his eyes tiny behind his thick lenses. Stashik wore the thickest lenses I'd ever seen on anyone who wasn't actually blind. Even with glasses, his vision was so poor he almost didn't pass the Army's physical. Even in the days when the war in Vietnam was heating up and the Army needed available bodies, Stashik nearly failed the physical, which would have put him in the same company as professional football players and politicians' sons.

"What's he like?" I said.

"Oh, he's a damn nice little guy, but we sure feel sorry for him. Everyone feels sorry for him."

I didn't understand why the D Trickers felt sorry for Halopowski. I'd seen him at shift change when D Trick replaced C Trick at the Hill. He didn't seem like someone we should feel sorry for; he was a gentle, soft-spoken and rotund little man with a round face and rosy cheeks, a human cherub with a smile that made his whole face light up.

"He's married."

"Shit, Stashik, a bunch of guys are married, and look at the treads, most of them are married."

"But, they're not married to Halopowski's wife," he said. "Just wait until you meet her. Poor bastard hasn't smiled since she got over here."

When I got to the Hill that night, I went to the Pit to meet Halopowski. He was glum, shuffling around like an old man, his shoulders stooped as if he were carrying a heavy burden, and his whole demeanor was downcast and joyless.

He was so gloomy that I turned around and went back to Violet, deciding to introduce myself later when he felt better.

"You meet Halopowski?" Grumpy John said. "He's no Big Clyde."

"No one's Big Clyde, not even Big Clyde, and I saw Halopowski, but I didn't say anything to him. Jesus Christ, the man looks like he's suicidal," I said.

"If I had his wife, I know I'd think about killing myself," Grumpy John said.

"Me, too," Shakey said.

"Not me, I'd harpoon the bitch," Hairy Ranger said.

"Christ, she can't be that bad," I said.

"She is. Believe me, she is. I saw her in the PX a couple of days ago, and she scared me," Hairy Ranger said.

I shook my head, put on my headsets, and prepared to listen in as the East German bureaucrats wrapped up work for the day. Conversation in the room started up again, but no one brought up Halopowski's wife.

My first encounter with her came two days later, after C Trick went on break.. We had worked six straight shifts of 3 p.m. to 11 p.m. After the sixth eve, we'd be off for 48 hours before working six 11 p.m. to 7 a.m. shifts, or mids. After the mids, we'd be off for 72 hours, before working six day shifts and being off for 72 hours, and then starting the whole series again.

I'd finished eves and was getting ready to enjoy my time off. It was a beautiful summer day, and I decided to go to a little Pakistani restaurant on Savignyplatz, off Kantstrasse and a few blocks from the Europa Center.

I didn't have a car and didn't want to pay extra to take a cab, so I decided to catch the military shuttle bus from the barracks to the main PX on Clayalle, near the U.S. head-quarters. The subway stop was just a block's walk away from the bus stop and for fifty pfennigs, or about twelve and a half cents, I could get there quickly and without the hassle of traffic.

The bus was filling up when I got on, and I saw Buffalo Head sitting by himself about halfway back. Buffalo Head was tagged with that nickname because his head — which was covered with very thick, curly dark red hair — was slightly oversized for his short, stocky body.

I had just settled in next to Buffalo Head when he gasped.

"Oh sweet Jesus, we're in for it now," he said.

"What the hell are you talking about, Buff?" I said.

"It's Halopowski's wife," he said, pointing out the window toward the front of the bus. I looked in the direction he was pointing and I saw her: Halopowski's wife.

She was an enormous woman, obese with great pendulous breasts so large gravity had pulled them toward the ground. With her bright red, curly and apparently unmanageable hair towering high above her ruddy face, she appeared to be twice as tall as her husband, who was hunkering down. While Halopowski was soft-spoken, she was a human foghorn, bellowing obscenities at the top of her lungs. He was polite, but she was rude, shoving her way to the head of lines and daring anyone to challenge her.

She was crude and rude, a mean-spirited harridan who was furious with the world and the people who were in her way.

Seeing her for the first time could be a shock — even if you'd been warned. I guess it was a lot like that first night on a new job. You'd gone through all the orientation, received all the training and listened to the old veterans tell you what to expect, but no matter how much training you'd received, the first problem to come up always was something for which you weren't prepared.

She moved like a fullback as she elbowed past other people lining up to board the bus. While one elbow was slamming like a piledriver into the side of a stunned Signal Corps master sergeant, the other was smashing into the back of a young Filipina, who looked as if she regretted marrying an American GI and leaving her native country.

Almost overlooked amid the turmoil was a small child who appeared to be dangling from her fat left arm like a piece of human jewelry. Trailing behind her, downcast and mumbling apologies to the other passengers who had been shoved, elbowed and verbally assaulted by his wife, was Halopowski.

When she reached the top step of the bus, she turned and glared at her morose husband.

"Come on here, quit dragging your ass," she said.

"Yes, Mona," Halopowski said, his voice barely above a whisper.

Looking fiercely at a young civilian-clad soldier sitting alone on the front seat, Halopowski's wife ordered the young man to get out of that seat because she needed it for her kid and husband, who by now was blushing with embarrassment.

"Christ, lady," the young soldier said, as he slid out of the seat and moved to another one across the aisle.

"I'm sorry. I'm sorry," Halopowski said, only to receive a sharp rap on the back of his head from his wife.

"Goddammit, stop being sorry all the time," Halopowski's wife said. "We needed this seat. I got this goddam kid and my feet are hurting. Why do I have to do every goddam thing? When you going to get some balls?"

Halopowski appeared to be shrinking right before our eyes.

"Man, she's a real piece of work, isn't she?" Buffalo Head said. "Ever seen anything like it? My God, if I were married to that, I'd put in for another tour of 'Nam."

"I heard Halopowski did, but he was turned down," I said.

"Talk about a life of shit," Buffalo Head said, shaking his head and looking sympathetically at the miserable little man sitting next to his wife. "Halopowski's wrecked. I bet he couldn't even blow his brains out if he tried."

Halopowski's life became more miserable by the day as his wife continued her reign of terror. No one was safe from her. She was an equal opportunity abuser, venting her con-

siderable and profane spleen on everyone, from the Turkish
guest worker who cleaned up the tables in the PX snack bar
to the company first sergeant, who darted out of his office
one day with Halopowski's wife close behind.

"Come back here, you fat shit! My husband's been on KP
three goddam times this fucking month! You trying to jerk
me around, you fat toad," she screamed.

The first sergeant, while overweight and a chain smoker,
was still swift enough to get away from her. Later sitting in
the NCO club, gulping beer, he admitted he was afraid she
would catch him.

"Jesus Christ, I hate to think what would have happened
if that bitch could run," he said. "I didn't dare tell her that
Halopowski volunteered for KP."

Days stretched into weeks, and Halopowski's wife continued to wage war against her neighbors in the military housing, with the PX employees, cab and bus drivers, the entire
Berlin subway system, the MPs who were sent to her home
because she was screaming at Halopowski and their baby,
and anyone else who crossed her path.

As his wife's reputation spread, Halopowski became more
withdrawn and morose. He seldom spoke to anyone, keeping his eyes on the ground as he shuffled around the site.

Her reign of terror ended in a burst of profanity, directed
at the unit commander, Halopowski's company commander
and the pair of uncomfortable military policemen who accompanied the officers to Halopowski's quarters.

The officers had come on a mission to save unit morale
and the good will of the other units that shared the housing — and probably the good will of the Germans, British
and French, who shared space in Berlin — by bundling
Halopowski's wife and baby up, putting her on a plane, and
flying her back to the States.

The skies turned blue with the profanity. Halopowski's
wife screamed curse words that even the veteran career officers had never heard used before. But cursing, stomping,
and screaming didn't stop the MPs from carrying out their
duty. She and her baby were put on the plane at Tegel Airport and flew off, never to return to Berlin.

A few days later, all of her belongings, packed in wooden

crates, were shipped back to the States to join her, and Halopowski moved back into the barracks.

The loss of his wife had a profound effect on Halopowski. He had a spring in his step, he laughed, he joked, he looked everyone squarely in the eye. He even whistled as he packed his belongings and moved into the barracks, just in time to become a suspect in the Case of the Phantom Shitter.

Bodily Functions in the Night

8 Prince was the Phantom Shitter's first victim. Moments after his alarm went off, Prince grabbed his soap, towel and shaving gear and headed for the shower room. As he opened the door and stepped into the hallway, he suddenly hopped back into the room, holding one foot off the floor. His eyes, which only minutes before had been sleep-filled, were wide open and wild.

"Sweet Jesus Christ! What asshole did this? Jesus Christ, this is disgusting! It's goddam disgusting! Fucking asshole!"

By now Hairy Ranger and I, who had shared the room with Prince since Doc had been promoted, were wide awake and staring at him as he continued to hop around on one foot.

"What the hell's the matter with you, Prince?" Hairy Ranger said.

"Man, I was trying to get a few extra Zs. What the hell's set you off?" I said.

"I stepped in shit," Prince said.

"Shit?" Hairy Ranger said. "Son, you're in a barracks, not a goddam barn. What do you mean, shit?"

"Shit! I mean S-fucking-H-I-T, shit. The kind that comes out of assholes. That kind of shit, you turd," a red-faced Prince said.

Hairy Ranger and I got out of our bunks and walked to the door. Looking down at the hall floor, we saw it. It was unmistakable. There, just outside the doorway, was a pile, with the color and odor of excrement. What had been a rounded pile had been flattened by Prince's bare foot.

"No doubt about it, Prince, it's shit," Hairy Ranger said.

"And you stepped in it," I said.

"Great. Just fucking great, but who the hell's the asshole who took a dump right outside the door?" Prince said.

"Is there anyone who has a reason to get even with you for something, Prince?" Hairy Ranger said.

"Of course not, you asshole, and what makes you think

I'm the one it was meant for? You two bunk in this room, too," Prince said.

"Yeah, but let's face it, Prince," I said. "Everybody likes the Ranger and me, but you've got that annoying habit."

"What the hell are you talking about? What annoying habit?" Prince said.

"Well, for instance," I said, then pausing as if to collect my thoughts. "When you come in Randy's, you don't just walk in, you have to stop under the light in the foyer, like you want everyone to see that you're there before you make your royal entrance. If you remember, that's why you're called Prince in the first place. Outside the Brits, just about everyone hates royalty."

"That's right, Prince. So it's got to be you that our Phantom Shitter's targeted," Hairy Ranger said.

"Fuck you both," Prince said as he walked, awkwardly because he was walking on the side of one foot, toward the shower. "Yeah, and screw the Phantom Shitter, too!"

Prince was right about one thing — he wasn't the only target of the Phantom Shitter.

Over the next several weeks, the Phantom Shitter left his calling card outside the door of Tub, a guitar-playing sergeant from Arkansas. Tub loved to crank up his Fender Stratocaster and belt out old Hawkshaw Hawkins numbers at the top of his lungs. Even without amplifiers and microphones, Tub's singing and playing would be loud, but with the electrical assistance it became positively ear-splitting.

Halopowski became the first prime suspect because the attacks didn't start until after he moved into the barracks. But Halopowski was cleared on the night the Phantom Shitter left his calling card outside Tub's door. Halopowski had been in the Scum with Chief, Doc and Grumpy John when Tub discovered he had become a victim.

Another unappreciated present was deposited outside the door of Catfish, a South Alabama redneck who bore a striking resemblance to his namesake. Catfish had a license to drive a trick bus but didn't have the nerve to drive the bus up the Hill when it was snowing. Catfish decided the road up the Hill would be too slick to drive, so he parked his bus at the foot of the Hill, pocketed the keys and set out of foot, leaving his 37 irate passengers to follow him through the snow. Their mood wasn't improved at all when the second trick bus roared past them on its way to the parking lot at the top of the Hill.

The shit-and-run tactics began to take their toll on the barracks.

Members of A Trick were positive that the Phantom Shitter was from D Trick, which was equally sure that he was from B Trick, which in turn blamed C Trick. The C Trick members denied vehemently that the Phantom Shitter was one of their own, but privately they agreed it was something a C Tricker probably would do.

There were several plans floated to capture the Phantom Shitter, but he always managed to escape detection.

"Of course, we're not catching the Phantom Shitter. We're not catching him because he's probably one of us," Hairy Ranger said.

"You admitting it's you, Ranger?" I said.

"Fuck you! It's not me, but it could just as easy be you. Hell, maybe Prince took a dump outside his door and tried to make everyone think it's someone else."

"But I was the first one to get a shit doormat. Why the hell would I be trying to make everyone think it's someone else when no one knew there was a Phantom Shitter in the first place?" Prince said.

"You got to admit the boy's got a point, Ranger," I said.

"Maybe it's a copycat Phantom Shitter," Ranger said.

"Copycat Phantom Shitter?" I said.

"Yeah, maybe the first couple of attacks were the real thing, but then someone else decided to settle an old score or two by leaving the Phantom Shitter's calling card."

"No, no, I think it's just one person. It's not likely C Trick's got more than one sick bastard like the Phantom Shitter."

"Jesus Christ, I'm getting the hell out of here. I can't believe I'm hearing this goddam conversation," Prince said angrily. He jumped up from his bunk and stomped out, slamming the door behind him.

After a few weeks, the Phantom Shitter's raids became less frequent and people no longer looked first before stepping out of their rooms into the hallways. As attention to turned to other things, the Phantom Shitter made his first — and last — mistake, which led to his identification.

Chief made the discovery early one morning as he headed for the latrine. About halfway down the hallway, he saw a pile in front of Rapid Roger's room. This pile was different, however, because the Phantom Shitter had stepped in it.

Chief rushed back to his room where Hairy Ranger and Prince and I were playing hearts with a beer-soaked deck of Bee cards.

"Come on, you guys, I've caught the Phantom Shitter. I know who the bastard is," Chief said as he burst into the room.

We rushed out of the room behind Chief, who showed them the pile of excrement and the tell-tale trail that led from where the Phantom Shitter had made his raid down the hallway and to the room occupied — alone — by Fat Kenny.

There was Fat Kenny, snoring contentedly in his bunk as he slept off a long night of barhopping. There was beer on his breath — and crap on his foot.

"What do we do with him?" I said.

"Give him a goddam blanket party," Prince said. "Just jerk the goddam blanket over his head and beat the crap out of him."

"Shit, Prince, that's what 'Gators do," I said.

"I've got an idea," Chief said. "Wait here and I'll be right back. Don't wake him."

Chief eased out of the room and ran down the hallway.

"What's he up to?" Prince said.

Hairy Ranger and I shrugged.

We didn't have to wait long because Chief, carrying a camera with a flash attachment, re-entered the room. Prince, Hairy Ranger and I moved out of the camera's range while Chief took a picture of Fat Kenny with the shit on his foot.

A few days later, a photograph of a sleeping Phantom Shitter was tacked to the bulletin board.

The YAK Crash

8 A sudden roar and the scream of jet engines caused me to start, slamming my knee against the bottom of the metal desk attached to the banks of radio receivers and tape recorders where I sat eavesdropping on East German bureaucrats. I jostled my cup of coffee, which splashed on my leg.

"Holy shit! What the hell was that?" I said as I pulled a paper towel out of the desk drawer and began wiping the coffee from my leg.

"Maybe the Phantom Shitter's got a plane now," Grumpy John said. "But it's probably the goddam Russians buzzing us again."

"What do you mean, buzzing us?"

"Hell, the assholes like to do it every now and then. You know, fly real low over our side of Berlin, just making a lot of racket. They haven't pulled this number in a few months — probably like to wait until summer. Anyway, they always come in real low over the Hill. I guess it's to let us know they know what we're doing up here. Nothing to it. Son of a bitch is probably landing at his base right now."

Chief said, "I don't think so, Grumpy. Sounded like that plane was coming from south of us. Hell, the fuckers always fly north to south over us. I'll bet it's coming back." He stood up and hung his headsets on the hook attached to his desk. "Come on, Blackie, let's go see a MiG."

I slapped my headsets on the top of my desk and followed Chief out of the dimly lit room with the hundreds of flickering lights. I had to blink when we emerged from the building. It was a beautiful summer day in Berlin, almost no clouds and the warmth of the sun's rays loosening the muscles which had grown tight from having to listen to the conversations of the East German government workers droning on and on about crop reports, breakdowns in factories, shortages of spare parts, and lack of hard currency, as well as gripes about the paperwork and Russians. Several C Trickers were leaning against the fence, smoking cigarettes and enjoying the warm sunshine.

"Hey, Big Ed," Chief said to a heavyset Russian linguist from Boston. "What was it?"

"One of those goddam new MiGs, with a pilot and navigator. Son of a bitch came from that way," he said, pointing toward the south, "and just disappeared. Man, that goddam plane was just screaming."

"Think he's coming back?" I said, squinting as I peered toward the north in the direction Big Ed said the plane disappeared.

"It wouldn't surprise me. Hell, I've never seen one make a south to north run over us."

"Holy shit! Look! He's coming back," Fang shouted, jumping up and down as he pointed toward the north.

A black speck in the distance began to grow rapidly as the Soviet fighter screamed low over Berlin heading straight for Teufelsberg. Within seconds we could see the plane clearly as it whizzed across the western sector of the city. We could see it was dropping lower and lower, the wings dipping as if the pilot were fighting to stay in control.

"Jesus Christ, he's going to crash," Fang said as the plane, now trailing smoke, roared past the Hill so low we could see the pilot and co-pilot in the cockpit fighting to maintain control of the aircraft. While we stood gaping, the plane veered sharply to the east, then disappeared from our sight in the direction of the Havel, a river inside the British sector of Berlin.

"Hey, any of you assholes see that goddam Russian jet?" Dirty Joe said with a shout as he threw open the door leading to the Pit. "Russian Marys picked up the pilots yelling about going down."

"It went down over there," Big Ed said, and pointed to the Havel. I couldn't be sure, but I thought I could hear the "doo-bee, doo-bee" sirens in the distance.

"Okay, break's over; everybody get your asses back to work — especially you Russian Marys," Dirty Joe said.

"Jesus, I'm glad to see you," Doc said when Big Ed eased back into his seat and reached for his headsets. "All hell's busted out with the goddam Russians. That plane went down in the Havel. We heard them talking all the way down and then nothing, nothing but static. The Russians are shitting bricks."

"It was a MiG, and we saw it going down, pouring smoke all the way. Just lucky it didn't crash into the Hill, for Christ's sake," Big Ed said.

"It wasn't a MiG, it was a YAK," Doc said, referring to a colorful aerobatics plane built by the Soviet Yakovlev Design Bureau. The YAK had been a crowd-pleaser at recent air shows around Europe.

"YAK?" Big Ed said. "I didn't know they had any of those in Berlin."

"Shit!" Doc said as the last few inches of recording tape fed through the recorder head. "Blackie, will you log out another tape for me?"

I turned to the green metal cabinet holding hundreds of reels of recording tape. I logged it in the book and used a red grease pencil to write the tape number on the reel. Then I handed it to Doc, who slapped it onto the recorder and fed the tape through the head to the take-up reel. He grabbed the microphone and almost shouted, "Beginning of tape, beginning of tape. This is tape number Sierra fifteen seven twenty; tape number Sierra fifteen seven twenty — Uniform Sierra Mike, Six Twenty Kilo; Uniform Sierra Mike, Six Twenty Kilo."

"Catch you guys later," I said and maneuvered my way past scurrying Russian Marys and traffic analysts on my way back to my banks of recorders and receivers. I didn't look forward to it; by now all of the East German offices knew a Russian fighter had crashed in West Berlin, and worried bureaucrats would be trying to find out if it we were going to war.

The East Germans were having a fit because the Russians were not sharing any information with either the East German military or the SED bureaucrats.

"They treat us like shit," a district leader in Leipzig told his counterpart in Potsdam. I punched each button as it lit up, checking to see which East German officials were on the lines. With a Soviet YAK down in the British sector of Berlin, the treads on the Hill thought Walter Ulbricht, the East German leader, might make a few calls himself. Ulbricht might have been a tough customer back in East Germany's early days, but by the time I found myself sitting on the Hill and eavesdropping on his government, he had become a tired old man. Even though the treads had convinced themselves Ulbricht would be making telephone calls, the old man kept quiet.

Although we got nothing useful from the East German officials, the Russian Marys couldn't keep enough blank tapes on their recorders as the Russians made call after call to Moscow to try to find out what to do, especially after the British sealed off the crash area and wouldn't allow the Soviet mission anywhere near the plane.

But the East Germans weren't the only ones not getting the information they thought they should be receiving. The British didn't share anything with their Berlin allies, so the National Security Agency civilians on the Hill suggested some of the German linguists switch to the British frequencies and monitor our allies.

"Hell, I'm not a British Mary; I'm a German Mary," Grumpy John said when Dirty Joe told him to start listening in on the British communications.

"What's the matter, Grumpy? Don't you understand English?" Dirty Joe said.

"Not that goddam Brit English."

"Well, just do the best you can," Dirty Joe said, a trace of irritation slipping into his voice.

I stepped back as Dirty Joe stomped out of the Pit, he whirled and glared at me.

"What the hell are you doing, Cooper? Aren't you supposed to be in Violet?"

"Nothing going on in there, Sarge. I thought I'd help out in the Pit."

He nodded, brushed past me and headed down the hallway toward the site commander's office.

"What's going on?" I said as I leaned on the back of Doc's chair.

"Brits won't let the Russians anywhere near the goddam plane," he said.

"Yeah, and it turns out the pilot crashed the plane in the Havel to keep from crashing into a bunch of apartment buildings," Big Ed said. "The Russians are calling them heroes."

"Sounds like they are to me," Doc said.

"They're still dead," Grumpy John said sullenly.

I shrugged and went back to Violet.

Grumpy John continued to monitor the British communications for the rest of the shift, cheerfully giving up his headsets to a bored D Trick short-timer who claimed he began forgetting all the German he ever knew on the day he went short.

By the time C Trick returned to the Hill the next morning, the British were raising the plane from the mud and silt at the bottom of the Havel. During the day, British divers carefully brought the bodies of the pilot and co-pilot to the surface, where they were placed in caskets and an honor guard transported them to the Russian mission.

It seemed very respectful and humanitarian; however, that wasn't the whole story, or at least not the story we heard when we got to work the morning after the plane crash.

"What's happening with the Russian plane?" I said when I relieved Heater, a tired A Tricker who always complained about mids.

"Not much. Brits are going to raise it sometime today and turn it over to the Russians."

"That's it?"

"Well, they did send divers down last night to remove some gear they'd never gotten a good look at."

"You're shitting."

He shook his head.

"I shit you not. Brits took some kind of new gear out of the cockpit, flew it to London to sneak a peek at, then flew it back here and stuck it back in the cockpit. Russians know what's going on and they're mad as hell, but they don't want to say anything."

"Of course, they know what the Brits were up to; they

listen in on them, just like we do."

"Well, the Brits don't seem to think we're listening to them. OIC's put out the word that no one's to ever, ever let the Brits know we've been snooping on them. You know, allies and all that. We're going to get whatever they got sooner or later, but someone in the Puzzle Palace wanted an early peek. East Germans are finding the whole thing funny, though. They jabbered all through mids about Russians being assholes ...."

"Yeah, treat the good old Germans like shit," I interrupted. "They were bitching and moaning about that all afternoon."

Heater handed me the headsets, stood up and stretched. He lit a cigarette and waved as he left.

The British raised the plane later in the day and turned it over to the Russians, who sent a huge truck to carry the jet back to its base, and everything returned to the regular routine on the Hill. Grumpy John went back to monitoring East German communications, although he stayed grumpy.

If the British ever suspected their allies on the Hill monitored their communications, they never said anything — at least not until a couple of weeks after the plane crash when Sergeant First Class Tommy Rigger, who was filling in as trick sergeant when Dirty Joe took a leave and went back to the States, decided to lecture a British Army sergeant about military correctness.

Hairy Ranger, Prince and I left Violet and headed across the compound toward the mess hall, which was operated by the 78th's cooks, when we saw the British sergeant, his shirt hanging out of his pants, which sagged over the tops of unpolished boots, and his long hair that covered the tops of his ears and touched the top of his collar, also heading for the mess hall. We were almost to the mess hall when the door flew open and Tommy Rigger, a hulking, beetle-browed tread, stepped out and clapped his fatigue cap squarely on top of his close-cropped head. Rigger's hair had been cut so close he had red stripes from where the clippers scraped his scalp.

Rigger's eyes opened in surprise when he saw the British sergeant slouching toward the door.

Sgt. Rigger learns the Queen's English

"Hey, you!" Rigger said, his voice booming across the compound.

Hairy Ranger, Prince and I stopped in our tracks and looked quizzically at Rigger.

"What you need, Sarge?" Prince said.

"Not you three assholes," Rigger said and glared at Prince. He took a deep breath and shouted: "Hey, you! Brit!"

The British sergeant stopped and slowly turned to look at Rigger.

"Yeah?"

"Yeah, what?" Rigger said, stepping closer to the British sergeant.

"What do you want?"

"You're just about the sloppiest goddam soldier I ever saw. Tuck that shirttail in, blouse those boots and get a goddam haircut."

The British sergeant smiled and cocked his head slightly to the side. He glared at Rigger and said softly, "If you'll look a bit closer, Sergeant, you'll see we're not in the same bloody army. Your regulations apply to you Americans, not to Her Majesty's forces."

Rigger looked as if he had been slapped.

"Look around you," he said with a shout. "We built this goddam Hill. It's all American equipment and men. We make the rules on this goddam Hill, and those goddam rules apply to you Brits, too. We share our food with you, we even put the goddam guards over there," he gestured toward the guardshack adjacent to the main gate, "to protect your secretive Limey asses."

"Secretive?"

"Yes, asshole, secretive. You thought you Brits were putting one over on your old American buddies with that bullshit with the Russian plane, but we were listening to every goddam word you said," Rigger said, his face now a fiery red. "And, just for the record, I outrank you."

"Christ, ol' Rigger's stepped in his own shit," Hairy Ranger whispered. Prince and I nodded.

The British sergeant spun on his heel and marched, rather than walked, back to the Quonset hut housing the British contingent on the Hill. Within seconds, the British site commander, followed closely by the sergeant who had been braced by Rigger, stormed out of the building and strode purposefully toward the U.S. sergeant, who began to display some signs of nervousness.

"I think someone's about to get reamed," I muttered.

"Yeah, and I can't think of anyone who deserves it more," Prince said.

Hairy Ranger, Prince and I leaned against the side of the mess hall, waiting to see what was about to happen. We didn't have to wait very long.

The British commander, a Royal Corps of Signals major, stopped directly in front of Rigger.

"Sergeant, who gave you the authority to harass one of my men?"

"Sir, I-I-I just thought his military appearance didn't

meet standards."

"Whose standards? Yours or Her Majesty's Army?"

"I-I-I, I'm not sure what ...," Rigger said with a stammer.

"Sergeant, I decide the correct appearance for a British non-commissioned officer, not you. You Americans might think you own the bloody world, but this installation is in the British sector and you are only here through the good graces of Her Majesty's forces. You will no longer address any British soldier unless you are directly approached by that soldier. Am I clear?"

Rigger gulped and nodded.

"What did you say, Sergeant?"

"Yes, sir," Rigger said sullenly.

"Sergeant, I can't hear you. What did you say?'

"Yes, sir."

The major smiled.

"And, I outrank you, Sergeant Rig-rah," he said, drawling as he spoke the sergeant's name. "Oh, and for another matter. You can be sure I will be discussing your behavior, as well as this unfortunate monitoring of Her Majesty's communications with your unit commander when I meet with him this afternoon. Now, you may leave."

The major stood quietly until Rigger completed his salute, stepped back and did an about-face before marching as rapidly as possible away from the withering stare of the British officer.

"Jesus Christ, did he get his ass reamed," I said. "Man, that Brit chewed him up and spit him out."

"Poor old Sergeant Rig-rah," Hairy Ranger said. "He might as well kiss his career goodbye. He'll be lucky if he doesn't get sent to one of those weather stations up by the North Pole."

Sergeant Rigger didn't go to the North Pole, but he certainly stayed well out of the way of the British contingent. A few days later, he sat quietly in the corner of the mess hall, when two British NCOs going through the line spotted him. Grinning, they walked across the mess hall directly toward his table. His eyes widened, and when he realized where they were coming, he almost jumped from his chair, grabbed his tray and cup, sloshing coffee on the floor and rushed past the two British NCOs toward the exit.

"Tootle-oo, Sergeant Rig-rah," they said in unison.

Sergeant Rig-rah didn't answer.

What it was, was fußball

9 It was nearly 3 a.m. when I walked into the Scum. I was looking forward to drinking one last beer before going to bed. C Trick was on break, and everyone had scattered throughout the city. Hairy Ranger, Shakey and Rapid Roger caught the British military train to Braunschweig, where they planned to spend as much time as possible touring the city's red light district. Doc, Big George, Tiny and Big Ed were on leave in Spain, so I was glad when Crooner asked me to go with him to a jazz club in the British sector.

If the 78th had been a movie, Crooner would have been the unit's sandy-haired Irish Catholic kid from Boston, a easy role for him to play because he was. When he was a youngster, he became fascinated with the vocal styling of Frank Sinatra, Mel Torme and Tony Bennett. Whenever he got the chance, he'd sing at picnics, parties, weddings — wherever a vocalist was needed. Not long after arriving in Berlin, I went with him one night to see Frank and The Captains at the Blue Note, a small jazz club in the British sector. He persuaded the group to let him join them for a couple of sets. On the way back to the barracks that night, I started calling him Crooner, a nickname that caught on quickly.

He hit it off with the members of the combo, and after Frank, a GI saxophonist who organized the group, rotated back to the States, the four remaining musicians — guitarist Hogie Kaminisky, bassist Siggy Lönnendecker, drummer Tommy Ackermann and organist Brill (Four Eyes) — asked him to be their vocalist.

It was a musician's night at the Blue Note. The audience loved them, so Crooner and the band decided to play as long as there was anyone left in the club. Shortly after 1 a.m., when I heard the opening bars of The 'In' Crowd, I decided to leave. The group's version of the song was an extended jam, with Hogie improvising wildly while Siggy, Tommy and Brill kept up a steady rhythm. Because the song was all instrumental, Crooner went to the bar and got a beer before joining me at the band's table, just to the left of the stage.

"Crooner, I think I'm going to ease out," I said.

"What for? We're cooking tonight," he said.

"I'm just tired. I think I'll head back to the barracks."

"Going to stop at the Scum on the way in?"

"Of course," I said. "It's a rule. You can't go in without stopping at the Scum."

"Well, don't forget to wake up Grumpy John," he said and laughed.

Nearly every night that he went out, Grumpy John would stop at the Scum for a last beer, promptly falling asleep in one of the booths. He often would stay there until another C Tricker would arrive, wake him up and walk him back to the barracks. It seemed that most of the time, the C Tricker who would wake up Grumpy John would be either Crooner or me. So we jokingly reminded each other to remember to wake up Grumpy John.

After leaving the Blue Note, I caught a bus to the Europa Center. I found a small Italian restaurant that was still open, and had an order of cannelloni and a carafe of Chianti. I rummaged through my coat pockets and found a Cuban cigar that I had bought a couple of days earlier at a tobacco shop near Stuttgarter Platz. I puffed on the cigar as I walked slowly along the Ku'damm. Except for a street sweeper moving slowly along the street, the normally bustling thoroughfare was nearly deserted. When I finished the cigar, I stubbed it out on the sidewalk and took a seat on a bench to wait for the bus. Within a few minutes, I climbed to the top deck of the bus, put up my feet and dozed off. I woke up just before the bus pulled to a stop at Ringstrasse, just a few blocks from Andrews Barracks. I started to stop in Linda's Lounge, but just before opening the door, I decided to go to the Scum and check on Grumpy John.

I chuckled to myself when I walked into the Scum. I could hear Grumpy John's snoring, a resonation of sounds that his rotund roommate, Big George, compared to jets taking off and landing.

"Hey, Grumpy," I said as I shook his shoulder.

He slowly opened his eyes, yawned and rubbed the back of his neck.

"What time is it?"

"Nearly four," I said.

"How long have I been here?"

"Christ, I don't know, Grumpy. I just got here. Come on, let's pack it in."

"No way," Grumpy John said. "I'm going to have another goddam Lion's Piss or whatever it is they serve in here, and I'm going to stay here until it's time to go to the chow hall."

"For crying out loud, Grumpy, that's another two hours."

"I don't give a shit. I'm going to have another beer," he said drunkenly. He pushed himself erect, swayed precariously before regaining his balance, and walked carefully to the bar. A moment later, he slammed two bottles of Löwenpils on the table, then slid into the booth across from me.

"Drink up, Blackie. Don't act like a goddam newk," he said, then turned up his bottle and took a deep drink.

An hour later, we crossed the street and were waved through the gate by a yawning military policeman. When we got to the mess hall, members of D Trick were going through the line. Grumpy John and I fell into line behind Stinky, a slight, balding maintenance man. He had a clipboard under his left arm.

"Hey, Blackie," he said. "You interested in getting off trick for a while?"

"If it'll get me away from Roadrunner, I sure as hell am."

"You won't even see him for three weeks."

"Who do I have to kill?"

"Nobody — at least not for this job. I'm supposed to get some guys to work at the Volksfest," he said.

The Deutsche-Amerikanische Volksfest had been going on every summer for several years. The Berlin Brigade brass thought it was a good idea to show the Berliners something about the States and build good will between the Germans and Americans. Every year, the festival featured a U.S. city. At the festival grounds, construction crews build false fronts on the tents that housed beer halls, exhibitions, games and souvenir stands. When everything was completed, it looked like a small part of a famous U.S. city was sitting in the heart of the U.S. sector of Berlin. I had been by the festival grounds a couple of days before, and I was surprised to see the French Quarter of New Orleans had been reproduced.

"What do I have to do?"

"Oh, you'll be one of the stage crew for the main beer hall. You and the other guys will change the sets and take care of the lighting, things like that. That okay with you?"

"I'll go for it," I said. "When do I start?"

Stinky didn't answer. He looked around the mess hall until he saw three empty seats together. After we took our seats, he pulled a form loose from the clipboard and shoved it toward me.

"Fill that out and bring it to the main beer tent tomorrow. We'll get started about ten. There'll be some rehearsals going on and we'll get a chance to see what we need to do."

I nodded, looked at the form, which was a release from regular duty. I folded it and put it in my shirt pocket.

It was almost ten when I joined a small group in the main beer tent. A two-level stage was at one end of the tent. At the other end was a scaffold filled with stage lights. It was cramped, with just enough room for a two-man lighting crew. Several sets of risers, to be used by a choir were stacked neatly to the left of the lower stage.

Other than Stinky, I didn't know any of the other stage hands, although I did recognize a 'Gator named Brennigan whom I'd met at a Berlin Brigade pinochle tournament a few weeks earlier. Stinky and I were the only ASAers on the crew.

"Hey, Brennigan," I said while Stinky was collecting the release forms. "What unit are you with?"

"Company F, 40th Armor," he said.

"Shit, you're probably happier than I am to land this detail."

"Goddam right," he said and laughed heartily.

"Hey, Brennigan, have you had any experience with lighting?" Stinky asked.

"Yeah, I ran lights at high school plays."

"Good, then you're our light man. I'll be your assistant. The rest of you will be the stage hands. There'll be some rehearsals this afternoon, so you can learn what you need to do," Stinky said. Then he pointed to a small table and some chairs just off the right side of the stage.

"That's for you. There's going to be schedule on it so you'll know what to do. I'll be back in a couple of minutes," he said and walked quickly out of the tent.

There were four of us, and we introduced ourselves. My three co-workers were Dick Cowsert, a cook with the 42nd Engineers; Jerry Edwards, a Signal Corps maintenance man; and Bill Line, an MP.

"Cooper, Cowsert, Edwards and Line. That sounds like a goddam law firm," Cowsert said.

"You know, it's going to be awfully damn hard to get a beer in this place when everything gets cranked up," Edwards said. "Why don't we ice down some beer in a garbage can. It'll fit under the table. The commissary's not too far away. We can ice down a couple of cases, and then we won't have to mess with the line."

"I can get us a garbage can, no problem," Cowsert said. "I'll bring it with me tomorrow."

"You have a car?" Edwards said.

Cowsert nodded.

"Why don't you two go get the can and beer?" I said. "Line and I'll hold down the fort."

Rehearsals went off with only a few problems. When the festival opened the next afternoon, the stage crew was in place at its table, with a case of beer iced down in the garbage can. For the next three weeks, we would spend every day changing sets, moving risers and costumes, and making sure microphones were in place and properly connected.

Stinky wanted to keep his crew fresh, so he let everyone take a night off now and then. On my first night off, I still went to the festival grounds, chipped in to buy beer and helped set up the risers for the Air Force Chorale, which came to Berlin from Ramstein Air Force Base in West Germany.

I was sitting at the table, drinking a cold beer, when I felt a tap on my shoulder. I turned around and saw Horst Sell, a construction worker on the Hill.

"Guten abend, Blackie," he said cheerfully.

"Wie geht's," I said.

He shrugged.

"What are you doing?"

"Nothing much. I just stopped by for a little while. I think I'm going to the Europa Center."

"Want some company? I've got the night off and I need to get out of here," I said. "You have a car?"

"No, I'm riding the U-bahn."

"Okay by me," I said, and I followed him out of the tent. The Oskar-Helene-Heim station was only a couple of blocks away and we hadn't been standing on the platform for more than two or three minutes when the train arrived.

After getting off the subway at the Uhlandstrasse station, we walked to the Europa Center and stopped at an imbiss, a sidewalk vendor's stand, where we bought currywurst, hard rolls and beer. We were sitting on a bench eating our currywursts when we noticed a crowd outside a department store.

"What's going on?" I asked.

"Let's go find out," Horst said, and we walked across the broad thoroughfare and joined the crowd. Instead of dresses or suits in the display window, there were several television sets, all showing a soccer match.

"Hell, Horst, it's just a soccer match," I said. I turned and started to leave, but Horst grabbed my arm.

"Wait, wait," he said. "It's the World Cup — we're playing England for the championship. Let's stay and see how it turns out. There's only about four minutes left."

Who the hell cares, I thought, then seeing the intensity of the crowd of people, their eyes glued to the sets, I realized that a lot of people cared about the match. I moved closed and stood next to Horst.

"What's the score?" I asked.

"Two to one, England."

The crowd was quiet, nervous because the West German defense was breached, setting up a three-on-one situation with only sweeper Willy Schulz between goalie Hans Tilkowski and English attackers Roger Hunt, Bobby Charlton and Geoff Hurst.

"Oh, shit," Horst said quietly as the Hunt passed to Charlton. However, Horst and the rest of the crowd suddenly cheered lustily when Charlton's kick went wide.

There was less than a minute left in the game when the West Germans moved downfield. Boos rained down from the English fans when the referee called a foul on Jackie Charlton, giving Lothar Emmerich a free kick. When his kick hit an English player in the back, Siegfried Held quickly moved to the ball and fired it toward goal, where it was driven into the net by Wolfgang Weber, sending the match into overtime.

The crowd grew quiet as the English took command at the start of the overtime. Midway through the first half of the extra time, Alan Ball centered to Hurst inside the box. Hurst's shot hit the crossbar and bounced down and out.

The crowd cheered, certain there was no goal. But the referee and linesman huddled and the goal was awarded. The English sealed the victory in the final seconds of the overtime when Hurst broke free from the defense and scored his third goal, giving England a 4-2 victory and the World Cup.

"I knew it," a slight, stooped white-haired man, his face flushed with anger, said to Horst. "The English bribed the referee. That was no goal — everybody could see that. Why couldn't that asshole of a referee see it?"

After a few minutes, the crowd drifted away, leaving Horst and me standing alone on the sidewalk.

"Was that it?" I asked.

Horst nodded. We started walking toward the subway station.

"It feels like shit, losing to the English again," he said. "You know, Germany's never beaten the English — or I don't think so. If we have, it was so long ago that I don't remember it."

"It's like Arkansas and Texas," I said.

"What do you mean?"

"Oh, it's a big rivalry. Arkansas can lose every game in the season, but if they beat Texas, then it's a good season."

"What are you talking about?"

"Sorry. The University of Arkansas and University of Texas football teams."

"American football?"

"Of course," I said. "American football, what other kind is there?"

"Football, like you just saw. That's football."

"That's soccer."

"No, no, it's football. That is what it's called all over the world and why there's the World Cup. Your football is only played in America."

"Maybe so, but soccer doesn't make sense to me. I don't have any idea what's going on," I said. I stopped to light a cigarette. I offered one to Horst, who pulled out a Marlboro. He held it carefully.

"May I have another one, for later?" he asked, smiling when I held out the pack again. He pulled another cigarette from the pack and dropped it into his shirt pocket.

"You know, I don't understand your American football either. I've seen the Army team play," he said. "Everyone's got all that armor and helmets. I don't see how they move in all that stuff. You know what it looks like to me?"

"What?"

"It looks like a bunch of people run over here and fall down. Then they get up and run over there and fall down."

"That's pretty much all it is, Horst," I said and laughed. "I have to tell you the truth. Before I joined the Army, I worked for a newspaper, and I had to write about football games. That's just about all I ever saw — a bunch of people falling down a lot. I guess the difference between your football and my football is your guys don't fall down as much. You know what we always say after we lose a big game?"

"No, what?"

"Wait 'til next year. We'll kick your asses next year."

"Well, we'll have to wait four years to kick the English asses."

We were back at the subway stop, where Horst would

have to catch the train on the way to his apartment in Charlottenburg. I was going to walk to the bus stop to wait for the A18 that would take me back to Lichterfelde.

"I'm sorry your guys lost, Horst," I said.

"Wait until 1970," he said and started down the steps.

"Hey, Horst," I shouted. When he stopped and looked back, I tossed the pack of Marlboros to him. He grinned and slipped them into his shirt pocket.

"Don't forget — 1970," I said.

He just waved and disappeared down the stairs.

A few minutes later, I climbed aboard the A18 for the 30-minute ride to Lichterfelde. I stopped at Linda's Lounge; however, before entering, I decided I'd go to the Scum and check on Grumpy John.

Crooner's probably with the band, so I'll have to check on Grumpy, I said. I let the door close and walked on to the Scum. When I stopped at the bar to order a beer, I saw Grumpy John sitting in his usual booth.

"Hey, Blackie, come join us," he shouted.

When I got to the booth, I was surprised to see Crooner sitting across from Grumpy John. He was reading a book and just glanced at me when I slid in next to him.

"Goddammit, I'm glad to see you, Blackie," Grumpy John said. "He's not any fun at all tonight, just sitting them with his goddam nose stuck in that book. Jesus Christ, what kind of guy sits and reads a book in the Scum anyway? You're missing out on valuable drinking time.

"Speaking of drinking, I think I'll have another beer," he said and laughed loudly. Then Grumpy John propelled himself out of the booth and, weaving precariously, made his way to the bar.

"What are you reading?" I asked.

"Cold Dogs in the Courtyard," Crooner said.

"Who wrote it?"

"Bukowski."

"The beat guy?"

"Yes and no."

"What do you mean, yes and no?"

"Well, he was sort of a beat, but he didn't hang out with Kerouac and the others."

"How's his stuff?"

"Not like anything else I've ever read," Crooner said. "He writes about shit stains on his underwear, hangovers and whores. Hell, he sounds like he ought to be on C Trick."

"Maybe he is and we just don't know it. Maybe he's really Prince."

"No, Bukowski's not Prince. Prince thinks too much of himself to ever admit that he has shit stains on his underwear. No, no, not Prince, no way."

"Well, we're just going to have to find out who's Bukowski."

Our conversation was interrupted by Grumpy John, who slammed two bottles on the table in front of us, hard enough that beer splashed on my arm and the cover of Crooner's book.

"Goddam, Grumpy, take it easy," I said brusquely. "Why don't you just pour it out on the table?"

"Fuck you if you can't take a joke," Grumpy John said and chuckled as he settled back in the booth. "Drink your beers, we've still got plenty of time to get drunk."

"Grumpy, who's Bukowski?" Crooner said.

"Isn't he that smartass little bastard Russian Mary, the one who's always trying to get people to call him Professor?"

"That's Lebowski, Grumpy," I said. "Crooner wants to know about Bukowski."

"Shit, if he's not that smartass Russian Mary, then I don't know who the fuck he is. I, I, I," he said, his voice trailing off as he leaned his head against the wall and began to snore.

"For Christ's sake, the son of a bitch's gone to sleep. I've got to hit the rack pretty damn soon. I have to work at the Volksfest, and it's going to be one long goddam shift if I don't get some sleep pretty soon," I said angrily.

"Don't worry about it," Crooner said. "You go on. I'll keep an eye on Grumpy. I want to finish my book anyway."

"Okay, I'll catch you later," I said and slid out of the booth. "Let me know if you find out who's Bukowski."

"Who knows? It might be you."

"Bukowski? Maybe I am," I said as I walked out of the Scum.

Volksfest

10 A few hours later, I was jolted out of a sound sleep by the persistent ringing of Shakey's alarm clock. Although Shakey's room was three or four doors down the hallway, I could always hear his alarm. It was louder than the alarms at a rail crossing, and only Shakey and his room mate, Grumpy John, could sleep through its ringing.

As I swung my feet out from under the cover, I could heard someone shout, "Goddam you, Shakey! Shut it off!"

But the alarm kept ringing. Then I heard the heavy steps of someone stomping down the hallway, a door opening, more steps and the alarm suddenly stopping.

"Jesus Christ, Hedgehog! What the hell do you think you're doing?" Shakey shouted. "You threw my clock out the window. You're going to have to buy me another one."

"I'll buy you another goddam clock, but I'm going pick the son of a bitch out myself," Hedgehog said. I heard the heavy footsteps again and a door slamming.

After a long, hot shower and a shave, I walked across to the PX, stopped at the news stand for a copy of the International Herald Tribune and went to the snackbar for breakfast. I had just placed my order when Hedgehog walked up behind me.

"We'll never have to hear that goddam clock of Shakey's," he said proudly.

"You're a good man, Hedgehog. I'm thinking about asking the Old Man to put you in for a commendation medal."

"Sarcasm's not one of your more likable traits, Blackie."

After breakfast, I took the shuttle bus to the main PX on Clayallee and walked to the festival grounds. When I walked

into the main beer tent, Brennigan was sitting at the stagehands' table. His feet were up on the table and he was reading an Overseas Weekly and laughing heartily.

"What's so funny, Brennigan?" I asked.

"This goddam piece in OW. It's one of the funniest goddam things I've ever read."

"What is it?" I asked, my curiosity was piqued.

"It's called the 'Lifer's Twenty-third AR.' You'll laugh you
ass off," he said, then he tossed the tabloid paper to me. "I'd
read it out loud, but I crack up too much. It's there on the
second page."

I opened the paper, skimmed down the columns and
found the article. I started reading it to myself, then I found
myself laughing as hard as Brennigan, which him laugh
even more, as I read aloud: "The Lifer's Twenty-third AR/
The Army is my crutch, I shall not think./ It alloweth me to
lie down on responsibility/It leadeth me blindly/It destroy-
eth my initiative/It leadeth me in the path of the parasite
for my country's sake/Yea, though I walk through the valley
of laziness, I shall fear no achievement."

I dropped the paper back on the table, sat down and
wiped my eyes.

"You know, it surprised me that this issue's at the PX
news stand," Brennigan said. "They pull stuff all the time. I
don't know how they let this one get through."

"It wouldn't do any good. Someone would have gotten a
copy."

He nodded, then swung his feet down from the table,
stood up and stretched.

"Let's go make the beer run," he said. "I borrowed my
roomie's wheels."

I followed him outside to the parking lot. A battered,
multi-colored Volkswagen van was the only vehicle in the
parking lot. It was once beige, but different colors had been
used to cover dents and the door on the driver's side was a
faded green. When I got around to the passenger side of the
van, I saw that door was blue.

"Interesting color scheme," I said.

"Gets us where we're going," Brennigan said and grinned.

We bought four cases of Beck's at the commissary, along

with several bags of ice. Then we drove back to the main tent and filled the garbage can to the top with beer and ice. There were four bottles that were left when the can was filled.

"Want one now?" I asked.

Brennigan nodded, and I opened two bottles and we began drinking the warm Beck's. Then we opened the other two warm Beck's, and were just finishing them when the rest of the crew arrived.

"Jesus Christ, it's only ten o'clock," Stinky said. "You two take it easy. I'm going to need all of you tonight. There's supposed to be some wheels out of Louisiana here tonight and I don't want us to screw up everything."

"Not to worry," Brennigan said. "We have everything under control."

"Well, just to make sure, I'm going to run the lights. There are some changes they want, and I don't have time to fill you in on everything. You'll be my assistant," Stinky said.

"Fine by me," Brennigan said.

Everything ran smoothly during the afternoon, although it seemed like Brennigan and I were drinking all the beer. By 7 o'clock, I was feeling pretty loose, as was Brennigan, who had left Stinky alone on the light platform and was working as a stagehand.

The big event of the night was the introduction of Louisiana Governor John J. McKeithen and New Orleans Mayor Moon Landrieu. The two politicians stood, waved and acknowledged the cheers.

"Goddam politicians are all alike," Brennigan said. "Hell, they act like they're running for mayor of Berlin."

"Christ, they're from Louisiana. They're probably getting votes right now," I said.

"Shit, Berliners can't vote in Louisiana."

"Dead people do, why not Berliners? McKeithen's probably already registered half of Berlin as Louisiana voters."

"Louisiana sounds like Chicago," Brennigan said. "Want another beer?"

When he bent over to pull the beers from the garbage

can, he let a fart, a long, rumbling explosion of gas that seemed to last for minutes.

"Damn, who stepped on that frog?" he said and laughed heartily.

"My grandpa used to say that when he cut one," I said.

While we were still laughing, Cowsert walked up. He stopped and sniffed, his nose twitching like a bloodhound trying to get a scent.

"Goddam, what have you two assholes be doing? It smells like a shithouse over here," he said.

"Brennigan's had a little gas problem," I said.

"Little, my ass. Jesus, it smells like someone curled up and died in his ass."

"God, what's that smell?" Edwards said as he arrived.

"Brennigan's farting," Cowsert said.

"Want a beer?" Brennigan said.

Edwards nodded and took a deep drink, then he grinned and said, "It still stinks, but I think I'll be able to handle it now."

The night was humid and stayed hot long after the sun had set. Brennigan and I were in an unofficial contest to see who could drink the most beer. It seemed that for every beer that Cowsert and Edwards drank, Brennigan and I had two or more. Both of us were sweating profusely, but we worked rapidly changing the sets, and everything was going smoothly until after the Man From La Mancha set.

Cowsert and I carried some costumes to the women's dressing room. That's when the heat and the beer kicked in, and I swayed and passed out. When I came to, I was lying on a sofa, covered with an Army blanket and with my shoes placed neatly on the floor. I looked at my watch and was surprised to see that it was almost seven o'clock — I had been asleep all night.

My head was pounding, my mouth was dry. I had a massive hangover.

"Jesus Christ, I need some coffee," I said and brushed my hair back off my forehead, smelling the strong odor of sweaty armpit when I did. "God, I need a shower, too."

No one was around as I left the women's dressing room.

I walked quickly to the main PX and boarded the shuttle bus back to Andrews Barracks. I walked past the mess hall, deciding I'd rather have a long, hot shower before trying to eat anything.

The day shift already had gone to the Hill and the mids shift hadn't gotten back to the barracks, so I had the shower room to myself. I turned on all the faucets, hot water only, and sat in the corner where the streams of hot water wouldn't reach me and let the steam fill the room. It wasn't the best steam room around, but it worked and after a few minutes, I was feeling good enough to turn off all but one faucet and take a normal shower.

After dressing, I went to the snack bar for a breakfast of scrambled eggs, toast and several cups of hot, black coffee. I had already eaten and was just sipping on my coffee when I saw Hairy Ranger, Rock Weed and Hedgehog, just off mids, get in the line to order something to eat. When they saw me, they started laughing.

What the hell? I thought.

Minutes later, Hairy Ranger and Rock Weed sat down across the table from me, while Hedgehog slid onto the chair next to me. All three were grinning broadly.

"Okay, what's the deal? You three assholes look like goddam hyenas," I said.

"Blackie, Blackie, it's all right. We understand." Hairy Ranger said, reaching across the table to pat me on the shoulder in mock sympathy. Hedgehog and Rock Weed actually giggled.

"Understand what?"

"Should I tell him?" Hairy Ranger asked. Hedgehog and Rock Weed nodded enthusiastically.

"Well, Blackie, everyone seems to think I should tell you. So, here goes," he said, pausing to take a drink of his coffee. "Last night, Shakey and I decided to go see if you're really doing all the work at the Volksfest like you say you are. Now, son, you have to realize how worried we were when we couldn't find you."

"Oh, shit," I said.

"We asked one of the 'Gators stagehands where you were. Well, he told us you got drunk and passed out in the women's dressing room. That's why we understand why you're so upset. Hell, I'd be upset to if I spent the night in a room full of naked women and didn't know about it."

Then they started laughing. They laughed so hard that I couldn't help myself, I started laughing, too. When I thought about what happened, it was funny. After all, I did spend the better part of the night in the room where women, most of them young, athletic and attractive, were changing clothes, and I missed it all.

At work that night, I did have to endure some teasing from the other stagehands and some mischievous looks from the young women. Although I continued to enjoy the beer from the garbage can, the rest of the Volksfest went off without any other incidents. Two weeks later, I went back to C Trick, which was now on swings.

As I walked down the hallway toward Violet, I nearly collided with Roadrunner.

"Sorry, Sarge," I said and stepped to one side to allow him to pass. He started to rush on down the hallway, but he stopped, turned and looked at me with a bemused expression.

"Hmm, Cooper, how was the sofa scene?"

"A waste of time, Sarge," I said.

I heard him laughing all the way down the hallway and into the site commander's office.

The Interlude

11 A late-summer front swept down from the Baltic, bringing a steady, soaking rain and a message that autumn was drawing near. By the time I pushed open the door to the Blue Moon, a small working-class bar in the northern part of the U.S. sector, it had changed to a steady drizzle, one that even in late August could chill you to the bones.

The Blue Moon, which was near the corner of Kadetten-weg and Brüderstraße, wasn't one of the bars favored by GIs, even though it was within easy walking distance of Andrews Barracks. But that made it more attractive to me on payday night. I tried to avoid the GI bars most of the time, and especially on payday night when the 'Gators were flush with money and spoiling for fights.

The crowd in the Blue Moon was all German, mostly construction workers and some students at the Free University. I slid onto a stool at the end of the bar, just under a neon Schultheiss sign, motioned to the waitress and ordered a shot of cognac and a beer. When the drinks arrived, I downed the cognac quickly, which sent a burst of warmth through me. Then I lit a cigarette, and sipped my beer.

I had just finished my first shift back on the Hill after the Volksfest, and I was still trying to adapt to dealing with Roadrunner on a regular basis. All I wanted to do was get away from everyone, be left alone and enjoy a few beers by myself.

A catchy tune by Los Bravos, a popular German rock band, was playing on the juke box when I sensed, rather than saw, someone standing behind me. I turned and saw a tiny black woman, not more than a couple of inches over five feet tall, standing there. She was wearing a long gray coat and a dark beret, looking around the bar as if she were supposed to meet someone.

"Looking for someone in particular?" I asked.

She looked at me and smiled.

"Well, I thought some of my friends were going to be here, but I don't think they are," she said. She pointed at the bar stool next to me. "Is it taken?"

"No, feel free. What do you want?" I said and motioned to the bartender, who was wiping the bar and emptying the ashtrays.

She glanced at the bottles on the shelves behind the bar, pursed her lips slightly and smiled, exposing even, white teeth.

"A cognac, I suppose," she said, and I noticed a curious lilt to her voice.

"Zwei cognac," I said and the bartender nodded.

I noticed two couples who had been sitting at the booth just inside the door were leaving.

"Why don't we move to the booth? You can see your friends when they get here," I said.

"If they get here," she said.

"Where are you from?"

"St. Croix. Have you been there?"

"No, but I'd love to. I love the beach and the ocean."

"Well, you know where I'm from, but I don't know about you."

"I'm from Arkansas. Have you ever been there?"

"No."

"It's certainly no St. Croix," I said. "What are you doing in Berlin?"

"I work for American Express branch at the main PX."

We finished our drinks and I motioned to the barmaid that we wanted two more. We chatted idly until those were finished.

"It doesn't look like your friends are coming," I said.

"I guess not."

"Look, it's getting stuffy in here," I said. "Would you like to take a walk?"

She looked at me curiously, then nodded.

The drizzle had stopped and the stars were shining when we left the Blue Moon. We walked along quietly, both deep in our own thoughts. We had walked for several blocks when I felt her slip her hand into mine. I clasped it and we continued to walk slowly through the darkened streets.

"I'm married," she said softly.

"I thought you might be," I said. "Where's your husband?"

"Wildflecken," she said, referring to the large Army training area in West Germany. Units from Berlin Brigade often went to Wildflecken for maneuvers.

"How long's he been gone?"

"Six days."

"You must miss him," I said.

"Not really. We haven't been getting along."

When I didn't say anything, she continued.

"I'm thinking that I'll go home, maybe see how things will look from there."

"When would you leave?"

"Oh, I already have my tickets, but I wouldn't leave until he gets back."

"Oh."

A brisk breeze signaled the return of the rain, which suddenly pelted us. I looked around for cover and saw a Catholic church across the street.

"Come on," I said. Still holding hands, we ran across the street and took shelter in the doorway of the church. When she shivered, I pulled her close to me and held her in an embrace as we leaned against the heavy wood doors and watched the rain.

It seemed to me the rain was going to stay around a while, so I used my free hand to reach behind me and check the door, which was unlocked.

"Let's go in and sit down until the rain eases," I said. "It's getting chilly and we don't need to just stand in the doorway."

"Okay," she said and followed me inside. We stood for a few minutes in the foyer, looking at the flickering candles lit earlier by the faithful. Suddenly she smiled broadly and grasping my hand tightly, pulled me toward the staircase leading to the choir loft.

We eased into the corner of the back bench in the loft, which seemed to be floating in the air far above the sanctuary. The altar seemed small and distant as we snuggled in the corner of the pew.

We sat quietly, locked in our embrace. I sensed her looking at me, and I turned to look into her eyes. She reached up and pulled my head toward her and we kissed, gently at first but then more insistently and she tugged at my belt, loosening it. I slid my hand under her skirt and she lifted her hips so I could slide her panties down. She stood and stepped out of the panties, bent forward, unzipped my pants and pulled out my now fully erect cock. As we kissed fervently, she sat astride me, guiding me inside her.

It was warm and moist and we moved slowly in rhythm, then faster and faster until we both shuddered with the pleasure of our orgasms. She collapsed against me and I held her tightly. I don't know how long we stayed locked in our embrace, but I opened my eyes and looked over her shoulder. I could see the Stations of the Cross mounted on the walls of the sanctuary. Then the rain stopped.

A few minutes later, we walked out of the church into the cool of the night. The stars were again twinkling. We walked and talked until the sky began to take on a pinkish hue. It was dawn.

"I've got to get home and get ready for work," she said quietly.

I stopped and looked at the street sign. It was Ringstraße. About two blocks away was a bus stop. When we got there, I leaned against the shelter and held her in my arms. We stayed that way until the A18 arrived. When the door opened, she reached up and pulled my head down and kissed me passionately.

"Goodbye," she said softly and the door closed behind her.

I stood there a few minutes, stunned. I never asked for her name, and she didn't ask for mine. I began to walk slowly down Kommandantenstraße toward Andrews Barracks. It was nearly light when I went through the gate and walked toward the mess hall, where the cooks were beginning to serve breakfast for the day shift.

When I walked in the mess hall, I saw Grumpy John. I took my tray and sat down across from him.

"Where have you been, Coop?" Grumpy John said.

"Just out and about," I said and sipped on my coffee.

"Well, where is out and about?"

"Nowhere in particular."

"No, asshole, where have you been?"

"I went to the Blue Moon and then I went to church," I said.

He peered at me over the top of his glasses.

"Smart ass."

A few days later, I went to the main PX. I went to the American Express office to exchange some U.S. currency for German marks. I didn't see a black woman in the office. She's probably walking along the beach and looking at the ocean, I thought.

Beer Guts and Belly Busters

12 I guess it was the fall when I first really noticed I had been gaining weight. Perhaps I didn't pay much attention because the Germans thought an expansive girth was a sign of prosperity. Of course, it isn't, but it makes a good excuse.

"Ach ja, zaftig," Inge the Barmaid would say as Big George and Big Ed would lift their bellies and drop them with a resounding thump on the table at the El Oso Club.

Big George, Big Ed, Fat Kenny and Duck weren't the only ones who had put on weight in Berlin. Except for those few fortunate individuals who could eat and drink as much as they wanted, without doing any exercise, Berlin was a place to gain weight — or get rather saftig.

One sure way to tell who had put on a few extra pounds was to look at the fatigues. After a year or so, the olive green would have faded to a light green. So, if you were carrying some excess poundage and had to have your uniform let out, there would be an inverted pyramid of darker green on the seat of your pants.

For those of us in the 78th ASA, gaining weight came easy and didn't really bother us at all, especially because it was happening to so many people around us. Unlike the 'Gators in the engineers, armor, artillery or infantry who were constantly in the field and exerting themselves physically, those of us in ASA spent our work days seated before a bank of radio receivers and tape recorders, smoking cigarettes, sipping coffee, and eating peanut butter sandwiches. The job was stressful, but it certainly wasn't aerobic.

In our unit, exercise was looked on with distaste, if not

outright horror. In the 78th, a beer belly was a sign of a robust personality, a person who enjoyed life to the fullest. A big beer belly served also as a sign of longevity. The bigger the belly, the longer its owner had been in Berlin. When I arrived in Berlin, I was a bit over five feet 10 inches tall and weighed 173 pounds. When I left three years later, after spending my time avoiding exercise, drinking as much beer as possible and not missing a meal, I was a shade over six feet tall and weighed about 230 pounds.

I probably would have gained weight even if I'd worked out regularly, because German food is frightfully fattening and Berlin was loaded with places to eat. On nearly every street corner was a vendor, much like the hot dog or pretzel stands in large cities in the United States, where you could buy your choice of German sausage, from the plain, unadorned bockwurst to the spicy currywurst, and from fried fish and potato salad to several varieties of bread and beer. If you didn't like the street vendors' wares, there were the little cafes found in every neighborhood, all of which offered similar menus — a variety of sausages, potato salad and a hard roll, with a dollop of mustard on the side, or a bowl of goulash or potato soup. Of course, Berlin had hundreds of full-scale restaurants, featuring menus from France to Greece to Turkey. As cities go, Berlin was a glutton's idea of heaven.

No one knew when the belly competition started in the 78th. It just happened. It probably began at Monster Happy Hour at the El Oso Club. Monster Happy Hour was held the last Saturday of the month before pay day. From 7 p.m. until midnight, all beer was ten cents at the El Oso Club. We looked forward to the five-hour happy hour because there would be a band playing, and there was always a good possibility that one of the German women who frequented the club would want some companionship later in the evening.

It was Monster Happy Hour when six or eight of us were sitting around the corner table, ordering our Beck's Beer by the case and stacking the empty bottles in the corner. Rock Weed told Big Ed that his stomach appeared to have developed its own personality.

Big Ed was proud of his beer belly, which was magnificent. It was marvelously round and stood proudly out before him, a beer belly of style.

"You don't just get a beer gut like this, you earn one," Big Ed said as he polished off another bottle of Beck's.

Rock Weed picked up his name on his first day on C Trick because as a "weed," or new arrival, he showed up wearing prescription sunglasses, tailored fatigues, a glistening shine on his boots, and an expressed desire to be a good soldier. While the newcomer was being shown his work station, The Chief, who was severely hung over, was sitting with his headsets hanging around his neck. He peered intently at the new guy.

"You look like a goddam re-up poster," Chief said.

"Jesus Christ, Chief, cut him some slack. He just got here," the Bunny said.

"You know, Chief's right, Bunny," Fat Kenny said. "He does look like a re-up poster."

"That, or a John fucking Wayne movie poster," Buffalo Head said.

"Yeah, look at the goddam sunglasses," Chief said. "He's off the goddam re-up poster, not the movie poster. A weed with sunglasses, for God's sake. A real fucking Hollywood star. Old Rock Weed."

Although it soon became apparent that Rock Weed wasn't a sergeant's dream, he never would be able to shake the nickname. Rock Weed he remained. The nickname was such a part of him that when he was promoted and his name was included on the list posted on the bulletin board, no one knew he had been promoted until he showed up wearing his new Spec 4 eagle instead of his PFC chevron.

Rock Weed tried his best to be like the rest of us — malcontents who didn't like the military, who tried to hold on to our civilian attitudes despite the best efforts of the treads to mold us into soldiers. But try as hard as he could, Rock Weed just wouldn't let himself go all the way; he kept in shape. He did pushups, situps, and ran a couple of miles three or four times a week. He watched what he ate and how much. He stayed trim and actually had to have his tailored fatigues taken in, not let out.

Rock Weed's observation that Big Ed's beer belly had taken on its own personality was disputed by Big George, a dark-haired New Mexican whose own belly was of rather substantial proportions.

"Shit, Ed's belly don't hold a candle to mine," Big George said. "It's just there. It's like a goddam sack of sand, for Christ's sake. Hell, anybody can put his stomach on the table, even you, Weed."

"The hell I can, Big George," Rock Weed said. "My gut's hard as a rock. It's a goddam washboard. I'm lean and I'm mean."

"A real re-upping machine," Other George said.

"Come on, Big George, you know you've just got a fat gut. That's all you got, just a fat, sloppy gut. But my gut, now there's a national treasure. People come up to me all the time just to look at it. Some people even want to rub it, like I'm Buddha," Big Ed said proudly.

The argument continued, with each Big contending his beer belly was the more magnificent creation. Fat Kenny tried to lay claim to top belly, but no one took him seriously because he was just fat all over.

"Well, I know how to settle this shit," Big George said. "Come on, Ed," he said, motioning for his friend to stand up and then maneuvering him to a spot just away from the table.

"Okay, you're there and I'm going to be over there," Big George said, pointing toward the other side of the dance floor. "When I count three, we'll run together and bump our bellies. We'll keep bumping them until one of us quits or falls on his ass. Okay?"

"Yeah, and get ready to dust your ass off, because I'm going to knock you on it," Big Ed said.

While Big Ed stood rubbing his belly, Big George stalked across the dance floor and took his position. Fat Kenny walked over to a spot about halfway between the two and started the count.

On the count of three, Big George and Big Ed thrust their bellies forward and rushed toward each other, the bellies smashing together with a resounding splat. Big Ed was bounced back, but he quickly regained his balance and rushed forward to slam his belly into Big George's again with another resounding splat.

Grunting fiercely, the two big men, looking remarkably like two bull sea elephants, continued to slam their bellies against each other until finally, with a tremendous surge, Big George heaved Big Ed over backwards, where he skidded into the pile of beer bottles.

Walking back to the table, nodding as he acknowledged the applause that broke out in the club, Big George picked up his beer, downed it, and looked at Rock Weed.

"Weed, Big Ed's right about one thing. You got to earn a belly like this."

A White Christmas

13 In most parts of the South, a white Christmas is just the title of a popular song. A white Christmas is something that you sing either, read or dream about. But, like the pot of gold at the end of a rainbow, you just won't find it.

But because Southerners grew up thinking that Christmas should be white, we all put cotton or white sheets under the Christmas tree, sprayed fake snow on our windows and pretended our Christmas was white.

That was why I began to get in the Christmas spirit very early during the first year I was in Berlin. In September, there were some snow flurries, those little teasers that would let us know that although it was just fall, winter was getting ready to make its appearance. The few flakes that dusted the tops of vehicles and covered windshields before melting was a message that, for the first time in my life, I would see a white Christmas.

As September faded and October turned into November, winter weather had Berlin in its grip. There was snow through October and November. For the first time in my life, I saw snow on the ground while I ate Thanksgiving dinner. While I enjoyed a white Thanksgiving, it was just the preview of the coming attraction.

My enthusiasm for a white Christmas wasn't shared by many of my Northern friends. To them, it was a common, and often unwelcome, occurrence.

"I hate white Christmases," Doc said. He was a New Yorker. "We always go to some relative's house for a big family Christmas dinner, and we get to shovel snow out of the driveway. Then we get to drive a couple hours to get to where a bunch of people I don't want to see are, and the heater always goes out about halfway there, so we freeze our asses off on the way. That's why I liked Christmas when I was in California. It was sunny, warm and definitely no snow."

But the griping about the annoyance of white Christmases didn't dampen my enthusiasm. I was still looking forward to my first.

A warm spell, accompanied by unseasonably sunny weather, caused the snow that had blanketed Berlin to melt away during Christmas week, throwing me into a fit of depression. The white Christmas that I had longed for, had expected to see, remained elusive. I felt like the youngster who got up on Christmas morning, ran to the tree to open the presents and found only socks and sweaters.

"Hey, Blackie, look at the street. No snow," Doc said as the bus carrying us to our jobs maneuvered through the morning rush-hour traffic on Christmas Eve.

"What do you expect, Doc? One thing I've always wanted is to have a white goddam Christmas and I've never had one. Why should I get one now? Hell, I could be sent to the goddam North Pole and all the snow would melt the day before Christmas," I said.

Buffalo Head, who was sitting in the seat in front of us, turned around. "Hell, you aren't missing a goddam thing. I've had enough white Christmases for me and you both," he said.

"Buff, it's just not the same damn thing. I want a white Christmas, and I need a white Christmas," I said.

"It doesn't look like this is going to be your year, Blackie. It doesn't look like it all," Doc said.

I scrunched down in the seat and glowered at the rising sun which was spreading its warmth across the city.

When we got to the Hill, I went to my work station in Violet, inside one of the Quonset huts jutting out from the central building housing three levels of dish-type antennas. During my shift, I would sit before the banks of tape recorders and receivers, looking at the blinking lights and watching the flickering monitor that meant some bureaucrat in the East German Communist Party headquarters in Leipzig was calling his counterpart in Magdeburg.

On Christmas Eve, while I listened to two workers in the East German agriculture ministry plan a New Year's get-together, the sun was disappearing behind a thick bank of clouds and the temperature was falling rapidly.

The two party hacks, one in Rostock and the other in Dresden, were trying to figure out an excuse to go to East Berlin for some serious partying when Doc came in and tapped me on the shoulder.

"Come outside for a sec, Blackie," he said.

I looked around and saw the relief man lighting a cigarette. Although he wasn't a German linguist, Fang had learned enough of the language to know if the conversation being monitored was important or if it were just routine stuff.

"Hey, Fang, got to break, okay?" I said, and handed him my headsets.

I followed Doc as he headed down the hallway, past the huge racks of tape recorders and receivers, and toward the exit.

Pausing before opening the door, Doc looked at me.

"Remember what you said about this not being your year, Coop?"

"Yeah," I said.

"Well, I think you might be wrong. Take a look at that sky," he said and threw open the door, giving me my first glimpse of the dark clouds that blanketed Berlin.

"My God, Doc, I think it's going to snow," I said. I walked out of the building toward the chain link fence that surrounded the installation. From where I stood on top of the mountain of rubble, I could see all of Berlin, and it was completely overcast in all directions, with no hint of sunshine.

"Doc, I don't think I've ever seen anything more beautiful. The sun's gone and I'm going to get my snow. I'm going to get my snow."

Every chance I got that afternoon, I would go outside to look at the sky.

"Hey, Fang! Take a break?" I would say.

"Yeah, Fang, fill in there, will you? Blackie's got to go look at the sky again," said The Pipe.

"I hope to Christ it does snow, Blackie, just to make you settle down," Fang said as he put on the headsets and began pushing buttons to monitor the signals.

The first few flakes began to drift slowly toward the ground as the trick bus was pulling away from the guard shack.

"Oh shit, it's snowing," Chief said. "I hope it don't stick."

"Why not?" Rock Weed said.

"Look up front, Weed. Who's driving the goddam bus?"

"Catfish."

"Yes, it's Catfish. That stupid Alabama redneck won't drive up the Hill if there's snow on the road, and that means we'll have to walk up the goddam Hill tomorrow," Chief said.

"Yeah, Chief, but look on the bright side. Blackie'll have his white goddam Christmas," The Pipe said. "That means he'll quit bitching and moaning, and we'll have a little peace and quiet around here."

"Oh wonderful, just wonderful," Chief said. "We'll have to hike up the goddam Hill through the snow, but Blackie'll be happy."

"You got it, Chief. If I'm happy, everybody'll be happy," I said.

And I was happy. The snow was coming down harder and I could see that it was beginning to stick to the cars parked along the streets, and the steep sloping tile roofs of the old houses. The city sounds — buses, subways, automobiles and people — became muted as the snow muffled the daily noise.

When the trick bus pulled to a stop in the barracks parking lot, I flew upstairs. I don't think I've ever taken a shower and changed clothes as swiftly as I did that Christmas Eve. But then again, I'd never been anywhere before in my life where it was actually snowing on Christmas Eve.

"Jesus, Blackie. What's the rush? Where the hell you going?" Grumpy John said when he dragged himself into the room.

"Out! Grumpy, I'm going out and I don't know where. I'm just going out and walk in the snow and see where it takes me," I said.

"You'll freeze your ass off in this weather if you're just walking around," he said.

"I don't give a shit. It's snowing and it's Christmas Eve. It's perfect for walking around."

"As the man said, 'Bah-humbug!'" Grumpy John said as he plopped down on his bunk.

"Well, what are you going to do, Grumpy?" I said.

"I'm going to sit on my ass until I get enough energy to walk downstairs and across that parking lot to the El Oso Club, where I'm going to have a few beers."

"You're going to miss the great snow," I said.

"Big hairy deal. I hate fucking snow."

"Goddam, I sure can see why you're called Grumpy John," I said.

"Hey, asshole, I deserve that name. You think it's easy being surly all the time? It ain't. You got to work at being grumpy."

"You be grumpy if you want. But I'm going to be happy and go play in the snow," I said, laughing as I stepped out into the hall.

I was almost to the stairs when Other George and The Pipe hailed me.

"Blackie! Where you headed?" Other George said.

Turning around, I saw they both were bundled up, with overcoats, sweaters and scarves. The Pipe even had on his Army pile cap, with the fur-lined flaps hanging loose. In the spirit of the season, he was puffing on a Meerschaum pipe with an exaggerated curve and Santa Claus carved into the ivory bowl.

"I don't know. I'm just going out and walk in the snow and look at things," I said.

"Sounds okay to me," Prince said. "What about you, Pipe?"

"Fine with me," The Pipe said, pausing to relight his tobacco. "Want some company?"

"The more the merrier," I said.

The snow was coming down harder as we headed out the

front gate. It was a gentle, but steady, snowfall. It wasn't one of those heavy snows that you know will turn into a blizzard. It was a powder that fell on us, light and feathery, not wet and heavy. The snow falling past the streetlights caused them to twinkle like artificial stars.

Habit, not thirst, sent us into the Scum.

"At least, the beer'll be cold," Hairy Ranger once said, when Shakey complained about the inadequate heat in the Scum.

"Of course it's going to be cold," Shakey said. "All they got to do is put the beer on the bar. It'll be colder there than in the refrigerator."

But on this Christmas Eve, the Scum didn't live up to its name. When we pushed open the door and walked in, it was quiet, even strangely warm.

"Damn, is this the Scum or are we lost?" Other George said, looking around the bar. The customers, normally so loud and rambunctious, were speaking in soft, muted voices. Several were just sitting quietly, appearing to be lost in their thoughts.

"I don't believe it. The Scum's civilized for a change," The Pipe said, as he tamped down a new load of tobacco and puffed furiously.

"I don't know about you, but I kind of like the new, improved Scum," I said.

"I'm not sure it's new and improved, but the it's definitely changed for the better tonight. I bet I can actually go to the head without worrying about getting knifed while I'm taking a piss," Other George said.

We had just finished our beers and were getting ready to leave when Little Monica, who sometimes filled in if the regular barmaid was sick, brought over another round.

"What's the deal, Moni? We didn't order anything," Other George said.

"Hans said to tell you 'Merry Christmas,'" Little Monica said, nodding her head toward the bartender.

Hans smiled a big toothy grin — the first time I had ever seen him smile — when we raised our glasses to him.

We spent a few more minutes in the Scum, sipping on the beers and chatting quietly about what we wanted to do when we got out of the Army. When we swallowed the last drops of beer, we all left a few coins on the table for Little Monica and started to leave. But we stopped at the door and looked at Hans, who peered at us over the top of his glasses.

"Thanks a lot, Hans. Merry Christmas," we said in unison.

"Fröhliches Weihnachten," he said, grinning. "Merry Christmas."

While we were in the Scum, the snow stopped, leaving the sidewalks and streets, the trees and shrubs blanketed in white. The streets sparkled from the reflections of the street lights, and it seemed as if fireflies were floating through the air down the street ahead of us.

The city was quiet. There were no cars roaring past us as was normal for this time of the night. Except for the buses, which continued their daily routine, there was no traffic. The cars, trucks and even the taxis had disappeared. A strange sense of calm, of peace, enveloped us and we found ourselves speaking softly, or just walking along immersed in our own thoughts.

We walked for hours that Christmas Eve, now and then stopping to sip a beer or a cup of steaming hot coffee. At each stop, proprietors, most of whom normally would be short-tempered at this time of the night, were caught up in the spirit of Christmas, and greeted us warmly when we came in out of the snow. On several occasions, when we prepared to pay for our drinks, the bartender would refuse our money, cheerfully reminding us that it was Christmas.

After several hours of wandering around the city and engaging in two or three snowball fights in the middle of streets, the sky cleared and flickering stars filled the heavens. It was no longer Christmas Eve when we turned back toward the barracks. As we passed the Scum, we noticed the lights were out.

"It must really be Christmas. The Scum's closed," The Pipe said. "I didn't think that place ever shut down for anything."

"The sun rises in the east and sets in the west and the Scum is always open. I guess you just can't count on anything anymore," Prince said.

"Well, it is Christmas, after all," I said.

"Yep, and a very merry Christmas to us one and all," The Pipe said cheerily.

"Listen to Tiny Tim over here," Other George said.

"Better Tiny Tim than Ebenezer Scrooge," The Pipe replied.

"Bah, humbug," Prince said.

As we neared the barracks, I thought about the evening. It had been magical. The snow had transformed this Christmas Eve into a wondrous occasion, a night when the moon beams reached down and touched me, when the stars sparkled more brightly than ever before, when my senses were more acute, and when there truly did seem to be a sense of peacefulness that was missing the rest of the year.

I stopped just before the door to my room. "Thanks for coming along, guys. Merry Christmas, and I mean it."

They grinned and said in unison, "Bah, humbug!"

But I couldn't be a Scrooge. I had seen a white Christmas and it was everything I had read about and everything I had hoped for.

The Many Moons of Fang

14 If nothing else could be said about him, everyone on C Trick agreed Fang always finished whatever he started. Even if he started something totally ridiculous, he would finish or die trying.

One frigid morning while Fang and I were waiting for the A18 at the bus stop on Kadettenweg, not far from the front gate of Andrews Barracks, he looked at me, his eyes bright with excitement.

"I'm going to master the bus system of Berlin," Fang said.

"What do you mean?" I said.

"I'm going to learn where every goddam bus goes, when it goes there and where you make connections. I going to know everything about the bus routes."

"For Christ's sake, why?" I said.

"Because it's spring, or it will be in a couple of weeks."

"Spring? Jesus Christ, Fang, there's still a goddam foot of snow on the ground. The Pipe hasn't even taken his Christmas decorations down. What do mean by spring? You know something the groundhog doesn't?"

"Everyone needs a project in spring, and I think this'll be one hell of a good project for me. Besides, unless the C.O. makes him take them down, the Pipe always leaves his Christmas decorations up until the Fourth of July."

"Why don't you just clean your room? Your wall locker looks like a goddam science project."

"That's no challenge, but mastering the bus system is. What if you want to go to a bar near Tegel and you're at the main PX? What bus do you take, and where do you transfer? What do you do?" he said.

"Easy," I said, "I'd just look at the schedule. There's one posted at every bus stop, you know."

"Hell, I know that," Fang said. "But, Christ, any idiot can read the schedule. Don't you want to just know which bus to take and where it connects with the other buses?"

"Good God, no," I said.

"Well, I do," Fang said, "and I'm going to master the whole bus system of Berlin."

"Yeah, Fang, sure you are," I said.

The word spread throughout the 78th about Fang's self-appointed mission.

"Hey, Fang," Dirty Joe said a couple of weeks later when we were on swings. "I'm going up to Neukölln to see my moose tonight. Which buses do I take?"

"Depends on where you leave from," Fang said. "If you're leaving from the barracks, take the A18 all the way to the Sportpalast, then transfer to the A23 and get off at the fourth stop. But if you're leaving from the housing, just ask your wife for the car keys and drive yourself there."

On days off, Fang would disappear, sometimes not show-ing up until just in time to clean up and get ready to go back to work. Everyone wondered where he was, but he wouldn't say. He would sit quietly on the trick bus to the Hill and smoke his cigarette.

After several weeks of this, I decided to find out what was happening.

"Where have you been going on your days off, Fang? We know you haven't been going out in the Zone, because you're not getting any orders cut. Just what the hell are you doing?" I said.

"I'm riding buses," he said.

"Riding buses? Where?"

"Well, I've mastered the buses in our sector and the Brit-ish Sector and now I'm learning the French Sector," Fang said. "Why don't you come with me? You might learn some-thing."

"I might learn something," I said, "but I sure as hell don't see what I'd be learning that's too bloody useful."

"Do you know which bus will take you from the Gleini-cke Bridge to Tegel and to the Havel at eleven at night?" he asked.

"Christ, no," I said.

"Well, I do."

Fang really did master the Berlin bus system. He probably knew it better than the city's transit authorities. He knew every little in and out, including which buses were the best connections if you were coming out of a club at midnight. He knew which drivers would wake you up at your stop and which ones would toss you off the bus if you were a bit too tipsy. There was nothing he didn't know about the Berlin bus system.

I didn't doubt Fang would do what he said he'd do next. C Trick was on mids and we were just sitting around drinking endless cups of coffee and smoking one cigarette after another when Fang announced his next project.

"I'm going to moon all of the major sites of Berlin!" he said proudly.

"What," Hairy Ranger and I said in unison.

"I'm going to moon all of the major sites of Berlin."

"For Christ's sake, Fang," I said. "I can almost understand why you'd want to master the bus system, but why the hell would you want to moon all the tourist attractions?"

"I didn't say every tourist attraction," he said. "I said all of the major sites in Berlin. There's a difference."

"Difference? What's the difference?" Hairy Ranger said.

Fang took a sip from his coffee and shook another cigarette out of the pack in his fatigue shirt pocket, lit it, and then leaned back in his chair before replying patiently.

"It's simple if you think about it. All the tourist attractions don't include all the major sites. What are the tourist attractions?"

"Well," I said. "There's the Wall. Everybody that comes to Berlin goes down to the Brandenburg Gate to look at the Wall."

"Charlottenburg Palace," Hairy Ranger said.

"Yeah, and the old Reichstag and the Gedächtniskirche and Dahlem Museum. Oh, and the Zoo," Other George said.

"Don't forget the Olympic Stadium, the Funkturm, and Spandau Prison," Fang added.

"Yeah, and the Strass queens at Stuttgarter Platz," Hairy Ranger chimed in.

"Okay. Okay," Fang said. "I know the Strass queens are a prime attraction for you, but they're not major sites of Berlin. I don't mean tourist attractions, I mean the major sites. I'm thinking about the Hill, the El Oso Club, the NAAFI Club, the Scum, the barracks, headquarters and the Colonel's house — you know, all the things that piss me off and make my life total shit."

"The Colonel's house. You got some kind of death wish or something, Fang? For Christ's sakes, you'd have to be a complete idiot to moon the Colonel's house," Hairy Ranger said.

"Got to do it," Fang said calmly as he lit another cigarette, stood up, stretched, and strolled out of the room.

"Think he's really going to do all that mooning?" Hairy Ranger said.

"Of course," I said.

"How do you know?"

"Because he said he is, and Fang always does what he says he's going to do."

We all kept a close eye on Fang for the next several weeks. Wherever he went, there would be two or three of us with him. He couldn't get rid of us. Whenever he looked up, there would be one of us right beside him.

"Jesus Christ," Fang said one day when Prince was shadowing him. "I can't take a shit without one of you jerkoffs right there to wipe my ass. What the hell are you doing?"

"We just want to make sure you do this mooning right, Fang," Prince said. "It's not that we don't trust you, but you need witnesses. What's the point of mooning everything in Berlin if there's no witnesses?"

Fang wasn't happy, but he sullenly resigned himself to our constant presence. Knowing that he wouldn't be able to do his hit-and-run mooning tactics as he had hoped, Fang began to plan his strategy. Like any good bandit or guerrilla, Fang knew that just mooning something was no good if you couldn't get away safely, so he planned his mooning attacks and escapes meticulously.

His first moon — of the bombed-out ruin of the Kaiser

Wilhelm Memorial Church on the Kurfürstendamm, the re-
tail center of West Berlin — was from a city bus. Fang knew
that there would be fewer passengers at mid-afternoon on a
Sunday, so he boarded double-decker bus, climbed to the
upper deck, where he was alone — except for the ever-present witnesses — and dropped his pants, pressing his ass
against the bus window as the bus pulled away from the
curb in front of the ruins of church. He quickly pulled up
his trousers and got off the bus at the next stop.

All of his moons, including the one on the Colonel's quarters, were carried off without a hitch until his mooning of
the Kongresshalle, or the Pregnant Oyster, as the Berliners
sardonically referred to the convention hall.

It was another Sunday afternoon and Fang was getting
pretty cocky. He had mooned every site on his list without
running into any problems. It was get the target, drop the
pants, moon, and get out. In many cases, Fang mooned and
was away from the scene before anyone had a chance to
react.

But on his last moon, he didn't move swiftly enough.

He waited until the tourists had finished taking photo-
graphs of the building. When the crowds thinned out, Fang
told me, one of his official witnesses, to get my car.

"I'll do the mooning and you have the car right there,
okay?" Fang said.

"No problem, Fang," I said as I walked off toward my car,
which was parked about a block away.

Fang watched as my battered green Volkswagen, which I
had bought for $75 about two weeks earlier, belched smoke
as it started. I gave it gas and moved away from the parking
space. He headed toward the front of the Kongresshalle.

When he thought the time was right, Fang unzipped his
fly, lowered his pants, aimed his rear at the front of the
building and shook it from side to side.

It was the moon of all moons. Down near the front entrance of the building, some people saw the little man who
was bent over with his bare ass pointed in their direction,
but he was too far away for them to grab or even identify.

A triumphant grin spread across Fang's face. I had arrived and was just a few feet way. He had the car door open.

"Come on, Fang! Goddammit! Let's get the hell out of here!"

Fang was delaying. He was making sure the last moon would be a most memorable one.

But he had dawdled just a bit too long. Before he could straighten up and get his pants back on properly, a tiny, wizened German grandmother who had been walking by whipped out her umbrella and whacked Fang solidly across his bare buttocks.

He was so surprised by the unexpected attack that he lost his balance and fell forward on his face.

"Jesus H. Christ! Let's get the hell out of here," Fang said, scrambling to his feet and jerking his pants up, only to find the pants legs tangled around his ankles, causing him to fall down again.

When Fang fell for a second time and the old German woman drew her arm back to take another shot at his ass with her umbrella, Hairy Ranger and Other George, who had been nearly rolling on the ground laughing at Fang's troubles, ran over, and each of us grabbed him by an arm and we propelled him — and his pants — into my Volkswagen.

"Way to go, Fang," Hairy Ranger said as I pulled away from the curb and we headed down the broad avenue toward safety. "You nearly got your ass kicked out there. That old lady was really pissed."

Fang by now had his pants pulled up and was tightening his belt.

Looking out the rear window of the Volkswagen, he grimaced, then smiled.

"Yeah, but I still mooned all the major sites of Berlin, didn't I?" he said proudly.

The Gold Weenie Award

15 After his success at mastering the Berlin bus system and mooning all the major sites in the city, Fang became depressed. He'd thrown himself enthusiastically into the two projects, and without a challenge, he began to sit morosely in the El Oso Club, drinking one beer after another without seeming to enjoy himself.

C Trick had finished eves, and on the only full night off before going on mids, Fang and I went to the El Oso. Fang drank more heavily than usual, finishing two beers in the time it took me to finish one.

"Damn, Fang, slow down, you're going to drown yourself," I said, as he chugged another bottle of Beck's.

"Don't give a shit. I'm depressed."

"What about?"

"All this shit," he said drunkenly, sweeping his arm out and around to show the entire club. "All this shit. Goddam Army bullshit. Look at that goddam asshole over there."

"Which one?"

"Which one can it be? That one in his goddam greens," Fang said, pointing in the direction of a enormous 'Gator first sergeant in his Class A uniform, complete with a full assortment of medals.

"What kind of chickenshit asshole wears his goddam Class-fucking-As in the El Oso?" Fang's voice rose in volume as he spoke and the first sergeant heard him.

"Oh, Christ, Fang, hold it down, will you?"

"Hold what down, Blackie? I want to know what kind of chickenshit asshole wears goddam Class As into this shit-hole?"

"Oh, Jesus, here he comes now." I saw the first sergeant

stand up, push his chair back and walk ponderously toward our table. I tried to ignore it, but I knew he didn't intend to go to the restroom, he planned to brace us.

He put his hands on our table and leaned heavily on it, the wood creaking in protest.

Fang didn't look at him, fumbling in his pocket for a pack of cigarettes.

"Soldier, I think you need to leave."

"Huh?" Fang had an air of drunken innocence.

"I've been listening to you, and I think it's time for you to leave."

"Are you the goddam manager or something?" Fang asked indignantly.

The first sergeant straightened up; I knew I had to do something fast or the MPs would be on their way in minutes.

"I'll get him out, Sarge. He's just having a few problems," I said, jumping up and grabbing Fang's arm. "Come on, Fang, let's go to Die Eierschale."

I deliberately chose Die Eierschale because I thought the bus ride might help Fang get sober. I guess I had another reason; I enjoyed sitting at the bar in Die Eierschale, talking with Ulli, a dark-haired, exotic university student who worked as a barmaid. I had been visiting Die Eierschale more frequently since I had met Ulli.

Fang nodded and came along with me. I looked over my shoulder and saw the 'Gator first sergeant standing by the table, his arms folded across his bemedalled chest, watching to make sure we actually did leave the club.

"Fuck him if he can't take a joke," Fang mumbled.

"Right, Fang, fuck him," I said.

Fang insisted on stopping at the Scum for a couple of beers, then followed by a couple of more beers at Linda's Lounge on Kommandantenstraße on the way to the bus stop on Ringstraße, about six or eight blocks from the barracks.

By the time the bus arrived, I had gotten a bit looped, but Fang, who had continued to drink two beers for every one I drank, had gotten positively soused.

"Fuck the Eierschale, Blackie. Let's go to the Hofbräuhaus," Fang said, his speech slurred. "I want to drink beer by the liter."

I still wanted to go to Die Eierschale, but I decided to wait until later, thinking maybe I should go along with Fang. We would ride the bus to the Europa Center, maybe sobering up a little on the way, and after getting off the bus across the Kurfürstendamm from the Kaiser Wilhelm Memorial Church, we'd walk to the Hofbräuhaus. However, Fang had other plans.

When we got on the bus, Fang pulled out some currency and bought transfers for both of us.

"Where're we going, Fang?"

"I have a better idea than the Hofbräuhaus," he said softly, closed his eyes and sat back in his seat.

A few stops later, we were on another bus, headed for the British sector, and I had an idea what Fang had in mind, especially when he swung out of his seat as the bus neared the stop on Stuttgarter Platz, one of the more prominent red-light districts in Berlin.

I followed along as Fang wove his way along the sidewalk to the Treffpunkt bar, a dive where softcore pornographic movies, mostly about buxom young women who liked to take off their clothes, stretch and breathe heavily, were shown on a white sheet tacked to a wall. After a while, one of the barmaids would offer to take you upstairs for a quickie.

We took seats at the bar, and each of us ordered beer and a shot of cognac. The bartender refused to sell a beer without the accompanying shot of liquor on the first round. It probably wasn't legal, but the Treffpunkt's bouncer had been a professional boxer, who rumors said had killed an opponent in a match in Hamburg. It probably wasn't true, but I certainly didn't want to take any chances, so I cheerfully ordered a shot of cognac.

Before I had finished my shot of foul-tasting cheap cognac, I saw Fang following a dark-haired barmaid, wearing a black dress so short it left nothing to the imagination, through beaded curtains in the doorway and up the stairs.

A tall barmaid, wearing a low-cut silky blue blouse and miniskirt, slid onto the barstool just vacated by Fang. She had long blonde hair with dark roots, a deep hatching of lines around her eyes from too many long nights in too many smoke-filled bars, and an oddly misshapen nose, which must have been broken and not reset properly. She smiled in a caricature of seductiveness.

"I'm leaving in a minute," I said before she could ask me to buy her a drink.

Her smile vanished and she glared at me. But her smile returned almost as quickly when she saw a 'Gator, easily recognizable by his PX clothes and military haircut, take a seat at the end of the bar. She glided toward the 'Gator, slipping her arm around his shoulder and whispering something to him that caused him to laugh and slide his hand down her back to rest on her rear end.

Suddenly over the noise of the jukebox, I heard Fang, his voice angry and drunkenly demanding his money, while a woman refused. I rushed to the doorway, pushed back the beaded curtain and looked up the stairs.

Fang stomped down the stairs, brushed by me and went outside. I looked up the stairs and saw the hooker straightening her miniskirt. When she got to the bottom of the stairs, I motioned to her.

"What's the problem?"

"He couldn't do it."

"What?"

"He was too drunk to do it, and he wanted his money back. It was his fault, and he don't get his money back."

I shrugged, and went back to my spot at the bar, drained the rest of my beer and went outside, where I saw Fang talking to two Berlin police officers. I started to join them, but then decided I didn't want to get involved.

The two officers stood patiently taking notes as Fang, his face red and his arms flapping like an angry bantam rooster, shouted about a whore stealing his forty marks. When he finished, the two officers glanced at each other, and one of them asked a question, which apparently involved me because Fang pointed toward me, making me wish I had stayed inside the bar.

While one of the officers stayed with Fang, his partner walked over to me.

"Do you know him?"

"Yes, we're in the same unit."

"Which unit is it?"

"Seventy-eighth ASA."

"Your friend says a whore stole his forty marks. Do you know anything about it?"

"She said he couldn't get it up and wanted his money back, and she won't give it back to him."

"He filed a complaint about it, so we had to call your MPs."

Oh, shit, I thought.

"Think I ought to hang around?"

The policeman nodded and went back to stand beside his partner. I walked over to lean against a light pole behind them, and wait for the U.S. MPs to arrive.

A few minutes later, the MPs arrived, and while the Berlin police officers went inside the bar to talk to the barmaid, Fang and I got into the back seat of the MP's car. I smoked a cigarette and stared out the window while the MPs drove through the darkened streets of Berlin to the MP headquarters at Andrews Barracks.

I didn't say anything, just waited for Fang to finish filling out his reports.

"Cooper!"

The MP sergeant of the guard's voice startled me.

"Yeah?"

"Get over here."

I stood and went to the sergeant's desk.

"What do you need, Sarge?"

"You're a witness. I need your statement, and then we'll get some photos."

"I didn't witness anything; I just happened to be there."

"Your buddy says you're a witness, so you're a witness."

"Shit."

I took a seat beside the desk and the sergeant slid a form toward me. I picked up a ball-point pen lying near his nameplate, and began to fill out the form. When I finished filling out the report, I signed my name beside an "X" that had been scrawled in blue ink on the bottom of the form. Then I followed an MP corporal to one side of the room, where I stood in front of a large light blue sheet of poster board tacked to the wall and waited for a sleepy private first class to take my photograph.

Fang and I didn't say much to each other on the walk back to the barracks. When we got to his door, he mumbled, "Sorry about all this shit, Blackie."

"Don't worry about it. I just don't know why they needed our pictures. Did they tell you why?"

"No."

"Never mind, see you later."

His door closed behind him, and I went on down the hallway to my room.

When I opened the door, Hairy Ranger was sitting on his bunk reading a John LeCarre spy novel.

"Where you been?" he asked.

"I'm not sure if I remember."

"How long were you and Fang at the stockade?"

"Good God, Ranger! How'd you hear about that?"

"Rapid Roger's the orderly tonight, and the MPs called and told him they had you and Fang. They said it was something about a fight with a whore."

"There wasn't a fight with a whore, and I just had to go be a witness for Fang."

"Well, what the hell happened?"

"Fang got drunk and almost got us thrown out of the El Oso, so we ended up at Stuttgarter Platz. He was shitfaced and went upstairs with one of the whores. I wasn't with them so I don't know exactly what happened, but the whore said Fang couldn't get it up and wanted his money back. Anyway, he called the cops, who called the MPs who took us to the stockade. We filled out a shitpot full of forms and then we walked back to the barracks. That's it. The end. Okay?"

"I'm sure Phantom's going to enjoy hearing it. You got a note from him on your rack."

Phantom was the company first sergeant, a tall, slightly stooped man with thick, bushy eyebrows and thin lips. Big Ed started calling him Phantom after the first sergeant seemed to appear suddenly like an apparition.

I looked to the corner of the room where my bunk had

been shoved against the wall. There was a piece of paper lying on the blanket covering the pillow. I walked over, picked up the note, unfolded it and saw the Phantom's scrawl.

"Shit, Ranger, what time is it?"

"About three."

"Goddam Phantom wants to see me at eight. I suppose Fang's got one, too?"

"Yeah, the Pipe told me Phantom left a note for Fang."

A few hours later, Fang and I stood in the first sergeant's office. Fang appeared to be nervous, not knowing what to expect, but I tried to appear indignant about the whole affair.

Phantom looked sternly at us.

"This is just about the silliest goddam thing I've ever heard of. Jesus Christ, filing charges against a whore because you're too drunk to get a hard-on. My God, men, that's something you don't talk about, much less file charges. "

"Sarge, I didn't file a damn thing, I was just a witness," I said in protest.

"Yeah, Sarge, I told the MPs he was just a witness."

Phantom ignored Fang, looking sternly at me.

"You were with him, weren't you?"

"Yes."

"You didn't stop it, did you?"

"Hell, I didn't think I had to. I didn't think the MPs were going to get involved."

"Well, if you had gotten him the hell out of there, they wouldn't have been involved."

"Hell, Sarge, I hadn't done anything; it just happened."

"Son, he's your buddy, from your trick. You guys have to take care of each other. Now, there's a bunch of paperwork and it's pretty damn embarrassing for all of us. Go on, get the hell out of here, both of you."

On the way upstairs, I glanced sideways at Fang. He grinned and said, "Like he said, you should have taken care of me, Blackie."

"You earned the Green Weenie, Fang."

"I think I've retired the damn thing."

The guys agreed with him. At midnight, after checking in

on the Hill, most of C Trick crowded into Violet to select the winner of the Green Weenie Award.

"All right, my roomie here's going to nominate Fang for the Green Weenie Award, but we can save some time," Hairy Ranger said. "Everyone who thinks Fang deserves the Green Weenie sound off."

The room reverberated with the roars of C Trick.

"Okay, okay, that's enough," Ranger shouted. Then he put his index fingers against his lips and whistled, a piercing whistle that cut through the noise and brought almost instant silence.

"I think Fang's got the Green Weenie. But because we don't think anyone else will ever be able to top him, we've already voted to retire it, so ...," he reached beneath his fatigue shirt, pulled out the box and handed it to Fang. "Since it's being retired, we decided to give you the Gold Weenie Award."

Fang opened the box, exposing a C-ration wiener, painted gold and lying on a bed of cotton. He grinned sheepishly, closed the box and put it in his pocket.

"Thanks, guys," he said and walked slowly from the room.

Fang never said, but I think he went to the restroom and flushed the only Gold Weenie Award ever presented.

Ulli

16 When I met Ulli, she was working behind the bar at the Die Eierschale, serving up drinks to the mixed crowd of American GIs and German students.

Like most young Americans arriving in Germany for the first time, we had a Hollywood-inspired image of German women — blonde, blue eyes, fair complexion, big busted, and outgoing. Ulli was far from that image. She was aloof, tall and slender, almost flat-chested, with thick, curly black hair and obsidian eyes. Sometimes, when she wore colorful German peasant dresses, she looked like a Gypsy.

Although Ulli may have looked like a Gypsy, she was German. I would learn later that she was from a small town in the Rhineland, where her family had lived for several generations. She was the first of her family to leave the Rhineland, choosing to move to West Berlin, where she found a small one-room flat in Kreuzberg, an old section of Berlin that was populated mostly by students, artists, and immigrant workers. She enrolled in the Free University. To make ends meet, she worked nights behind the bar at the Die Eierschale.

On the night that I met Ulli, she was cleaning beer glasses in the sink behind the bar. Most of the bars in Berlin had a double sink for cleaning the glasses, allowing the bar to get by with fewer glasses because they could press used glasses back into service faster. One side of the sink had scrub brushes attached in an upright position to the bottom of a sink filled with soapy wash water. The beer glasses would be shoved down over the scrub brushes and vigorously moved up and down. Then they would be moved to the other side of the sink and immersed in the rinse water, before being used again.

I was alone the night that I met Ulli. Earlier in the evening, I had been with a group that had scored free tickets to a jazz concert at the Berlin Sportpalast. After the concert, I split off from the group, and drifted around the city, finally arriving at Die Eierschale about midnight.

It was the first time I had been to the bar, and it was crowded. I thought that I'd go down the street to another bar that I knew would be less congested. But while I was deciding what I wanted to do, I saw a somewhat looped young man get off a stool at the end of the bar, next to the wall under a neon light that kept flashing "Trinkt Shutheiss Bier." I watched to see if he was just going to the men's room, but when he brushed by me and went out into the night, I walked rapidly across the room and settled onto the stool.

I liked the spot at the end of the bar, because I could lean back up against the brick wall and watch everything that was going on in the pub. It was a big room, with two large windows looking out onto a courtyard in the front. There were two long tables in front of the windows and several smaller tables scattered throughout the large room. There was a hallway that led to the front entrance. The hallway had hooks mounted on the walls for hanging coats or umbrellas. On the side of the room opposite the windows were several booths, which had small tables, that offered at least a sense of privacy.

The bar was in the corner of the room, extending about fifteen to twenty feet from the wall toward the center of the room. Between the end of the bar and the booths was a doorway opening into a hallway. To the left was the kitchen, and to the right were the restrooms and a stairway that led to the bar owner's living quarters.

When I took my seat on the stool in the corner, I noticed a tall, slender, dark-haired young woman washing beer glasses in the double-sink behind the bar.

She glanced at me. "Moment mal," she said, indicating she'd be with me as soon as she finished washing the glasses. As soon as she had rinsed the last glass and placed it behind her, she got a towel to dry her hands, and walked over to where I was sitting.

When I first saw her, I thought she was Turkish, because Germany at the time had a shortage of workers and there seemed to be hundreds of the dark-haired, dark-eyed guest workers in Berlin. But when she got closer and spoke, I could tell she wasn't Turkish or Gypsy or Romanian, she was German — just one who didn't fit any of the stereotypes.

I stayed the rest of the night on that stool at the end of the bar, sipping on my beer and watching Ulli. I learned her name when the bar's owner, who had been working in the kitchen, peered around the doorway and called out to her as she went about her duties.

She was friendly, but somewhat aloof, as if there were an invisible wall between her and the patrons. Unlike some barmaids in other bars who would giggle when men grabbed their behinds, Ulli gracefully dodged the hands of the men, Americans and Germans alike. It was like she had some kind of radar, because she always seemed to know where a hand would be and managed to avoid contact.

Because the bar was so crowded and Ulli and the other employees were working so hard, I wasn't in a hurry for a refill. I decided to wait until there was a lull in the activity before getting another beer. While waiting, I noticed that other patrons at the bar would shout at her, bellowing her name and what they wanted.

"Ulli, ein Bier, bitte! (Ulli, one beer, please!)"

"Hey, Ulli, bring me another beer, okay?"

"Noch eins. (Another one.)"

"Hit me again."

"Bier."

"Beer."

For as long as I was there, the mixture of German and English continued, with Ulli quietly filling the orders. I don't know if she appreciated me because I didn't bellow her name and shout out my order, but she would look in my direction now and then to see if my glass was empty. When I had finished the first glass, she looked at me, raised her eyebrows and tapped an empty glass with her index finger.

I nodded and she put the glass under the tap, filled it to

the brim with the foaming, frothy brew, and placed it on the bar in front of me. From then on, I never had to say anything, because Ulli would look at me, and if my glass were empty or near-empty, she'd raise her eyebrows. I'd nod and she'd pull another for me.

After that first night, I began to go to the Die Eierschale more frequently, stopping by two or three times a week. I even began to think of the stool at the end of the bar against the wall as mine, and I would be slightly irritated when I came in and found someone else using it. I would wait impatiently until the interloper left, then I'd rush over and grab it before someone else could.

After I became a semi-regular at the Die Eierschale, I would find a glass of beer waiting for me when I came in. Ulli, from her spot behind the bar, could see out the front windows into the lighted courtyard. She would see me as I walked up the sidewalk to the front entrance. It became a pleasant little ritual — I would come in the bar and the glass of beer would be waiting for me.

Ulli and I had very little conversation. Running the bar kept her busy most of the time, and I'd always been painfully shy, having to fight a constant battle with my demons to meet and deal with new people. But gradually, I became more comfortable, and Ulli's pleasantness broke down those walls of silence and we would engage in friendly conversation.

Often on those nights when business was light, Ulli would pull up a stool across from me behind the bar and we would sit and talk or, if there were another other people with me, play Chicago, a dice game. The game used three dice, which were shaken in a cup and then slammed down on the bar or table top and the points tallied. Each player had to score more points than the previous player. Play would continue until someone couldn't better the previous score. To make the game even more interesting, the loser had to buy a round of drinks.

I enjoyed sitting across the bar from Ulli and talking to her. She would tell about the courses she was taking at the university, and we would talk about music, movies, books, and politics. Occasionally after she got off work, I would walk her to the bus stop, and we would laugh and talk until the bus came that would take her to her flat in Kreuzberg.

Although her job at Die Eierschale kept her too busy to be a member of the German student groups that were part of the wave of rebellion that swept university campuses around the world in the Sixties, she knew all of the groups, their leaders, and their goals.

Her awareness of the student movement was demonstrated about six months after Berlin was shaken by the death of Benno Ohnesorg, a university student shot to death by Berlin policeman Karl-Heinz Kurras during a demonstration against the Shah of Iran, who was visiting the city. Benno Ohnesorg was just in the wrong place at the wrong time. He wasn't even part of the protest. He was on his way home and just happened to show up when the demonstrators and police began to scuffle. Also, it would be revealed years later that Kurras, who would be acquitted on murder in connection with the shooting, was a spy for the Stasi, East Germany's secret police.

One of the student leaders, Rudi Dutschke, used the death of Benno Ohnesorg to consolidate the various student groups and there was a series of demonstrations against the Vietnam war, nuclear weapons, police brutality, and censorship.

Red Rudi, as he was called in the Berlin newspapers, became as prominent in the student movement in Germany as the Chicago Seven would be in the U.S. His picture was on the front page of the Berlin newspapers, and he was the subject of many interviews by journalists from all around the world. Even a couple of pubs where he and some other student leaders would hang out were declared off limits to GIs by the U.S. military commander. Rudi had become quite a celebrity.

It was late fall in Berlin. The days were getting shorter, the nights were crisp and cold, and it rained frequently. Die Eierschale was nearly empty when I arrived, so I took my favorite spot at the end of the bar next to the wall. It was quiet, giving Ulli time to clean glasses, arrange the liquor bottles, and generally do a little bar-type housekeeping.

I had eaten supper at the snack bar and before I left the

PX, I stopped in the bookstore and bought a copy of News-week, which I rolled up and stuck in the pocket of my rain-coat. With Ulli busy and no one else around to talk to or play Chicago with, I pulled the magazine out of my raincoat pocket, rested my back against the wall and put my feet on the stool next to me and began to read.

I was intent on my magazine when I heard Ulli calling.

"Blackie, come here, bitte," she said.

I looked up and saw her standing by a table in the far corner of the room. There were several young people at the table, obviously Germans because they all had hair that crept down past their collars and over their ears. I marked my place in my magazine and walked over to stand next to Ulli.

"Blackie, I want for you to meet someone we have talked about," she said. "This is Rudi Dutschke." She placed her hand on the shoulder of the slight, dark-haired young man sitting at the end of the table.

"Pleased to meet you," I said, and shook his hand, which he had extended to me. "I've certainly read a lot about you."

"Not pleasant reading, I assume." He chuckled.

"Absolutely not. But then, from what I read, you're trying to destroy civilization as we know it," I said.

"It's hard to get the truth out about what we're doing when the ruling class owns the press. But then, you Ameri-cans should know about that," Rudi said.

"You don't have to tell me," I said. "I was a sportswriter for a newspaper before I joined the Army."

"Why are you in the Army if you were working for a newspaper?" he said.

"It's kind of strange, but joining the Army probably has kept me from getting my ass shot at in Vietnam," I said.

"How?"

"Well, I was going to college during the day and working for the paper at night. I didn't really want to go to college just then, but as long as I was in school I wouldn't be draft-ed. Anyway, I quit going to classes and I was probably going to fail everything and lose my deferment, which would mean I could be drafted," I said. "I was afraid that if I was drafted, I'd be sent to Vietnam and I didn't want to go."

"Did you oppose the war?" Rudi said.

"Yeah, but I guess I was too chickenshit to go to Canada or Sweden, you know. So, I went down and enlisted in the Army because if I enlisted, I could choose where I'd go — and I damn sure was going to make sure it wasn't Vietnam. Anyway, here I am."

"Tell me something else," Dutschke said. "What do your friends think about the war?"

"I really don't know about anyone else, but I don't think we have any business being in Vietnam," I said.

Rudi nodded seriously. Then he pushed his chair back and pulled on his raincoat. He began shaking hands with all of the people at the table.

"I am sorry, but I have to go home now. We're having a committee meeting and I must be there," he said. Then, extending his hand to me, he said, "I am pleased to meet you. Maybe we'll have a chance to sit and talk again."

We never did, although I saw Rudi Dutschke several more times at the head of student demonstrations. On April 11, 1968, as he was getting on his bicycle outside a student gathering-place, Rudi was shot in the head by Josef Bachmann, a neo-Nazi who was inspired by the assassination just days earlier of Dr. Martin Luther King. Dutschke didn't die, but he suffered brain damage and had to spend months and months in therapy in England. He later taught in England until running into visa problems. He and his family relocated to Denmark, where he died, drowning in the bathroom after suffering a seizure.

After Rudi Dutschke left, I went back to my seat at the bar, where Ulli joined me a few minutes later.

"You see, Blackie, I do know what's going on at the University," she said.

"I knew you did, Ulli."

"You did, but some of your American friends didn't. They think I'm just another barmaid," she said.

"Big deal. Most of them think I'm crazy. Hell, even my own family thinks I'm unstable," I said with a grin. "Don't worry about what they think. We're all just here for a couple of years anyway. Nobody's going to miss us when we're back in the States."

"Oh, some of you will be remembered," Ulli said softly.

I looked at her closely, but the moment, if there were one, passed swiftly, because another patron at the other end of the bar called out for another beer and Ulli moved down to serve him.

Things were as they were before, until a couple of weeks later.

Ulli was different. She seemed withdrawn, maybe even depressed, and didn't have the usual wide smile of greeting for the customers. She did have a beer sitting on a coaster where I always sat when I got to my stool and she smiled, but there was no joy in her smile.

"Is something wrong, Ulli?" I said the first chance I got.

"I can't talk about it now," she said. "Maybe later."

"Is there anyway I can help?" I said.

"I don't think so. No. Maybe. I don't know."

"If I can do anything, let me know, okay?"

"I will."

"You sure about that?"

"Yes," she said.

She continued to go about her nightly routine, but it was as if she were in another place and another time.

"What's the matter with Ulli? She's not herself," Prince said, as he settled onto the stool next to me. He leaned over the bar and found the cup and dice, then settled back on his stool. He looked toward Ulli.

"Hey, Ulli, want to play some Chicago?"

"No," she said, without looking up.

"Jeez. What gives? She depressed or something? You and her have a fight, Blackie?" Prince said, shaking the cup and slamming it down on the counter. "Three fives, what a way to start," he said, looking at the dice and then sliding the cup over to me.

"No, we haven't had a fight, for Christ's sake. How could we have a fight? We don't have anything to fight about," I said.

I shook the cup, listening to the dice rattle inside and then flipped it over on the bar top. Lifting the cup I saw a pair of fives and a deuce.

"You been getting any of that, Blackie?" Prince said, leer-ing.

"Jesus Christ, Prince, it's none of your goddam business," I said.

"Hey, Blackie, don't get your bowels in an uproar. I didn't mean anything, but you are spending a lot of time down here, and every time I come in, she's over here in this corner with you," Prince said.

"That's bullshit, Prince. I just enjoy talking to her and she likes to sit over here because she knows I'm not going to try to put my hand up her skirt."

"Don't tell me you haven't thought about it."

"Of course I have. But I'm not going to. She's not on the make. She's just working here while she's in school," I said.

"Well, you're a dumbass if you don't at least try, Blackie. I know if it looked like she liked me, I damn sure would try to get her in the sack."

"But you're not me, are you now?" I said.

It was almost closing time.

Prince, noticing the time, leaned toward me. "I'm going to the Scum. Want to come along?"

"Yeah, got nothing else to do," I said.

"Well, wait for me, I got to go drain the lizard," he said with a laugh.

As I tugged on my coat and drank the last few drops of beer from my glass, Ulli came down to my end of the bar.

"Could you give me a ride home tonight, Blackie?" she said softly.

"Be glad to," I said and sat back down on the stool just as Prince got back from the restroom.

"Hey, Prince, something's come up. I'll pass on the Scum," I said.

"What is it?"

"Ulli needs a ride home and she lives up in Kreuzberg," I said.

"I'm not that hot on the Scum myself. Why don't I ride along, too?" Prince said.

"Since no one's asked you, I don't guess you will," I said.

"Yeah, yeah. Looks like old Blackie's got a shot at getting laid, so I'm left to walk halfway across Berlin by myself in the middle of the night."

"Screw you, Prince. It's only three blocks to the Scum. Hell, I've seen you crawl farther than that," I said.

"Well, if you get any, let me know," Prince said with a laugh. He slapped me on the shoulder and headed out the door.

The door had barely slammed shut behind Prince when Ulli, now wearing a red beret and denim jacket and carrying a loaded bookbag, came through the door to the hallway and walked over to join me.

"I'm ready now, Blackie. What was that all about with the Prince? He was laughing so hard when he left," she said.

"He wanted a ride."

"Why didn't you offer him one?"

"I've had enough of him for one night. Besides, he's just going down to the Scum," I said.

"Well, you still could have given him a ride that far."

"The walk'll do him good," I said, reaching down and taking her heavy bookbag. "Ignore the mess in the car," I said as I unlocked the passenger-side door of my battered old Volkswagen. "I promise there's nothing alive in it."

She laughed and slid into the seat and reached across to the driver's side and unlocked my door.

We didn't talk much as we drove through the silent streets of Berlin, winding from Lichterfelde past Tempelhof, until we arrived at the old apartment building in Neukölln, where Ulli had been living since she arrived in Berlin.

While Ulli was getting her bookbag, I got out and walked around to the passenger side and opened the door for her. I took the bag and carried it for her to the door, as she hunted through what looked like dozens of keys until she found the one that unlocked the building's main door.

"I have too many keys, I think," Ulli said. "I need another one for the door on my floor and another one for my flat."

We stood there for several moments, before I broke the silence.

"I guess I got to go. There's a bunch of guys waiting for me at the Scum."

"Yes, I know," she said, making no move to go upstairs.

"Are you all right, Ulli? What's bothering you?"

"Yes — no, no, I'm not all right," Ulli said. "I need some-

one to talk to. Will you stay with me for a little while, Blackie?"

"Sure, I'd be glad to."

"Are you sure you don't mind? What about your friends?"

"They'll never miss me, Ulli."

We climbed the four flights to her apartment, which was
at the end of a hallway. It was a single room, with a tiny
alcove in the left corner near the door. In the alcove were
a small refrigerator, stove and sink. A single bed, covered
by a thick, colorful comforter was under two tall windows
that looked out over a small courtyard. A dining table and
three chairs sat against the wall on the left side and directly
across from it was an overstuffed sofa. Next to the sofa was
a book shelf, which seemed to be sagging under the weight
of all the books.

Movie and concert posters, including one for the American rhythm and blues legend Ray Charles, were tacked
to the wall alongside several posters endorsing the Social
Democrats in Berlin municipal elections.

"Ray Charles?" I said, pointing to the poster.

"I love Ray Charles," Ulli said. "I went to see him at the
Sportpalast last summer."

"Well, so did I!" I said. "I got a free ticket at the PX."

"Where did you sit?" she said.

"Right up behind the band. What about you?"

"Oh, I was way back near the exit. I had to use my
friend's binoculars to see good," she said.

"Hit the road, Jack."

"What?"

"Hit the road, Jack — you know, the song. I love it when
Ray Charles does that song."

"Me, too," Ulli said. "You want some coffee? I'll make
some."

"Fine," I said, and went over and sat on the sofa while
Ulli measured out the coffee in the pot and put it on the
flames. Within minutes, the wonderful aroma of percolating
coffee filled the room.

"You want anything in your coffee? I have some sugar,
but I'm out of cream," Ulli said.

"I take it black."

"Black for Blackie," she said with a smile, as she put two teaspoons of sugar into one cup and began to stir it. When she was finished, she dropped the spoon in the sink and bringing the two cups of hot coffee, joined me on the sofa.

We sat quietly, sipping on the coffee. After a few minutes I leaned over and put my cup on the floor.

"What is the matter, Ulli? I know I haven't known you a long time, but I've never seen you like this," I said.

Ulli also had put her cup on the floor. "My father has died."

"When?"

"Today. No, no, it's today now. He died yesterday. My mother called me just before I went to work," she said.

"I'm so sorry, Ulli. But why did you go to work? Why didn't you go home?"

"I wanted to, but all of the flights out to home had left. I would have to wait anyway, and I didn't want to just sit in this apartment and wait. I think I would have gone crazy just sitting," she said.

"It must have been a hard night, going to work and putting up with all of us at the bar."

"No, no," she said, "really, it helped."

"You must have been close," I said.

"We were once. But we weren't very close at all for the last few years. He didn't like my friends. He didn't want me to come to Berlin. He didn't even want for me to go to the university; he wanted me to stay at home and be a nice little German mother and have lots of babies. We fought a lot."

"But you loved each other, didn't you?" I said. "I mean, my mother and I don't get along at all, but we still do love each other."

"I did love my father," she said solemnly. "But we had just had another big fight over me being in Berlin and working at the bar at night. We argued really bad and he hung up on me. Blackie, when he hung up on me, I wished he were dead."

"Now he's dead and I can't tell him I loved him. I didn't want him to die," she said.

Then she broke down and fell forward with her head on

my lap. As she sobbed, great wracking sobs that came from deep within her, I stroked her hair and told her to cry it out.

Ulli cried and cried until there were no tears left, just a gasping for breath. Finally, she sat up and brushed her dark hair back from her face. She leaned over and put her arms around my neck and hugged me tightly. I hugged her back and kissed the top of her head.

Pulling her close, I kissed her on the lips, feeling her return my kiss.

Then she leaned back and looked intently at me. "Blackie, are you wanting to sleep with me?" she said.

"Of course, I do," I said, and for a brief moment I saw a sign of disappointment in her eyes. "But I'm not. It's not the right time, Ulli."

"Thank you. You are my friend, like I knew," Ulli said. "But you will stay with me for the rest of the night, will you?"

"I'm here for as long as you need," I said. "But what you need right now is to get some rest."

We spent the rest of the night on the sofa, with Ulli snuggling against me, as if she were seeking warmth and comfort.

We must have dozed off, because I became aware of the sun's rays streaming in through the tall windows behind us.

"Ulli, Ulli," I said, shaking her shoulder gently. "It's morning. I've got to go."

She yawned, and smiled at me.

"You can't leave until you've had some coffee," she said. "There's a pastry shop right down the street. Why don't you go get us something while I make coffee?"

She made coffee and I walked to the shop where I bought us each a breakfast pastry. When we had finished our breakfast, I got ready to go back to the barracks, because I knew she would be leaving soon for the airport.

As I opened the door to leave, Ulli wrapped her arms around me and hugged me tightly.

"Thank you, Blackie. Thank you for being here for me. I will never forget how much you have been my friend," she said.

"I'm glad I could be here, Ulli," I said and started down the hallway. At the stairway, I stopped and looked back to the apartment. Ulli waved and smiled at me. I returned the wave and she went inside the apartment and closed the door.

The day seemed to drag on endlessly, with the minutes seeming like hours and the hours like days, until I had to catch the trick bus to the Hill. I had just settled into my seat next to the window when Prince sat beside me.

"Missed you at the Scum, Blackie. Where'd you and Ulli go?"

"I took her back to her apartment. We had coffee and just sat around and talked."

"Did you get any?"

"No, and it's not any of your goddam business anyway, Prince."

"Yeah, yeah, sure. Come on, Blackie, what's she like?"

"Prince, we didn't do a goddam thing but sit and talk. Her father died, for Christ's sake. She just wanted a friend to talk to," I said.

"Hell, she could've talked to me if she wanted to talk to someone."

"The hell she could. She couldn't talk to you. All she could do is fight you off," I said.

"God, I don't believe you, Blackie. Damn fine-looking woman takes you home with her and all you do is sit and talk. I'm afraid you're hopeless, old son," Prince said, and then he moved out of the seat beside me and took the vacant seat beside Chief.

Prince leaned over and said something to Chief.

"Leave me alone, asshole, I don't give a shit what he did or didn't do," Chief said.

I didn't see Ulli again. When I went in the Die Eierschale that night, I found out she had been in earlier that day and quit her job, collected her pay, and left. She dropped out of the university and moved back to her hometown.

A few months later, just before my birthday, I received a birthday card that had the postmark of a small town in Germany. In it was a note: Thank you for being my friend.

It was signed: Ulli.

A Place of My Own

17 After Ulli left Berlin, I stopped going to the Eierschale. It didn't happen suddenly. I continued to stop in, take my seat by the wall, drink a few beers, and play Chicago. But it wasn't the same, and I just didn't enjoy myself anymore. Over a few weeks, my visits to the the Eierschale became less frequent until finally I just didn't go there at all.

About the same time, I got tired of the barracks and its lack of privacy. Single soldiers were supposed to live in the barracks, but I knew several guys who had apartments off the base, and I decided to get my own place.

Prince was the reason I made up my mind to go out and find an apartment.

I was sitting at my desk, writing on a stack of postcards I had collected on my walks around Berlin. They were typical tourist postcards, most of them showing the sites of the city, and I was scribbling notes to my parents on the backs of the cards when I felt someone looking over my shoulder. I whirled around, startling Prince.

"Jesus, Blackie," he said. "What's the matter?"

"You were breathing down my neck, that's what," I said.

"I was just trying to see what you were doing," he said.

"What for? It's none of your goddam business what I'm doing."

"I didn't mean anything by it, for crying out loud. Jesus Christ, it's no big deal."

"Maybe not to you, but it's a big deal to me. Hell, I'm trying to get these postcards ready to mail, and there you are, breathing down my goddam neck," I said.

Prince was oblivious to my annoyance.

"Who're you writing?" he said.

"My folks," I said, and continued to scribble messages on the card. When I finished, I tossed the card onto a stack, grabbed another card, and began scribbling on it. While I was writing, Prince walked over and looked at the stack of postcards. Slowly, he turned over two or three postcards. He looked at them closely, then got another one, and looked at it. He shook his head.

"These are all to your folks," he said.

"I told you that," I said.

"Why have you written all these different postcards to your folks?"

"Goddammit, Prince, it's really none of your business," I said. "But I'm going to tell you, just to get you off my goddam back. My folks expect to get a card or a letter from me every goddam week. You know, they go bonkers if they don't get a letter or something from me every week."

"So?" Prince said.

"So, asshole, I was looking at a rack of postcards down at the Zoo station one day, and I got an idea. I bought four or five postcards, and I wrote some little bullshit message on each one, and stuck them in my locker. I mailed one of them every week. They were happy, and I got all of the letter writing taken care of at one time. When I run out of cards, I buy a bunch more, and I do the same thing again."

"But you don't really tell them anything," he said, pointing at one of the cards. "It's just some crap about this being Congress Hall and how the Berliners call it the Pregnant Oyster. Hell, you're not writing real letters home."

"I know that," I said. "But if I wrote what I'm really doing here, you know, hanging out with hookers, smoking, getting drunk, getting stoned, getting laid. If I wrote about all that, well, they don't want to know that. They want to think their little baby boy's going to chapel on Sundays, reading his Bible everyday, saluting the flag, and being a shining example of Southern Christian manhood. They don't want to know that I'm different than I was before I came over here, that I like to smoke and drink and chase women. So I let them keep thinking that."

"But they are your folks," Prince said. "It doesn't seem right to write all the letters ahead of time."

"Prince, they were part of my life, and they'll be part of it again. But, goddammit, they aren't part of this life, and I don't want them to be. For the first time ever, I have my own life, and I damn well intend to enjoy every minute of it."

I stood up, gathered the postcards, tossed them on the shelf of my locker, and pulled out a jacket.

"Now, if you don't mind, I'm getting the hell out of here," I said as I pulled on the jacket.

"Want some company?" Prince said.

"Christ, no. I want to be left alone," I said, and I rushed from the room, leaving a gaping Prince in my wake.

I was in such a hurry to get away from the barracks that I didn't even bother to get my car. I kept my head down as I strode rapidly down Kadettenweg. When I reached the intersection with Ringstrasse, I ignored the waves and shouts of the Hairy Ranger, Chief and the Pipe, who were standing at the bus stop. I crossed the street, and continued to walk down Kadettenweg.

I was about two blocks from the bus stop when I saw a small sign attached to a wrought-iron gate. "Room for rent," the sign read.

I looked more closely at the house. It was a massive, three-story brown brick building with a red slate tile roof. On each floor, facing the street, a door opened onto a small balcony. A brick wall surrounded the lot, and I could see a neat flower garden and a patio.

I removed the sign, pushed the gate open, and walked up a flagstone walkway to the entranceway, which featured double doors with heavy brass hinges and ornate scrollwork. I lifted the heavy, wrought-iron doorknocker, and released it, letting it clang loudly.

Within seconds, I heard movement inside the house, and I stepped back from the door.

The door opened, and a short, stout woman, with a halo of white hair framing her round face smiled at me.

"You would like to see the room?" she asked, nodding at the sign in my hand.

"Yes, ma'am," I said, with a slight nod.

"It is on the top floor. Wait here while I get the key," she said as she stepped back from the door, and disappeared down a hallway leading to the back of the house.

She didn't close the front door, and I peeked inside the house. There was a foyer, with a door on the left side and a hallway, where the woman had gone, straight head. A staircase that led to the upper floors was to my right. A small door, which looked like it might be to a closet, was under the staircase.

I stepped back when I heard a door slam, and footsteps approaching. It was the woman, and she had a ring of keys in her hand.

"Come, I will show you the room," she said.

We climbed the stairs to the third floor. At the top of the stairs was a heavy, wood door, with a transom. She tried two or three keys before the lock turned. She pushed open the door, and we found ourselves standing in a small foyer. To our right was a short hallway with a door at the end. Another door was directly in front of us, and a third door, which also had a transom, was to our left.

She motioned to the left, and I followed her. Again, she had to try two or three keys before the lock turned, and we entered a huge room. Just inside the door to the right was an enclosed fireplace. Beside the fireplace was an iron poker, a long-handle brush, a small box of kindling, and a bucket of coal.

A heavy armoire, with a mirror mounted in the door, was against the wall on the left, and a small bed, covered with a thick comforter, was pushed against the wall in the right corner. At the foot of the bed was a heavy wood trunk, with a brass lock and leather straps. Also against the wall on the right side was a small table and chair.

The end of the room featured French doors that opened onto a balcony, offering a view of nearby houses and the street. There was a recess in the left wall, and I saw a small refrigerator and a two-burner stove.

"Is it to your liking?" she said.

"Very much," I said. "How much is it?"

"One hundred and sixty marks a month," she said.

"I'll take it," I said, and reaching into my wallet, I counted out the money, which she folded neatly and slid into a pocket of her blouse.

Her key ring jingled loudly as she removed four keys and placed them on the table.

"This one is to the front gate," she said, pointing to one of they keys. "The others are to the front door, the door to this floor, and to your flat. The bathroom is down the hallway on your left, and the coal is in the basement. I will clean your bedding once a week. If you need anything, just tell me. I am Dagmar Heinrici, and I am on the first floor. I own this house."

"Thank you. I'm Don Cooper, and I think I'll be fine," I said.

"I hope you enjoy it here, Herr Cooper," she said as she walked toward the door.

"I'm sure I will," I said. "Thanks."

I pulled open the French doors, and walked out onto the balcony. As I leaned on the railing, I could see that my landlady spent many hours in her garden. There were several flower beds, with flagstone walkways leading from one bed to another. The lawn was neatly manicured, and I thought I could see some fruit trees near the back of the house.

"Beats the hell out of the barracks," I said to myself as I went back into the room.

I walked back to the barracks, and went straight to my room. I pulled my old suitcase out from under the bunk, and packed several changes of civilian clothes, a couple of books, and a couple of towels and washcloths. Then I went to the PX, where I bought a razor, blades, toothbrush, toothpaste, and soap.

I loaded the suitcase and toiletries in my car, and drove away from the barracks toward my apartment.

A few minutes later, I was sitting on the bed in my new apartment, my clothes hanging in the armoire, my books stacked on the table, and reading a copy of BZ, a popular Berlin tabloid. I was feeling remarkably content, enjoying the solitude and the feeling like I was a civilian again.

I was on break and didn't have to go back to work for two days, and I intended to be a civilian, stay away from the GI bars, and just relax. I didn't want to see any of the other guys on C Trick. I didn't want to go to any of the places where they might be or do any of the things that we always did when C Trick was on break.

I had wanted to relax, and relax I did. I spent my two days just reading my books, taking walks around the neighborhood, and eating at a small restaurant on Curtiusstrasse, about two blocks from the apartment.

When I walked into our room, Prince, who was in his underwear and holding his shaving kit, looked at me.

"Where the hell have you been?" he said sharply.

"Nowhere in particular," I said.

"What have you been doing?"

"Nothing special," I said.

"Who have you been with?" he said.

"Nobody, Mother," I said.

"Mother, my ass!" he said with a snort. "You're shacked up with someone, aren't you?"

"No."

"If you're not, then where the hell have you been?"

"In East Berlin, selling secrets to Ulbricht, what do you think? It's none of your goddam business, Prince. Get off my ass," I said. I pulled a set of fatigues out of my locker and began taking off my civilian clothes.

"You can be as mysterious as you want to be, asshole, but I'll find out what you've been up to," Prince said from the doorway. He left the room, slamming the door hard behind him.

I knew Prince was right. Sooner or later, someone on C Trick would find out what I was up to, and everyone would know about my off-base apartment. But until then, I intended to enjoy my life away from the Army.

For the next two weeks, it was ideal. After finishing work, I went back to the barracks, changed into my civilian clothes, climbed into my car, and drove to my apartment. I stayed in my neighborhood, going to the bakery for bread, buying papers at a sidewalk news stand, drinking beer in the pub just two blocks from the apartment.

I even ran into Karin, the streetwalker with flaming red hair who worked around Savignyplatz, at the little restaurant on Curtiusstrasse. I had just taken a sip of coffee and

begun to read Die Welt when I felt a touch on my shoulder.
I looked up and saw Karin. I almost didn't recognize her,
probably wouldn't have recognized her if it hadn't been
for the hair, because she was wearing a pair of blue jeans
and a baggy, black sweatshirt. Without her tight miniskirt,
boots and makeup, she looked younger, more like a college
student.

"May I join you?" she said.

I motioned to the empty chair across the table from me.

"Want some coffee?" I said.

She nodded, and I signaled the waiter.

"I almost didn't recognize you, Karin," I said, watching
her as she stirred sugar in her coffee.

"Because I'm not in a miniskirt and wearing a lot of
makeup?" she said with a grin.

"I just didn't expect to see you here. I thought you probably lived up in the British sector."

"No, no. I don't want to live near where I work. That's my
other life," she said. "I was surprised to see you here. Not
many GIs come to these little places."

"I have a little apartment a couple of blocks away. I just
like to get away from the Army as much as I can. Sometimes, the guys just get on my nerves, and I just want to get
away from everyone."

"I'm taking some courses at the university," she said
proudly. "I'm going to do something else."

"What are you taking?"

"Art. I think I'd like to teach art sometime."

"I'll probably go to college when I get out of the Army," I
said.

"What will you take?"

"I don't know. I worked for a newspaper, so maybe I'll
take journalism. I don't really know yet."

She smiled.

We sat in the restaurant, talking and drinking coffee for
nearly an hour. I learned about her three-year-old daughter, how she started out as a nude model for a photographer
and drifted into prostitution, and how she decided to get
out of the business and enrolled in the Free University to
start a new life.

I talked about growing up in a small town in southwest Arkansas, and how I joined the Army to make sure I wouldn't be drafted and sent to Vietnam.

It hadn't seemed that we had been in the restaurant for nearly an hour, but she glanced at her watch, quickly drained her cup of coffee and stood up.

"I've got to go. I've a class in a few minutes."

"Hope it goes good," I said. "It was good seeing you — you know, like this, Karin."

"Petra. My name's really Petra. I just use Karin at work. I'll see you again; maybe you can show me your apartment," she said and smiled. I watched her as she walked out of the restaurant, walking purposefully like a young woman who knows what she is going to do with her life, and not with the exaggerated swing of a streetwalker's hips.

I wouldn't see her again, although I went to the restaurant about the same time whenever I got the chance. Later I would go to Savignyplatz, but she had vanished, and a big blonde streetwalker said she heard Karin had left the business.

I knew she was taking courses at the Free University, but I never tried to find her; I guess she really wouldn't want to be reminded of her former life.

I became a part of the neighborhood, and other residents would wave and shout greetings when they saw me. I got to know my third-floor neighbor, Matthäus Fassbinder, an artist and student at the Free University who helped me begin to understand something about the brilliant colors of his abstract paintings. It almost made me forget I was in the Army.

But that sense of being a civilian didn't last long.

It was the last night of my break, and I was tired after spending most of the day going through the Dahlem Museum and an art gallery in Charlottenberg where Udo had some paintings on exhibit. I was sitting on my bed, reading a biography of Douglas MacArthur that I had checked out of the base library, and sipping on a beer when I heard footsteps approaching my door. There suddenly was a rapping on the door. I opened the door cautiously. There, grinning like two hyenas, stood Hairy Ranger and Prince.

"Oh, shit," I said.

"No shit," Hairy Ranger said as he and Prince pushed past me into the room.

"Where's your shack job, Blackie?" Prince said with a leer.

"There's no shack job, and what the hell are you two ass-holes doing here?" I said.

"Is that any way to be talking to your roommates?" Hairy Ranger said. "We've been worrying about you, what with you disappearing all the time and not telling anyone where you're going. You really shouldn't have parked that green piece of shit you call a car out front for the whole world to see. All we had to do was ask your landlady if you were in, and she was more than happy to tell us."

"We've decided to give you a housewarming," Prince said.

"I don't want a housewarming, I want to be left alone," I said petulantly.

Hairy Ranger pulled the chair away from the table, sat down, and began looking at the books. Then he leaned back in the chair, and locked his hands behind his head.

"What you reading?"

"A book about MacArthur."

"Why?"

"I don't know. I just like to read history."

"Bores the shit out of me," Prince said.

"Anything interesting?" Ranger said.

"Well, there's something funny in here," I said and thumbed through the pages until I found a quote. "Here's what MacArthur said about military service."

"Oh, give me a break," Prince said.

"No, no, it's pretty damn funny. Do you want to hear it or not?" I said.

"There's no reason to get pissy. Go ahead and read the damn quote," Prince said.

"Okay, this is something MacArthur said in 1927. 'Every male brought into existence should be taught from infancy that the military service of the Republic carries with it honor and distinction, and his very life should be perme-ated with the ideal that even death itself may become a boon when the man dies that a nation may live and fulfill its destiny.' What do you think about that?"

"I think every day spent in the Army is a day in my life that's wasted," Hairy Ranger said. "Actually, it's just as good that we found you. Roadrunner checked the barracks last night, and asked where you've been. He suspects you've gone over the Wall or something."

"All you had to do was tell him I was out on pass somewhere," I said.

"We did, but you still need to check in now and then, just to make Roadrunner think you still live in the barracks. He's after your ass anyway over that Eckford name tag, and you don't need to give him any excuse to haul you in front of the old man," Prince said, referring to the company commander.

"Jesus Christ, that was over a year ago," I said.

"Yeah, but Roadrunner's like a goddam rogue elephant, he never forgets," Prince said.

"You have any beer in there?" Hairy Ranger said, pointing toward the refrigerator.

"There's three or four Beck's," I said. "Help yourself."

"Don't mind if I do," he said, and walked across the room, bent over and took two beers from the refrigerator and opened them. He handed one to Prince and took a big swig from his bottle.

"Want to hit a couple of clubs now that we've found you?" he said.

"Not really, but I guess I will because it's the only way I'll be able to get rid of you," I said.

"See, Prince, I told you. He still enjoys our company," Hairy Ranger said with a grin. "I'll bet he'll even offer to drive."

"Hell, I guess I have to, unless one of you jerkoffs got a car today," I said. "Let's go."

I pulled on a coat, grabbed my keys, and led the way downstairs and out to the street, where I was surprised to see Grumpy John, smoking a cigarette, and leaning on my car.

"What the hell is he doing here?" I said.

"When we found out your place's on the third floor, Grumpy decided to wait down here. He said he won't walk up any stairs unless he lives there," Hairy Ranger said.

"Damn right. Stairs aren't good for my health," Grumpy John said.

"Only because you're usually so goddam drunk when you try to climb them," I said.

We piled into the Volkswagen. I turned the ignition, the engine coughed and sputtered, and with a scraping of the gears, I pulled away from the curb.

I had been staying away from the GI bars, preferring the more peaceful atmosphere of the local pubs. But my companions were in a mood to be rowdy, so we headed for the KBS Bar, which was notorious for its bad beer, hookers, and fights between 'Gators.

"Let's stay near the door. If there's a fight, we can get the hell out of here," I said.

"Chickenshit," Prince said.

"You're damn right I'm chickenshit. I hate bar fights," I said.

"Blackie's right. I got caught in the corner here one night, and if the MPs hadn't gotten here so quick, I probably would have gotten the shit kicked out of me," Grumpy John said.

"Grumpy, you know 'Gators are like dogs. They only attack if they sense fear," Prince said. He pushed the door open. We followed him inside.

The noise nearly deafened us. The juke box was turned up full blast, blaring a twangy country song. The bar was packed, and harried waitresses tried to serve drinks while managing to dodge the hands that kept trying to slide up their skirts.

"Jesus, Grumpy, let's just get the hell out of here," I said.

"Everything's okay. I've been here lots of nights when it's worse than this," he said. "We'll be okay if we stay together. See, the Ranger and Prince already found us a table," he said, pointing toward the corner of the room.

Hairy Ranger and Prince were waving for us to join them at the table, which had been occupied by two drunken 'Gators. The 'Gators had passed out, and just grunted when Hairy Ranger and Prince had rolled them out of their seats onto the floor.

"Welcome to the fun house," a grinning Hairy Ranger said, and gestured expansively around the bar.

"Welcome to the war zone," I said.

"Blackie, see what you've been missing by going to all those art galleries and museums on your time off," Prince said. "You've missed the real Berlin, the smelly armpit of life."

"Give me a break, Prince, I've been in the Scum just as many times as you," I said.

"The Scum's nothing, It's strictly minor league. This is the big league of scummy bars," Hairy Ranger said. "It's got whores with diseases that don't have names yet; it's got fights; it's got bad food; it's got the worst beer in Berlin. It's Grumpy John's kind of place."

"Why's it Grumpy's kind of place any more than the Scum?" I said.

Prince pointed toward the opposite side of the bar to some small cubicles with drawn curtains.

"It's Grumpy's kind of place because he can get a whore to give him a blowjob while he drinks his beer," he said.

"Speaking of Grumpy, where the hell is he? Getting a blowjob already?" I said.

"I'm right here, asshole. This round's on me," Grumpy John said, slamming a beer down in front of each of us before taking his seat.

I took a sip of the beer and grimaced.

"You're right about one thing. This is bad damn beer," I said. "What the hell is it?"

"Its name is Löwenpils, but we call it Lion's Piss," Hairy Ranger said. "It's bad enough that we thought we should buy a case of it for Catfish, except that dumb redneck probably likes it."

I took a big gulp of the beer, hoping that I had just about drained the bottle. But I was disappointed to see it was still about half full.

"I've got to go to the head," I said.

"Good luck, there's about a million 'Gators in there," Prince said.

I took my bottle of beer with me, thinking I would dump the contents in the commode or wash basin in the restroom. As I worked my way down the wall toward the rest-room, I saw Prince turn and shove his hand under a buxom blonde waitresses' skirt and between her legs. He laughed when the startled waitress jumped, spilling beer on two 'Gators at the next table.

"Jesus, he's going to get a fight started," I muttered to myself.

The restroom was just as crowded and noisy as the rest of the bar, with men jostling each other and nearly slipping on the urine that had splashed onto the floor.

I had just relieved myself and was heading for the door when I heard the fight break out behind me. I looked back and saw the room was in pandemonium, as men pushed, shoved and threw punches wildly. I was startled when one massive 'Gator saw me and rushed in my direction.

Without thinking, I swung the beer bottle I was holding and brought it down solidly across the bridge of his nose. Blood was gushing from his nose when he hit the floor sod-denly.

Before anyone else could move, I darted from the rest-room, ran to our table and shouted to Hairy Ranger, Prince and Grumpy John.

"Let's get the hell out of here. The 'Gators are going to kill me," I said, and I ran for the front door, with Hairy Ranger close behind.

I got to the car and jumped in.

"What the hell's going on?" Hairy Ranger said.

"I just brained a 'Gator with a beer bottle."

"You what?"

I told him what happened in the restroom, and he began laughing.

"You're probably right about getting the hell out of here. But Grumpy John and Prince aren't in any mood to leave, and I think I'll stay with them. I'll tell them why we are sud-denly on foot. Oh, I'll find out if you killed the 'Gator."

As it turned out, the 'Gator, a big corporal from the Com-pany F, 40th Armor, just had a broken nose and blackened eyes. Although nothing ever came of it, I never went back to the KBS Bar, and I had recurring dreams that I was being stalked by a big 'Gator with a broken nose.

Smilin' Jim and Rock 'n' Roll

18 On a good day, Smilin' Jim was surly, but on most days, he was hostile.

Before he was transferred from an ASA installation in West Germany near the Czech border, Smilin' Jim was interviewed by a reporter from Overseas Weekly about some problems the enlisted men were having with the treads. Although Smilin' Jim wasn't identified in the article, he was described as a disgruntled Spec Five, which unfortunately for him was all the identification that the treads needed, and he suddenly found himself on the military duty train for Berlin and the 78th ASA, arriving a couple of days after I brained the 'Gator at the KBS bar.

Smilin' Jim may have been out of place in the ASA unit in the Zone, but he fit right in with the 78th — most of us were disgruntled.

One thing, however, that made Smilin' Jim lose his surliness was rock 'n' roll. He loved rock 'n' roll, especially the music from the '50s. When he heard Little Richard, Chuck Berry, Buddy Holly, Gene Vincent, Eddie Cochran or the pre-Army Elvis, Smilin' Jim's scowl would disappear, his foot would begin to tap to the music and his face would light up with an ear-to-ear grin.

He loved rock 'n' roll, but that love didn't include the Beach Boys.

He would tolerate the Beatles and grudgingly admit he almost liked the Rolling Stones; however, he genuinely detested the Beach Boys, although he didn't dislike the California band as much as he disliked Bobby Vinton.

"Goddam Bobby Vinton nearly killed rock 'n' roll," Smi-

lin' Jim said whenever "Blue Velvet," "Mr. Lonely," or any
of Bobby's tearful ballads started playing on the jukebox at
the El Oso Club.

"How the hell did Bobby Vinton nearly kill rock, Jim?" I
said.

"Goddam, Blackie, where the hell were you in 1962?"

"High school," I said.

"Well, so was I, but didn't you listen to the goddam radio?" Smilin' Jim said.

"Off and on."

"What did you listen to?"

"Wolfman Jack out of Del Rio."

"Well, no wonder. The Wolfman played decent stuff, but
most stations were playing that Bobby Vinton bullshit. Everytime I turned on the radio in Philly, I heard nothing but
Bobby Vinton and his fucking 'Blue Velvet,'" he said. "Give
me a break. Over and over I'd hear that goddam piece of
crap. That's what I mean. Bobby Vinton was doing fucking
Lawrence Welk rock."

Smilin' Jim's distaste for Bobby Vinton was apparent a
few nights later. I was loading my laundry into the battered
1951 Volkswagen I had bought four or five months earlier,
before driving back to my apartment. Smilin' Jim was coming down the steps of the barracks when he spotted me,
waved, strolled over and leaned on the top of the car.

"What're you up to, Blackie?" he said.

"Heading back to my place with my laundry," I said, motioning to the folded clothes in the back seat.

"I'm heading over to the El Oso for a few beers. Want to
join me?" he said.

"Sure, I'll have a couple," I said, slapping the car door
shut.

A few minutes later, we were sitting near the jukebox,
sipping our beers, when a 'Gator sergeant dropped a coin in
the machine and punched a couple of numbers.

"Bet you he plays Green, Green Grass of Home or Distant
Drums," Smilin' Jim said, referring to two tearjerker country ballads that were extremely popular with the Southerners — well, most Southerners. I never liked country music.

"Shit, Jim, that's a gimmie. I'm not going to take that bet.

Of course, that redneck'll play them," I said.

But when the record dropped onto the turntable, the sounds that came out were the lush strings and the syrupy voice of Bobby Vinton singing Mr. Lonely, his ballad about a lonely soldier far from home.

Smilin' Jim endured the song with all the pleasure of someone getting a root canal without anesthesia. He gritted his teeth and glared across the room at the 'Gator all the time the song was playing. After what seemed to us an eternity, Bobby Vinton finally stopped singing about being a lonely soldier. The record stopped and another dropped into place.

It was Blue Velvet.

Grimacing, Smilin' Jim reached behind the jukebox and punched the reset button, stopping the record.

The 'Gator looked up when his song stopped. He stood up, reached in his pocket for another coin, and strode purposefully across the room to the jukebox. He inserted the coin, made his selection, and returned to his table and resumed his conversation with his friends.

Blue Velvet started again. Smilin' Jim again reached back and hit the reset button.

When the song stopped again, the 'Gator looked dumbfounded at the jukebox.

While the 'Gator was staring at the jukebox, trying to figure out what was wrong with his song, I got up and stood by the machine. I fumbled around in my pocket for a coin, inserted it, and selected the Beatles' Day Tripper.

The 'Gator sat there staring intently at the jukebox as the Beatles number played in its entirety. When the last chords died out, the 'Gator again walked across the room, again inserted a coin, and made his selection.

Bobby didn't even have a chance to begin singing before Smilin' Jim hit the reset button. This time, the 'Gator saw his little maneuver. Enraged, he jumped up, knocking over his chair with a crash, and stormed across the room toward us with his buddies close behind.

"Just relax, we can handle them," Smilin' Jim said. He leaned back in his chair and folded his arms across his chest.

"The hell we can," I said and looked around for the nearest exit.

"Just what the hell do you think you're doing, asshole?" the irate 'Gator said. His face was red, and the veins in his forehead were so swollen they looked like they were going to explode. He stood over Smilin' Jim, clenching and unclenching his fists.

"I don't care for your taste in songs," Smilin' Jim said.

"What the hell are you? A goddam music critic?"

"As a matter of fact, I am, and I just couldn't stand to listen to anymore of that crap you were playing. I did everyone a favor by shutting that shit off."

"You sorry sack of shit, I'm going to kick your ass," the 'Gator said with a snarl.

"Come on, Jim, let it go. Let's get the hell out of here before we get our asses kicked," I said, pulling at his arm.

"Fuck, no. I'm trying to sit here and enjoy my beer and this goddam 'Gator has to screw it up by playing that bullshit. We shouldn't have to listen to that bullshit!" Jim said.

Fortunately for us, the club manager had seen the confrontation and he rushed up before it could escalate.

"Break it up. I said, break it up," he said.

"He was screwing around with the jukebox," the 'Gator said, pointing at Jim. "He kept stopping my record."

"I don't give a shit who started anything. I just want this to stop. You got that? Now get your asses back over to your table," the club manager said. The 'Gators, mumbling among themselves, slunk back to their table, from where they glared at Smilin' Jim.

"Now, I think you two ought to take a hike, because those boys won't stay quiet much longer," he said.

"Good idea," I said, grabbing my jacket. "Come on, Jim, let's go."

"Fuck them, I'm staying," Smilin' Jim said.

"Oh for God's sake, Jim, it's not worth the bother. Let's get out of here before those goddam 'Gators get hot again. I don't intend to get my ass kicked and I damn well know they'll do it if we hang around here."

"No, goddammit, I'm staying."

"No, you're not," the club manager said. "Your buddy's right. Let it slide and go somewhere else. I don't want to have to fill in reports for the MPs if there's a goddam fight in the club. Now just be cool and go somewhere else. Hell, by tomorrow night everything'll be okay."

"Well, fuck 'em if they can't take a joke," Smilin' Jim said. He stood up, drained the last few drops of beer from his glass, lit a cigarette, and pulled on his jacket. Then, throwing his shoulders back, he marched out of the club, with me trailing behind and looking back over my shoulder to see if the 'Gator or any of his buddies decided to carry on the discussion outside.

We weren't being followed as we walked across the parking lot toward the barracks.

"I got to stop at my room and get another pack of smokes," Smilin' Jim said. "Then let's go to the Scum."

"Okay by me," I said.

As we climbed the stairs to the third floor, we heard the raucous sounds of a party. Just as we reached the top of the stairs, we saw Chief burst out of the huge squad room near the center of the old pre-World War I barracks.

"Blackie, Jim, come on and join us. We're having a party!" Chief said.

We looked at each other and shrugged.

"Might as well," Smilin' Jim said.

"I'll be there in a sec; I got to go get some smokes," he said.

"Why don't you get a pack for me, too? I'll pay you for it," I said, pausing before the squad room door.

The party was going full tilt when Smilin' Jim got back.

It was Doc's birthday and the party just happened. C Trick was on break, the treads were all gone, so Chief and several others chipped in and bought several cases of beer at the commissary and sneaked them upstairs to the unused squad room. Prince brought his stereo and nearly everyone brought a favorite album to provide the musical entertainment.

Junior Walker and the All-Stars were blasting from the stereo when I walked in the room. As I pulled a beer out of one of several ice-filled trash cans scattered about the room, I noticed Smilin' Jim sitting with his back against the wall, smiling and keeping time to the music.

The album finished and Prince lifted it off the turntable and put it back in its jacket.

"What are you going to play now?" Smilin' Jim said as Prince put another album on the turntable.

"Oh, just one of mine," Prince said.

"Oh no," I said as the first sounds of the Beach Boys' Little Deuce Coupe came out of the speakers.

"Keep an eye on Smilin' Jim," I said to Chief. "Son of a bitch could have gotten us killed at the El Oso over a record some 'Gator wanted to play, and he hates the Beach Boys."

"What was it?" Chief said.

"Some Bobby Vinton crap," I said.

"Christ, I don't blame him. Person ought to be maimed for playing that shit in public," Chief said.

"You're not going to be a whole hell of a lot of help, are you?" I said.

"Don't worry, Blackie, nothing's going to happen. Hell, that's Prince, not some fucking 'Gator."

Smilin' Jim scowled all through the first side of the album. When it finished, Prince, who had been talking to Shakey and Hairy Ranger on the other side of the room from the stereo, walked back and turned the album over.

"Hey, Prince, how's about playing something different?" Smilin' Jim said.

"I just want to hear the second side. No big deal," Prince said.

"No big deal, my ass," Smilin' Jim said.

"Prince, Smilin' Jim really hates the Beach Boys," I said when the second side started playing.

"Fuck him. It's my record and my stereo," Prince said.

"It's your ass then. But I'm telling you, Jim really, really hates the Beach Boys."

"Who gives a shit? He don't like the music, he can take a hike. He don't tell me what music I'm going to play on my own goddam stereo," Prince said.

"Believe me, Prince, he will," I said, and I walked away, leaving Prince standing there with a quizzical look.

I leaned against the wall not too far from where the now-unsmiling Jim was sitting and decided to watch what I was certain was going to happen.

The record finished and Prince strolled up casually and glanced at Smilin' Jim who continued to sit on the floor with his back to the wall.

"Going to play something else, Prince?" he said softly.

Prince ignored him and just turned the album over and started to play the first side again.

"You really ought to play something other than the Beach Boys, Prince," Smilin' Jim said, this time a little more forcefully as an eerie smile that crept across his face.

"Kiss my ass, Jim. You should've brought your own record," Prince said scornfully.

Smilin' Jim stood up and calmly brushed dust off the seat of his pants.

"I guess you're right, Prince. I should've brought my own record. I really should've," he said quietly. "I hate the Beach Boys. They make me want to puke, but it's your record and you can play it if you want to. But," and he paused for what seemed an eternity, then suddenly slammed his hand down on the turntable, "I don't have to listen!"

Jerking the album off the turntable, Smilin' Jim spun around like a discus thrower and sailed the album through the window and out onto the parking lot.

Prince's mouth dropped open and his eyes widened as Smilin' Jim leaned into his face.

"I said no more goddam Beach Boys!" Smilin' Jim said.

A shaken Prince could only stand and watch as Smilin' Jim rifled through the albums and found one to his liking, which he put on the stereo and then again sat on the floor and rested his back against the wall as Wilson Pickett began to sing about Mustang Sally.

Tapping his feet to the music and closing his eyes, Smilin' Jim was smiling again.

Dirty Joe and His Moose

19 Dirty Joe loved his wife, but he also was crazy about his moose, as he called his girlfriend.

His wife was Norma, a mousy little woman who had the same look of resignation worn by the woman in Dorothea Lang's famous Depression photograph, Migrant Mother. Norma was unexceptional in any way, except for her ability to conceive.

"Hell, all I got to do is walk by her with a hard-on and — bang! — she's pregnant," Dirty Joe said. Dirty Joe was proud of Norma's fertility and his efforts over the years at keeping her pregnant — efforts that apparently paid off, because Norma had two babies during the three years she and Dirty Joe were in Berlin. Dirty Joe often seemed to be as proud of Norma's fertility as he was of the sergeant first class stripes on his sleeves.

Although Dirty Joe loved Norma and her fertility, he didn't really like the five children and spent as much time as possible away from the home.

During one of his late-night wanderings to avoid going home and listening to the constant bickering of his nearly unmanageable youngsters, Dirty Joe arrived at the Blue Moon, where he ran into the two Monicas.

Just as rock stars, jocks, and other celebrities have their groupies, the two Monicas were soldier groupies. They loved America and American soldiers. They were indiscriminate in their fascination with American GIs. It didn't matter if you were short or tall, lean or stout; if you were a member of the American military, the two Monicas found you fascinating and were anxious to share their favors with you.

The two Monicas were easily identifiable by their nicknames. The larger of the two was called Big Monica, and her smaller friend was called Little Monica.

Big Monica was a buxom blonde, nearly six feet tall and weighing about 170 pounds. Little Monica, also a blonde, was barely over five feet tall and weighed about ninety pounds. While Big Monica was constantly watching what she ate, although she never watched how many beers she drank, Little Monica could eat everything in sight, wash it down with gallons of beer, and never gain a pound.

The two Monicas were almost inseparable. They worked together at the giant Siemens plant, they lived in adjoining apartments in the Zehlendorf section, they shared their meals, and, until Dirty Joe swept Big Monica off her feet, their men.

When Dirty Joe claimed Big Monica as his full-time moose, it left Little Monica at a loss. She tagged along when Dirty Joe and Big Monica went out, but she was uncomfortable, a tiny waif-like creature huddled in a corner of a booth across the table from the lovebirds. She looked annoyed as Dirty Joe would reach inside Big Monica's blouse and play with her big breasts, and she looked distraught as Big Monica would giggle and slide her hand up Dirty Joe's leg until she was playing with his crotch.

Dirty Joe, of course, lived up to his name. Shakey and I wandered into the Blue Moon and sat down a table near the booth where Dirty Joe, Big Monica, and a surly Little Monica were sitting.

"Hey, look at my moose. She loves to play with my dick," Dirty Joe said.

Big Monica giggled, but she didn't move her hand. Little Monica glared at her table companions and mumbled something under her breath as Dirty Joe pulled down Big Monica's blouse and began to suck on her nipples.

"Good God, right in front of the whole world," Shakey said. "What are they going to do next, start screwing on the table?"

"Knowing Dirty Joe, there's a good chance they will," I said.

Dirty Joe and Big Monica, with the ever-present and ever-gloomy Little Monica tagging along, continued to put on their public shows of affection for several weeks. On almost every night they could be found in the Blue Moon, the Goldene Sonne, or one of the other neighborhood bars frequented regularly by the members of the 78th, exchanging passionate kisses and fondling each other. As always, Little Monica would be sitting with them, glaring at them and mumbling under her breath.

Dirty Joe seemed particularly proud of himself and his relationship with Big Monica.

One night on the trick bus after a swing shift, Dirty Joe began to compare the sexual habits of his wife and Big Monica. His comments came during a conversation among some of the guys who were deciding what to do when they got back to the barracks. Most of us were going to change into civvies and hit a couple of the bars before daylight.

"What are you going to do, Dirty Joe?" Rock Weed asked.

"I'm going to have a coupla beers and get my moose to give me a blow job," Dirty Joe said.

"Why don't you just go home and get your old lady to give you one?" Rock Weed said.

"Shit!" Dirty Joe said. "My old lady don't give no blow jobs. She says ain't no way she's going to suck cock."

"Hell, Joe, she sure didn't tell me that," Hairy Ranger said.

"You sorry asshole! You stay the hell away from my wife, you worthless cocksucker!" Dirty Joe yelled. He lunged for a laughing Hairy Ranger. Dirty Joe was livid; his face was fiery red and contorted as he wrestled with Grumpy John, Shakey, and me in an effort to get to Hairy Ranger.

We finally got Dirty Joe calmed down and back in his seat, a job that was made more difficult because Hairy Ranger was laughing so hard.

Even though he had calmed down and decided he wasn't going to kill Hairy Ranger, Dirty Joe's night out with Big Monica had received a death blow. Dirty Joe was in such a foul mood that he and Big Monica bickered all night — much to the joy of Little Monica, who smiled for the first time since her friend had taken up with Dirty Joe. The bickering between the two ended when Dirty Joe jumped up, upsetting his glass of beer which spilled in Big Monica's lap.

"Fuck you, you goddam fat whore. I'm sick of your shit," Dirty Joe said and stomped out of the Blue Moon, slamming the door violently behind him.

Everyone sat stunned at his outburst. Little Monica pulled a handkerchief from her purse and began to dab at the beer in her friend's lap. Big Monica said nothing, just tapped Little Monica on the shoulder and the two slid out of the booth and left.

"Look's like the bloom's off that rose," Shakey said.

"Yeah, I guess Dirty Joe's going to remember he's married," I said.

"No way, Dirty Joe'll be back here tomorrow night with Big Monica. It'll be just like nothing ever happened," Grumpy John said.

"I think you're wrong, Grumpy. Big Monica was really pissed about being called a whore," I said.

"Shit, she's probably been called worse than that," Grumpy John said.

"This was different. She really was hung up on Dirty Joe," I said.

"I'll tell you what," Grumpy John said, tapping on the table. "I bet you that they'll be back tomorrow night, and everything'll be just like it was before their fight."

"You're on. But what's the stakes?" I said.

"If you're right, I'll buy your beer all night. But if I'm right, you buy my beer. Okay?" Grumpy John said.

I reached across the table and shook his hand.

"My God, I can taste a cold Beck's now," I said.

We kept an eye on Dirty Joe during the day, hoping to see if there were anything about his demeanor that would give us a clue about what would happen. But, we just couldn't read him.

When we got off work, Grumpy John, Shakey and I headed to the Blue Moon. We were at our favorite table when Dirty Joe came in alone. He got a beer and wandered over to our table and sat down.

"Where's Big Monica?" Shakey said.

"I got rid of that snake," Dirty Joe said. "I don't know how I could've kept her around anyway. Jesus Christ, I couldn't believe how her pussy smelled. She must never wash that thing."

"Speak of the devil, Joe, smell what just walked in. It's Big Monica. Maybe you can talk her into washing up," I said.

Dirty Joe turned around to look at the entrance. As he was turning, Big Monica, screaming curses in German, pounced on him, knocking him out of his chair and onto the floor. She scratched and punched at him as the now desperate Dirty Joe tried to regain his feet and get away from the very angry big German woman.

"Help me, for Christ's sake, the bitch's crazy," Dirty Joe said, as Big Monica slammed his head into the table leg. "For God's sake, get her off me!"

"Should we?" I said to Grumpy John and Shakey.

"I don't know, it's a pretty damn good show," Grumpy John said. "He got himself into this shit, maybe he ought to get himself out of it."

"Yeah, but what if the MPs come in?" Shakey said and looked at me. "You could get your ass in a sling without your pass."

"Goddam right, we got to stop this shit now," I said. The Bunny, the company first sergeant who earned his nickname because of his bouncing style of walking, had jerked my pass for two weeks after he found I had substituted my own duty roster for his on the company bulletin.

The duty roster had been up for several days before anyone realized that it wasn't the Bunny's. I had retyped the duty roster, only I had put Catfish, Rock Weed and a couple of guys from A Trick on KP every day for the month. No one knew it wasn't the official duty roster until Rock Weed went in and complained that he had been on KP for four straight days.

When I redid the duty roster, I had used the typewriter in the day room, except I had taken it upstairs to my room, and forgot to return it when I had finished. Although the Bunny was certain I was the culprit, I denied any knowledge of the duty roster switch. After much fuming, The Bunny jerked my pass because I had taken the typewriter out of the day room without permission.

When Grumpy John and Shakey said they were going

to the Blue Moon, I slipped out a hole in the fence. When the MPs went into a bar to break up fights, they generally checked the IDs and passes of everyone in the bar — even people who weren't involved in the disturbance. If I were caught without my pass, I probably would be slapped with an Article Fifteen and restricted to the barracks for another couple of weeks. That meant I would have to slip out the fence every night to go back to my apartment, running the risk of getting into even more trouble.

We reluctantly grabbed Big Monica's arms and pulled her off Dirty Joe.

As she struggled to get loose, Dirty Joe stood up, dusted himself off, and looked at Big Monica.

"You are one crazy bitch, Monica," Dirty Joe said, wagging his index finger in the angry woman's face. Before Dirty Joe could move his hand, Big Monica leaned forward and clamped down on his finger with her teeth.

"Omigod! Jesus Christ, she's biting my finger off," Dirty Joe said. With a tremendous jerk, he pulled his finger out from between Big Monica's teeth. If her biting hadn't brought blood, Dirty Joe's jerking it out of her mouth certainly did, because blood was streaming out of his finger.

"Jesus H. Christ! The bitch tried to bite my finger off. Jeez, it hurts," Dirty Joe said, wrapping a napkin around his bleeding finger.

"Yeah, but think how lucky you are you didn't stick your dick in her face," Shakey said.

Dirty Joe glared fiercely at us as we all began laughing.

"Fuck you! Just fuck all of you!" he said as he stormed out of the bar.

It probably was just as well that Dirty Joe stomped out, because all of us were laughing until tears rolled own our cheeks. Little Monica, who had been so morose for so long, was laughing so hard that she was gasping for breath. After a moment, when she looked as if she were thinking about tracking down Dirty Joe and pounding on him some more, even Big Monica began to laugh.

She certainly had the last laugh, because Dirty Joe's bitten index finger became infected. It swelled up enormously and he had to go to the infirmary for a stitch in his finger and a tetanus shot in his butt.

Duty Trains and Golden Showers

20 After the fight with Big Monica, Dirty Joe changed his pattern, rushing home to Norma and their children as soon as C Trick got off the Hill. He stayed away from the Scum and the other bars where he had been a regular, choosing to take Norma and the kids to Disney movies at the PX theater and to eat hamburgers in the snack bar.

One night after C Trick went on mids, Fang swore he saw Dirty Joe and Norma eating escargots at the French officers club, but no one believed him.

"Hell, Fang, I could believe you saying you saw Dirty Joe eating a chili dog at the snack bar or even fish and chips at the NAAFI Club (British PX), there's no way I'll ever believe he took Norma to the French officers club."

"I tell you I saw him."

"Bullshit, Fang! You've heard Dirty Joe say he hates the French ..."

"Frogs, he calls them Frogs," Hairy Ranger interrupted.

"Yeah, yeah, Frogs," I said. "I don't think he's even been up to the French sector, and even if he did, he wouldn't eat at the French officers club."

"I can just see him looking at his plate and yelling at the waiter, 'You're out of your mind if you think I'm going to eat goddam snails,'" Hairy Ranger said and burst out laughing.

"See, Fang, you got to be mistaken. It had to be someone else," I said.

"No, goddammit, it was Dirty Joe; I'm sure of it," Fang said, and stomped out of the room.

"It could have been Dirty Joe, you know," Ranger said softly.

"Not too damn likely."

"Why don't you ask Dirty Joe if he was eating snails at the French officers club."

"Because all he'd say is 'What's it to you, shithead?'" I said. "I don't need the aggravation."

"Well, we're going to have to talk to him pretty damn soon if we want to make the pilgrimage to Bremen. We've got to get him to sign our passes."

I nodded. Break would be coming up in a couple of days and we needed Dirty Joe's approval before we could get our three-day passes to Bremen. Ranger, Rapid Roger and I planned to go to Bremen and tour the Beck's brewery — or make the pilgrimage to worship before the throne of the beer god Beck, as we joked about our trip to the home brewery of our favorite German beer.

Leaving Berlin on a three-day pass, or any leave, took considerable planning. U.S. soldiers had to either fly out, which cost money most of us didn't have, or take one of the military duty trains, which cost nothing. The British duty train pulled out about 7:30 a.m., while the U.S. train left about twelve hours later. But no matter which train we took, we still had to have flag orders in English, French, German and Russian before we could travel through East Germany.

The trains stopped at Potsdam, just outside Berlin, to allow an East German crew to join their Western counter- parts in the locomotive's cab. Why the Russians and East Germans thought an East German crew needed to ride along baffled me, because where did they think the train would go? Anyway, the train always stopped in Potsdam, later at Magdeburg (for no apparent reason) and again at Helmstedt on the border between East and West Germany. At Helmstedt, the East German crew got off board and the military train went on to Frankfurt am Main in the south, or toward Bremerhaven in the north.

"Let's go find Rapid Roger and get Dirty Joe to sign our requests," I said, and I took my headsets off and flipped them on the little table mounted to the bank of receiv- ers and radios where I spent every shift eavesdropping on East German bureaucrats. I had been doing it so long, I recognized the voices of several of the East Germans, from gravel-voiced Horst in the Leipzig office of the Agriculture Ministry in Leipzig to the soft-spoken Magda in the Volksar-mee. I imagined her as a tall blonde whose breasts strained against the fabric of her severely cut military uniform.

"Hey, Grumpy!" Hairy Ranger yelled, waking up Grumpy John, who had been sprawled across three chairs he had pulled together in a makeshift bed. Grumpy John opened his eyes and glared at us.

"What the hell do you want? I hope you assholes know I was about to get a blowjob from Claudia Cardinale," he grumbled, referring to his favorite actress.

"Keep an eye on the place for a while; we've got to go see Dirty Joe," Hairy Ranger said.

Grumpy John just waved and closed his eyes. I swear he had begun to snore before Hairy Ranger and I got to the door.

We found Dirty Joe in the break room, pouring a cup of coffee and munching on a peanut butter sandwich. Seeing Hairy Ranger and me, he pushed the green can of peanut butter across the counter toward us.

"Thanks, no," I said. "Sarge, could you sign our requests for passes?"

"Where you want to go?"

"Bremen."

"We're making a pilgrimage to the Beck's brewery," Hairy Ranger said.

Dirty Joe grunted, then felt the pockets of his fatigue shirt for a pen. He didn't find the pen in his shirt pocket, but he pulled one out of his pants pocket and scribbled his signature on our requests, which we snatched back before he could change his mind.

"Thanks, Sarge," I said, and started to leave the break-room. I cringed when I heard Hairy Ranger suddenly blurt, "Sarge, did you eat snails up at the French officers club?"

"What's it to you, shithead?"

"Nothing, nothing. Just wondered," Hairy Ranger said, and we rushed back to Violet.

Two days later, Hairy Ranger, Rapid Roger and I were on the U.S. duty train bound for Bremen, and three days of free beer at the Beck's brewery. We settled into our compartment, waiting for a bored second lieutenant who served as the duty train officer and an MP corporal to come around to collect our flag orders and ID cards. The Soviet military personnel at the Marienborn checkpoint later checked the IDs and orders, probably logging down the names of everyone who traveled through East Germany.

"I'm going to the head," Rapid Roger said, swinging out of his bunk. He popped open a little attaché case and found his ID card and flag orders, then snapped the attaché case closed and placed the card and orders neatly on top. "Turn in my stuff if I'm not back before the treads get here."

Rapid Roger was one of those people who didn't seem to fit his nickname. Just like the hulking soldier who was called "Tiny," Rapid Roger moved methodically in everything he did, from tuning through the dial to intercept East German radio communications to eating his meals. If he weren't so methodical in his actions, Rapid Roger would have just been slow, but his slowness took on the air of someone who had thought out every move beforehand.

When we first met, Rapid Roger, a balding and sandy-haired Ohioan, was simply Roger, a typical Midwesterner. Somewhere along the way, he became fascinated with France and all things French and overnight he was Rozhay. But to most of us, he remained Rapid Roger or, when we felt like it, Ro-jay.

The bored second lieutenant, with the MP corporal in tow, slid open the door to our compartment and took our orders and ID cards. He seemed particularly annoyed when he got three sets of ID cards and orders but only found two people in the compartment.

"Where's your buddy?"

"He's in the head," Hairy Ranger said.

"Tell him when he gets back, he'd better be here when the ID cards are returned. I'm not supposed to give them to anyone else. I'm not supposed to accept them from anyone else either, but I'll let it go this time."

"Yes, sir," Hairy Ranger and I said together.

"Jesus, what a shitty job," I said.

"Whose?"

"That second looey. Hell, he probably busted his ass to

get through OCS, thinking he'd get a platoon in Vietnam, be a hero and win all kinds of medals. But look what happens. He ends up as a goddam conductor on a duty train, just riding back and forth across East Germany."

Hairy Ranger started to say something, but Rapid Roger suddenly burst back into the compartment, his face flushed and his eyes wide with excitement.

"Look what I found in the head!" he said, and pulled a small brown book out from under his shirt. I could see "CONFIDENTIAL" in bright red ink stamped on the cover.

"What is it?" I asked.

"It's the radio operator's code book. I found it in the head!"

"Goddammit, Ro-jay, what the hell are you doing with it? You idiot, he's going to miss the damn thing," Hairy Ranger said, his voice barely above a whisper.

"I guess he just forgot it, so I took it. It's no big deal. I'll give it back later."

"Jesus Christ, you asshole, they could think you stole the goddam thing," Hairy Ranger said and glared at Rapid Roger.

"Hell, I didn't steal it; I found it. I just haven't turned it in yet," Rapid Roger said.

"Goddammit, Ro-jay, why didn't you just leave it where it was? The treads probably'll think we're East German spies and want to shoot us or send us to Leavenworth," I said.

"Piss off, I'll turn it in when we get to Bremen," Rapid Roger said, and tossed the book under his bunk. "Now, if you two assholes don't mind, I'm going to catch some Zs."

Hairy Ranger and I didn't say anything; we just settled into our bunks to sleep away the trip through East Germany. I had just drifted off when I was startled by rapping on the compartment door. I heard Ranger, who had the bunk below me, slide open the door and suddenly someone turned on the light.

"What's the deal?" I asked.

"Hey! What's the hell's going on?" Rapid Roger said loudly.

"Shut up, soldier!"

I rubbed my eyes and looked in the direction of the voice.

It was the second lieutenant, only now he didn't look irritated, he looked angry. Without saying a word, he stepped in the compartment, bent down and picked up the codebook, which Rapid Roger had tossed under his bunk.

"You three come with me."

"What's the deal?" I asked, but he ignored me and then I saw two very large MPs standing in the corridor. This could be a serious situation, I thought.

I trailed closely behind Hairy Ranger as we walked down the corridor toward the MP car.

I tapped Hairy Ranger on the shoulder and whispered, "Deny everything. Deny everything."

He nodded.

The second lieutenant and the MPs escorted us into a compartment in the last car on the train. This compartment didn't have bunks, it had two long seats on opposite sides of the compartment.

"Sit down and don't say anything," the second lieutenant said. Hairy Ranger and I sat on the seat facing the front of the train, while Rapid Roger, his face ashen, took the seat across from us. The second lieutenant glared at us, then left the compartment and one MP took a post directly in front of the window, while his partner stood in front of the door. I had no doubt the .45s strapped to their hips were loaded, so I decided to stay as quiet as possible.

An hour later, the two MPs marched us off the train and into the station at Helmstedt. Within minutes, we boarded another duty train, again under guard, for the trip back to Berlin. About the time we should have been getting off the train in Bremen, we found ourselves sitting, under guard, outside the Criminal Investigation Division office in the Berlin Brigade headquarters, which also served as the U.S. consulate's office.

A man, with a military-style haircut, wearing a dark suit, white shirt and narrow black tie, came out of the CID office. He tapped Rapid Roger on the shoulder. Rapid Roger jumped up and followed him into the office.

An hour later, two more men, looking almost identical to the one who took Rapid Roger, came out of the office.

"You," one of the men said, pointing at me, "come in

here."

I followed him into the CID office, down a short hallway and took a seat in a chair across from a tiny metal desk in a small windowless room. Other than the desk and chair, the room had no furnishings and nothing on the walls.

"You know you're looking at some serious jail time?" he asked.

"What for?"

"We know you took the codebook."

"What codebook?"

"The one we found in your compartment."

"I didn't know there was a codebook in there. I hit the rack as soon as I got on the train."

"The train commander said you were awake when he picked up the flag orders."

"I went to bed right after that."

"You didn't go anywhere?"

"Where could I go?"

"You didn't go to the head?"

"No, I went to bed."

"Did you see one of your buddies go to the head?"

"No, I was asleep."

"You'll make it easier on yourself if you tell us the truth."

"I am telling you what happened. I went to sleep, the MPs woke me up. I don't know anything about a codebook."

"You plan on sticking with that story?"

"It's what happened."

"Humph," he snorted. He shoved himself away from the desk and stomped out of the office, slamming the door behind him. I took a deep breath. It seemed as if I sat alone in the room for hours before the door opened and the CID agent came back in and leaned on the desk.

"We're letting you go back to your unit. We've been in touch with your C.O., and he'll deal with you."

I nodded and tried to appear nonchalant as I left the room. I almost bumped into Hairy Ranger coming out of a small room directly across the hallway from where I had been interrogated.

"You okay?"

He nodded and grinned, a lopsided grin of relief.

"Let's get the hell out of here," I said.

"What about Rapid Roger? They're still holding him."

"They can have him."

The Phantom stood on the steps leading into the company when we got back to the barracks.

"Captain wants to see you three," he said grimly. "You wait in the day room until your partner in crime gets here."

"Any idea how long it'll be before he gets here?" I asked.

"CID just called, so it shouldn't be too long."

"Sarge, what's up? Blackie and I didn't do anything," Hairy Ranger said, a trace of indignation having crept into his voice.

"Your good buddy told the CID he found the codebook and brought it back to the compartment and the three of you looked it over. Why didn't you three think about turning the damn thing in?"

"I was asleep," I said.

"Me, too," Hairy Ranger echoed.

"Good try, men, good try," Phantom said and chuckled. "Just wait in the day room until Captain Weldon's ready for you."

Hairy Ranger and I decided to pass the time by playing some eight ball, but we couldn't concentrate on the game and we finally quit. Hairy Ranger sprawled on the sofa in front of the television mounted on the wall and tried to get interested in a German soap opera. I sat on the window sill and stared out across the parking lot toward the ruins of former S.S. barracks. Because the Army never needed the additional barracks, the Engineers battalion erected an eight-foot-high chain-link fence around the old building and padlocked the gate, opening it only when a detail went in to mow the grass.

"All right, you two, captain's ready for you," the Phantom's voice startled me.

Hairy Ranger and I followed the Phantom into the company commander's office, where we saw an ashen-faced Rapid Roger standing nervously in front of Captain Weldon's desk.

Hairy Ranger and I snapped to attention in front of the captain. He looked at us and grinned.

"Well, you three have really screwed up this time. If I didn't know you three, I'd think you were trying to steal the codebook, but I've assured CID you aren't spies, you're just goddam morons," he said. "What in God's name were you thinking about when you took that codebook?"

I saw Hairy Ranger open his mouth as if he wanted to protest, but he thought better of it and clinched his jaws.

"Well, you're pretty damn lucky that I could talk CID out of charging you with something, but you're not getting off scot-free. The train commander doesn't want you three on the duty train anymore, and I think it's a pretty damn good idea. So, you three are banned from the duty train for as long as you remain in Berlin. The only way you can ride the duty train is if you're being transferred to the Zone or if you're dead and we're shipping your body out. Got that?"

"Yes, sir," we said in unison.

"Fine, now get the hell out of here," Captain Weldon said, casually returning our salutes. We spun on our heels and marched out, in as much semblance of military bearing as we could muster.

We remained silent as we climbed the stairs to C Trick's area on the third floor, but when we got to the first room, where Rapid Roger bunked with the Pipe, Hairy Ranger whirled and shoved Rapid Roger against the wall.

"You piece of shit! You ran your goddam mouth to the CID!"

"N-no, n-no, guys, I didn't say a thing," Rapid Roger stammered.

"The hell you didn't, asshole," I said. "The goddam CID told me exactly what happened when they got me in their office. They knew who took the goddam codebook, who looked at it, everything."

"That means you had to run your goddam mouth," Hairy Ranger said.

"They were going to send me to Leavenworth," Rapid Roger wailed.

"Jesus Christ, you asshole! Don't ever admit anything to the goddam treads. Just deny everything, even your name. Fuck him, Ranger, I don't even want to see that worthless son of a bitch," I said, and then I walked as rapidly as I could toward my room at the end of the hall. As I opened the door and entered the room, I heard Hairy Ranger say, "Fuck you, Ro-jay," and then the click of his cowboy boots followed me into my room.

"Hey, Blackie, we still have our passes. Let's go to the trick party."

"Shit, I'd forgotten about the beer wall. It's fine with me, I just don't want to take Ro-jay with us."

"He'll probably mope around the barracks for the rest of break anyway. Your car running?"

"Yeah, Tiny fixed it. It was just a broken plug wire," I said. I had bought the 1951 Volkswagen from Hammerhead, a diddy-bopper from Minnesota who rotated back to the States. I guess the old car had been green a few years before, but by the time I bought it for $75 and a bottle of cognac from the French PX, the green had faded to a dirty gray and it probably had more rust than paint. Hammerhead said the gear shift snapped loose one night so he used a pair of vise-grip pliers to change gears. I intended to get a new gear shift out of a junked VW that had been abandoned in the alley behind the Scum, but I never did, so I drove around Berlin shifting gears with a pair of pliers.

The party had been going on for several hours when Hairy Ranger and I arrived, so holes had begun to show in the beer wall. C Trick created the beer wall at its first party in the Grunewald to keep the Germans from joining the party. All of the guys on the trick pooled their money and bought about 140 cases of Beck's from the commissary. When we got the beer unloaded by a small lake in the forest, we were stunned by how much beer we had. We also saw how interested the Germans, who were sunbathing by the lake, had become in us. So Tiny and Buffalo Head suggested making a wall of beer between the Germans and us — a "beer wall to keep the Doobs out," as Tiny said.

Grumpy John saw us first.

"Hide your codebooks, here come the spies," he shouted drunkenly and began laughing. The others saw us and welcomed us with insults.

"We'll put up with your shit, just give us beer," Hairy Ranger said, reaching into the garbage can where bottles of

Beck's cooled. He passed the beer to me, then pulled out a bottle, opened it and took a deep drink, nearly emptying the bottle.

"What'd they do to you guys?" Fang asked.

"Threatened to send our asses to Leavenworth, but decided to just ban us from the duty train," I said. "While Ranger and me were sitting there, denying everything, that shithead Ro-jay was spilling his guts. Asshole probably said we took the damn book."

Chief looked at us blearily.

"Where's Ro-jay now?"

"Chief, I just don't really give a flying fuck where he is. We could have been worshipping in Bremen, but instead we had our asses reamed by the CID and we're stuck in the middle of the woods with you shitheads," I said.

"Fuck him," Hairy Ranger said harshly.

Chief grinned, and whirled around, nearly falling down. He held his beer bottle high and shouted, "All right, C Trick! What about Ro-jay?"

"Fuck him!" everyone shouted at the top of their lungs, drawing wide-eyed looks from the startled Germans.

I lost count of how many beers Hairy Ranger and I drank that evening, but it seemed like everytime I looked up someone handed me a bottle, and I didn't turn down one. But the lack of sleep and stress caught up with us, and I saw Hairy Ranger nodding.

"Ranger, let's go while I can still see," I said.

He nodded and we eased through the trees to the car. I started it, gunned the engine and backed into a tree.

"Shit," I said as I wrestled with the vise grip pliers, trying to shift into low, finally getting the balky transmission to cooperate on the third try.

Our overtaxed bladders began to hurt as we raced through the Grunewald, but we decided we didn't want to stop because a German policeman might see us relieving ourselves on the side of the road, and then we'd have to face Captain Weldon again, so I shoved the accelerator to the floorboard and we raced to the barracks.

"Goddam, I've got to piss like a racehorse," Hairy Ranger said.

"So do I; we're almost there," I said as I swung out around a city bus onto Finckensteinallee, racing past Randy's, a bar owned by a retired Air Force sergeant who'd married a German woman and decided to stay in Berlin.

"First damn time I've been by here that I didn't stop in Randy's for a beer," I muttered.

"Don't stop, I can see the gate," Hairy Ranger said, leaning forward in the seat.

I slammed on the brakes, skidding to a stop at the gate. The guard, glanced up from the magazine he was reading in the guard shack. He recognized me and just waved us through. I gunned it and raced toward the ASA barracks, tires squealing as I slid across the brick street and into the parking lot. I parked near the end of the dimly lit lot, and we jumped out of the car.

"I can't make it. I've got to go now," Hairy Ranger said, and darted toward the dark corner of the barracks, with me just a few steps behind him. We began relieving ourselves on the barracks wall. I thought I heard some shouting, but I didn't pay any attention; my overtaxed bladder was finally getting relief.

"What the hell do you think you're doing!"

I quickly zipped up, turned and squinted, trying to see who called.

Dirty Joe, a furious Dirty Joe.

"What's the problem, Sarge?"

He pointed, and I looked down and saw a small window at the base of the wall.

"Oh, shit," Hairy Ranger said.

We bent down and saw the electric fan, blowing directly into the Sergeants' Club. The club had been opened a few months earlier as a place where the NCOs could go and have a few more drinks after the El Oso Club closed. We could see Roadrunner and the Phantom trying to wipe off the piss spray.

"Oh, shit," we chorused.

The next morning Hairy Ranger and I stood before Captain Weldon for the second time in two days.

"I hope this isn't going to be a habit," he said.

We didn't say anything, and I don't think he expected us

to because he immediately began reading the Article Fifteen, which is military equivalent of a misdemeanor, telling us how we'd demonstrated a "callous disregard for the well-being of others."

He didn't say Hairy Ranger and I got the Article Fifteen for peeing on NCOs, but he could have.

Ma's Army Cooking

21 Army mess halls aren't places where you sit in a relaxed atmosphere and enjoy a meal. You're herded through lines rapidly, watching incredulously as surly servers slap the food onto the meal tray. Then you find a place to sit and wolf down your food as rapidly as possible and leave, making room for the next person.

The meals, while meeting the nutritional standards laid down by the Department of Defense, just couldn't be compared to the home cooking most of us had been used to before we left civilian life. Our mothers would have watched in horror at how we ate, gobbling down whatever was on our trays as fast as we could.

"Slow down. No one's going to take your plate away," my mother would say when I began to eat faster than she thought was proper.

"Hurry up! You ain't the only person in here. There are other people who got to eat, too!" the mess sergeant would say when I didn't eat as rapidly as he thought was necessary.

I always thought the mess sergeants probably once took pride in their cooking, thinking of themselves as chefs in fine restaurants. However, their abilities to put nourishing meals on the tables weren't considered as important by the higher-ups as their ability to feed hundreds of soldiers as quickly as possible. Also, their cooking skills were generally unappreciated by the hundreds of soldiers who were forced to eat so fast that they couldn't even remember what they had eaten just minutes after leaving the table.

Because of pressure from above and lack of appreciation from below, the mess sergeants became surly and defensive, taking even the most simple question about the food as an insult.

I made the mistake once of pointing at the hamburger steak about to be dropped onto my tray.

"Is it medium or well done?" I said to Walrus, the grossly overweight mess sergeant.

"You the cook, soldier? You let me worry about how it's cooked. You just eat it. Okay?" Walrus said, and slapped the meat onto my tray.

After dealing with the surly male mess sergeants for nearly three years in the ASA, Buffalo Head, Prince and I thought things might be different that day we went into the mess hall for the pre-swing shift meal and saw the new mess sergeant, Master Sergeant Bessie Raines.

We were wrong.

Bessie Raines might have been a woman and she might have been called "Ma," but she was no one's mother.

Ma Raines was as surly, as irascible, and as offensive as any mess sergeant, man or woman, who ever lived. She was a large woman with huge breasts resting on a massive belly, a bulbous nose, and eyes that looked like two black dots. Although she was big, her legs were surprisingly spindly, making her look something like a boiled egg balanced on two toothpicks. She didn't have a voice, she had a foghorn, a blaring sound that could cut through the noise of a couple hundred soldiers jabbering away during their meal.

Because of her size, her voice and her general surliness, Bessie Raines was an intimidating presence in the mess hall.

Chief quit going to the mess hall when he knew Ma would be on duty. Very little frightened Chief, but the mess sergeant terrified him.

"Goddam woman scares me to death," he said when I asked him why he was buying all of his meals at the PX. "She's going to kill someone one of these days. You ever look at her when she's holding a knife? She looks like she'd just as soon slice your gut open as look at you. Hell, she'd probably rather slice your guts open than look at you."

"Oh, for Christ's sake, Chief, she hasn't killed anyone yet," I said.

"You don't know that. Whatever happened to Sanders? He just disappeared."

"Goddammit, Chief, you know as well as I do what happened to Sanders. He was shipped back to Leavenworth for robbing a jewelry store."

"Do you really know that? Did you see the MPs take him away?" Chief said.

"No, I didn't."

"Then you don't know that Ma didn't kill him and feed him to us. I'm just not going to eat in that mess hall as long as that woman's there. No way," Chief said.

Grumpy John and Other George also said they were afraid to go into the mess hall when Ma was on duty, and especially when she was at her favorite place — at the garbage cans where soldiers cleaned off their metal trays.

"I got to tell you, when I go up there and Ma's standing right there, it's like walking through a minefield," Other George said. "I mean, you just don't know when she's going to go off."

"She's a few bricks shy of a load," Grumpy John said, as he pushed open the door to the mess hall.

"Oh, good God, there she is," I said, nodding toward the back of the mess hall where the garbage cans were sitting. There, feet firmly planted, and with an air of unbridled hostility, stood Ma.

"You and the Ranger are pretty good at pissing on treads, why don't you just go over there and take a leak on her leg?" Grumpy John said.

The memory of my recent Article Fifteen remained fresh, and the loss of part of my pay was the main reason I had been eating more of my meals in the mess hall.

"You're out of your goddam mind, Grumpy," I said. "I'd sooner take a shit on the Colonel's birthday cake. Christ, he'd just send me to the stockade, but there's no telling what Ma would do."

We moved along the line, barely even noticing the food being ladled onto our trays, and keeping an eye on Ma. We continued to watch her as we ate. When we had finished our meal and swallowed the last few drops of coffee, Prince strolled by our table. Although he had finished his meal,

Prince's tray still held an apparently untouched mound of mashed potatoes.

"Watch out for Ma, Prince," Other George said.

"Screw Ma," Prince said with a sneer.

"Not me, I'd rather bite a bear's butt than screw around with Ma," Grumpy John said in a whisper.

We were watching intently as Prince approached the garbage cans and prepared to dump the mashed potatoes. But before he could dump the uneaten food, he was startled by Ma's voice booming in his ear.

"What's the matter with them goddam potatoes?"

"Uh, nothing, nothing at all. I just really wasn't that hungry," Prince said.

"If there ain't nothing wrong with them, then you better goddam well get hungry enough to eat them," Ma said.

"Right, sergeant. Right," Prince said, backing away from the massive and irate mess sergeant. He quickly sat down at the closest table and began to gobble down the mass of potatoes as Ma hovered over him.

"You're goddam right there's nothing wrong with them potatoes. I sweat my balls off to feed you pissants and you ain't going to throw any of my food away," Ma said before spinning around on her heel and stalking off toward her office.

It began to seem that food and Ma really didn't go together.

A few days after Ma terrorized Prince, Buffalo Head and I, along with about 100 others, were in line for lunch. It was one of those lunches that none of us wanted, but because it was a couple of days until pay day, we didn't have enough money left to buy a meal at the PX. We were in line and not too happy about the meal selection, which was one of the most unappetizing lunches imaginable — wieners cooked in some unidentifiable red sauce, scalloped potatoes featuring rubber cheese, and some bland pudding that resembled library paste.

"I think we should've gone to the PX," Buffalo Head said with a sigh as he looked bleakly at the wiener concoction.

"Remember your choices, Buff. You can have a decent meal or you can have a lot of beer," I said.

"I know, I know. But, goddam, what a piss-poor choice. Have you looked at those goddam weenies? They look like dicks cooked in blood, for Christ's sake," he said.

Before I could make my own assessment of the food selection, the Bunny bounded past us, cup in hand, on the way to the huge mess hall coffee pot, where Ma was filling her own cup.

"Hey, Bessie, you old bitch! Been getting any lately?" The Bunny said.

"No, Sarge, I been on the rag," Ma said.

There was deathly silence in the mess hall, as 200 eyes looked at Ma, then looked at the wieners floating in the red concoction.

"Oh, Jesus God, I can't handle this. Fuck the beer money, I'm going to the PX," Buffalo Head said. He spun out of the line and returned his tray to the big rack and darted toward the door. I was only about a step behind him. As we pushed open the door and stepped out onto the sidewalk, we heard the scuffling of feet behind us. Looking back, we saw nearly every person who had been in line with us close behind.

There wasn't an official boycott of the mess hall, but most of the C Trickers just stayed away, preferring to pay for our meals at the PX snack bar. We had been on the unofficial boycott for several days when Chief interrupted Hairy Ranger and me while we were shooting pool in the day room. It was almost noon when Chief sauntered in and leaned against the table.

"I'm heading over to the mess hall. You coming?" he said.

"But, Chief, I thought you don't go to the mess hall. You finally realize that Ma's just disgusting, not a murderer?" I said.

"She can't kill me now. Ma's gone. The old bitch's been shipped out to the Zone. I can go to the mess hall anytime I want to now," Chief said happily as he trotted down the steps.

Shakey

22 Shakey came by his nickname honestly. The slight, balding, nearsighted Spec Five was a walking definition of nervousness. He was an artist of twitches and jerks, piecing together a tapestry of nervousness and agitation as complex and, in its own way, as beautiful as a finely woven Navajo blanket.

"Shakey, did you have these seizures before you went to Vietnam or have you always been epileptic?" Hairy Ranger said as we watched Shakey twitch and jerk while pouring a cup of coffee in the Hill's break room.

"What do you mean, Ranger?"

"Well, Jesus Christ, Shakey, you jump and twitch all the time like you're sitting on a time bomb or something. I thought maybe you'd been through some tough times over there. After all, it's not like Berlin — they're actually shooting at people in Vietnam."

"I wasn't shot at. I'm just kind of nervous. Runs in the family," Shakey said.

"You sure you weren't shot at? You were at Phu Bai," I said.

"Don't you think I'd know if I were shot at? That's something that a person would remember," Shakey said.

"Not always," Rock Weed said solemnly. "I remember reading about a guy in a bar in Denver who was shot in the head and he didn't know about it until he went to the doctor a couple of days later to see about his headaches. Doctor nearly shit when he found a bullet in the guy's head."

"For Christ's sake, the guy was probably drunk," Shakey said.

"Weren't you ever drunk when you were in Vietnam?"

Hairy Ranger asked.

"Of course I got drunk in Vietnam. You had to get drunk to handle Vietnam. Just like I had to get drunk before I could handle the swill Ma Raines used to serve up before they shipped her to the Zone," Shakey said.

"Well, that's it. You got shot at when you were drunk, but you just didn't remember it. But, your subconscious remembers it, and you're nervous because of it," Hairy Ranger said.

"Ranger, did your mother have any children that lived?" Shakey said.

The verbal sparring ended when Roadrunner darted into the break room, hitched his pants, looked at his clipboard, and cleared his throat.

"Shakey, Captain Weldon's picked you for this month's courier scene," Roadrunner said. "You need to go to head-quarters to get your paperwork. You can catch a ride with the supply truck."

With that, Roadrunner hitched his pants again and darted out of the break room and headed toward the Pit.

Shakey quickly drained his coffee and tossed the cup in the sink.

"Well, assholes, I got to go. See you in a month," he said as he left.

"What'd he mean he'd see us in a month?" Rock Weed said.

"He's got courier duty for the month. He's going to be spending most of his time riding back and forth between here and Frankfurt on the duty train with a briefcase hand-cuffed to his wrist," I said.

"What briefcase?"

"There's a lot of shit that has to be sent to ASA brass in Frankfurt that they don't want to put in regular mail, so they have a special courier carry it all by hand on the train. He takes a briefcase full of stuff to Frankfurt and gets an-other one there to bring back here. The damn thing's hand-cuffed to him when he leaves and is taken off when he gets there," I said.

"Sounds like something out of James Bond to me," Rock Weed said. "Does he carry a gun?"

"Yeah, he'll have a .45," I said.

"Oh my God, Shakey with a .45. Jesus Christ, he'll probably shoot himself."

"He'll just have the .45. He won't have the clip for it. The damn gun's just for show."

"It sounds kind of boring to me. Hell, all he's going to do is ride back and forth between here and Frankfurt. He probably won't be in either place long enough to enjoy himself," Rock Weed said, stifling a yawn.

"You don't just get off the train and then get right back on one going back," I said. "The duty train from Berlin gets to Frankfurt about eight in the morning and it doesn't leave there until eight that night. You got all day to yourself after you deliver your briefcase and before you pick up the new one."

"When do you grab some Zs?" Rock Weed said.

"On the train, asshole," I said.

"Well, I still don't think it's such a good deal," Rock Weed said.

"It is if you count the stuff you can score from the Russian guards and then sell to our guys. You've seen all the guys who wear Russian Army belt buckles with their civvies, haven't you?"

Hairy Ranger and Rock Weed nodded and I continued.

"Anyway, the Russian guards will trade anything they got for a new copy of Playboy and some PX cigarettes. All the couriers take along a couple copies of Playboy and a few packs of cigarettes, and when the train stops at Potsdam and Marienborn, you can swap them for Russian belt buckles or hats or whatever. Christ, you probably could get a goddam Russian rifle if you asked. Those Russians love Playboy and our cigarettes."

"What's so special about our cigarettes?" Rock Weed said.

"It's pretty obvious you've never smoked a Russian cigarette," Hairy Ranger said. "The goddam things are about a foot long, but only two inches is tobacco and that's like shredded inner tubes. There's no filter, just that long tube that you pinch in a couple of places. Jesus Christ, they're awful. There's no goddam wonder the Russians are so damn gloomy. You'd be, too, if you had to smoke those things."

"You ever smoke one of them, Blackie?" Rock Weed said as he peered owlishly over the top of his coffee mug.

"Yeah. But not here. I went on a cigarette-of-the-week jag in Monterey. There was a tobacco shop downtown that had cigarettes from all over the world. Every Saturday morning, I'd get up early and I'd go down there and buy a pack of cigarettes from a different country. I bought some from Turkey, Israel, Holland, Finland, Japan — you know, all over. Anyway, I tried some Russian cigarettes and they were pretty fucking awful. After I bought them, I went and had a cup of coffee and when I fired up that goddam Russian cigarette, I swear to God they looked like they were going to run me out of the restaurant. The thing smelled worse than old tires burning. I think I ended up giving them to some goddam Russian weed."

I didn't see Shakey until after he had been on courier duty for a couple of weeks. He was sitting in the PX snackbar, staring glumly at a plate of French fries while he munched slowly on a hamburger.

"Hey, Shake, how's the courier's life?" I said as I eased onto the chair across from him.

"I'll be glad when this crap's over. It's not worth a shit, Blackie," he said sullenly.

"Aw, come on, Shakey, what's the problem? You're off the Hill. You got your days to yourself. What's the matter?"

Before answering, Shakey paused to take a long drink.

"Nothing's going like it's supposed to. First morning I get to Frankfurt, right after I turned in the briefcase, I went to the mess hall to get some breakfast and there was Ma Raines. They sent that old bitch to Frankfurt, for Christ's sake. If you can imagine it, her food's even worse there than it was here."

"I thought they sent her to Herzo or one of those 'Gator-infested shitholes down near the Czech border. Hell, I hope Chief doesn't get courier duty. He'll shit if he sees her waiting for him in the Zone."

"Yeah, that's bad enough, but here's the real kick in the ass. You know how the Russian guards are always trying to get cigarettes and 'Playboy'?"

"Yeah, they grab up that stuff as fast as we can get it to them," I said.

"Well, someone's getting it to them pretty damn fast," Shakey said.

"What do you mean?"

"I mean that every damn trip — it don't matter if it's from Frankfurt or if it's from Berlin — someone's already made the swaps with the Russians. Every time I've showed them a Playboy, they've already got it. Every time I've gotten ready to show off my cigarettes, I see they're already smoking a Marlboro or Winston or some other damn PX cigarette. The whole courier deal's been a big, goddam waste of time. I feel like I've been screwed, blewed and tattoed," Shakey said.

"Damn shame, Shakey," I said. "It's a sad state of affairs when an honorable courier has his little black-market operation screwed up by some unscrupulous asshole who's doing the same thing you're wanting to do."

Mr. Greyhound

23 When I first met Jude Patout, I didn't know he'd be one of the reasons why I would be busted. It wasn't his fault — I was to blame for my own run-in with the authorities. But he was the snitch who turned me in.

I had first met Jude Patout when I arrived in Berlin. It was a typical January day — cold and overcast. I had just gotten off the military duty train from Frankfurt and was looking for the ride to Andrews Barracks.

As I looked around, I spotted an Army bus. The door was open and the driver, an overweight young man with sleepy eyes and a mustache, was sprawled in the seat, with his feet on the dashboard, smoking a cigarette and reading a copy of Playboy.

"Hey, driver," I said, tapping on the side of the bus.

"Driver, my ass. That's Mr. Greyhound to you, fellow," he said.

"Is this the bus for the 78th ASA?" I said.

"Just what's the sign on the goddam side of the bus say?"

Sure enough, there on the side were those familiar white, stenciled letters: 78th ASA SOU.

As I clambered aboard and stowed my duffel bag on the rack overhead, the driver slammed the door shut, fired up the diesel engine, and roared away from the train station.

We rode through the neighborhoods of southern Berlin in silence, except for when the driver looked in the mirror.

"You know, I got to get a goddam dog for the side of my bus," he said.

A few minutes later, I was in the company clerk's office, processing in and becoming an official member of the 78th.

"Who the hell was that driver?" I said to the clerk

"Did you get the Mr. Greyhound routine?" he said.

"Yeah, and he said he wanted a dog on the side of his bus."

"That was Jude Patout. He's a crazy Cajun from some swamp in Louisiana. He pulls that Mr. Greyhound on all the weeds. He's really a maintenance man or some crap like that up on the Hill. Everyone who's got a bus license has to go pick up weeds now and then, but he's the only one who thinks he's a Greyhound driver."

I would see Patout play Mr. Greyhound whenever he drew the duty of driving the trick bus to the Hill. Somehow he had gotten a Greyhound driver's hat that he wore when he drew the trick bus driver detail. We'd be waiting in the barracks parking lot for the buses to carry us up to the Hill, and Patout would roar up in his bus, slam on the brakes, and slide to a stop in a cloud of dust, or mud, depending on the weather.

He would have that Greyhound hat firmly planted on his head, and before pulling out, he'd call out our destination, just like he was on a cross-country bus trip.

"Welcome to Greyhound's C Trick Express," he'd say. "We'll be making stops at the main PX, Site Four and Site Three. Our cruising speed will be approximately fifty clicks and our estimated time of arrival is 22 minutes. My name is Mr. Greyhound. Now sit back and enjoy your trip."

The Mr. Greyhound routine came to a screeching halt on the day the unit commander decided to be one of the guys and ride up to the Hill on the trick bus. The colonel was an imposing figure, made even more so because of his reputation. During the waning days of the Korean war, the colonel, then a captain commanding a company of infantry, had personally led the last-reported bayonet charge by the U.S. Army in combat. The willingness of the man to stick a big knife on the end of a rifle and run screaming at people who were shooting at him with machine guns, mortars and anything else that makes a big bang, certainly made us leery of crossing him.

We were sitting on the bus and Patout had just started his Mr. Greyhound bit when the colonel mounted the bus, and glared at Patout.

"Stow that goddam stupid hat, soldier!"

"Yessir!" Patout blurted and shoved the bus driver's hat under the front seat, slapped his regulation Army fatigue cap squarely on top of his head, started the bus engine, popped it in gear, and headed off to the Hill.

Mr. Greyhound was never heard from again.

Not long after the disappearance of Mr. Greyhound, Patout decided he would re-up and collect the VRB, the re-enlistment bonus paid for his military job description, and buy a Jaguar XKE sports car. His decision was met with derision and as he was driving up to the Hill, he was ser-enaded by his passengers.

"Re-up, for the VRB!/Re-up, for an XKE,/Re-up!/I'd rather throw up,/Than be a lifer, a beggar, a tread!"

Although he didn't say anything, we knew that we were getting to Patout, because the back of his neck turned fiery red and he whipped the bus through turns that would send his passengers slamming into each other, and deliberately ran through potholes to make us bounce and jar our teeth.

Patout's decision to re-enlist was an indirect cause of my bust.

A few weeks after he re-enlisted, it was late fall in Berlin. It was cold and damp, and I came down with a bad cold. The trick was on mids, so I went to the infirmary as soon as the shift ended to get some cold medicine.

The Army doctor listened to my heart, took my blood pressure, and then gave me some pills to take for the cold.

"These pills should do the trick. Take one every four hours and you'll see quick results," he said.

I had just given up my apartment on Kadettenweg, and moved back into the barracks, so I went straight to my room and went to sleep. After sleeping until about six that evening, and grabbing a hamburger at the PX, I went to a movie, making sure that I took my cold medicine. The movie was over about 9:30 p.m., so I decided to go to the El Oso Club for a couple of beers before getting ready to catch the trick bus to the Hill for the mid shift.

Hairy Ranger and Shakey, who had just finished his month-long courier duty, were already at the El Oso when I got there. I joined them and drank a couple of beers before we decided it was time to get ready for work. Everything was fine until the bus was about a mile from the Hill.

I felt lightheaded and giddy.

That feeling passed and by the time I was checking in at the guard shack, I was back to normal, or at least I thought I was.

Still nothing was apparently wrong until I walked into the wing where I worked, sitting before a 24-channel module with a dozen tape recorders. The room was dimly lit and there seemed to be hundreds of blinking lights sending shock waves directly into my brain.

I flipped out. All I could think about was getting rid of the lights. If I got rid of all the lights, the pain would stop. I began to hit at the tape recorders, pulling at the tapes. I must have ripped thirty or forty tapes off the recorders, before Hairy Ranger and Fang were able to get me under control.

Shakey grabbed an empty box and began tossing the broken tape reels into it.

"Hey, Prince, put tapes on those machines before the Roadrunner gets in here," he said.

Prince went to work rapidly, slapping reel after reel in place.

While all this was going on, Patout, who was going down the hall on his way to the maintenance shack, looked in and saw all the bustle of activity.

"What's going on?" he said.

"Nothing, Greyhound, nothing," Hairy Ranger said. "It's just Blackie. He's sick, but he'll be okay."

All the damage had apparently been corrected, and Shakey had dumped the broken tapes before Roadrunner came in for his first round. He didn't spot the box of broken tapes, but he did spot me, pale and shaken, sitting with my head resting on the little desk at my work station.

"Hmm," Roadrunner said, his prominent Adam's apple bobbing up and down. Roadrunner was a hyperactive tread who started every conversation with a long, low, drawn-out "hmm."

Roadrunner and I did not get along. I had been promoted to Spec Five after he had run out of reasons to block it, although he could always find plenty of reasons why I should have the latrine scene or the break room scene. For Roadrunner, everything was a scene. We all were pretty sure that when he passed away, he would just be trying out the death scene. After I got the promotion, Roadrunner and I had an uneasy truce. I stayed out of his way and he generally tried to ignore me. In the last six months, I guess we hadn't exchanged more than a dozen words, with most of my conversation being "Yo!" when he called my name at roll call.

But that night, Roadrunner must have been in a particularly good mood because when he saw I was sick, he told me to get out to the guard shack and catch the supply truck back to the base.

I went gladly.

Everything seemed to under control. I was off the Hill, the broken tapes had been replaced, and Roadrunner was unaware that anything had happened.

Unfortunately, mids are long and boring. It's hard to stay awake on mids, which are eight tedious hours during which you consume numerous cups of coffee and smoke one cigarette after the other. When the shift ends, you're completely wiped out and frequently forget things.

This mid shift was no different. Shakey and Hairy Ranger were completely wiped out, and they forgot to dump the box of broken tapes, which was discovered by the Groad, the obese trick sergeant for D Trick, which had the day shift.

It was apparent that they had been left over from the mid shift, so it was a matter of finding out what had happened.

We were routed from our sound sleep by a horde of treads, the company commander, the first sergeant, the trick sergeant, the platoon sergeant, and a group of NCOs and officers from the headquarters.

"Sabotage. Someone's sabotaged the Hill," a major from headquarters said. The major had never even been to the Hill, because if he actually were to go to the Hill he wouldn't be able to kiss ass at headquarters and could miss out on a promotion.

All of us who worked in Section Violet, where the offense occurred, were questioned.

We went into the enlisted man's standard operating procedure when confronted by higher-ups about something's wrong — we admitted nothing, denied everything, and spoke in generalities.

"Did you know about the sabotage?" Roadrunner asked.

"I heard about it," I said.

"Do you know who did it?" Roadrunner said.

"Nobody's mentioned any names to me," I said.

"Did you see anybody hiding those tapes?" the first sergeant said.

"I was sent back with the supply truck," I said.

"Why did you go back with the supply truck?" the major from headquarters said.

"I was sick," I said.

"He was sick," Hairy Ranger said.

"You didn't see anyone committing the sabotage?" the major said.

"I wasn't watching; I was sick," I said.

The treads were getting frustrated. They knew that we knew, but we were stonewalling. We could hold out as long as they could. Hairy Ranger was confident that we'd get restricted to the barracks for a week or so, then the whole thing would blow over.

"You'll be off the hook, Blackie," he said.

"Yeah, everything'll be okay," Shakey said. "They won't be able to get anything out of us."

They were, however, able to get something out of Jude Patout.

The recently re-enlisted former Mr. Greyhound remembered seeing me with Hairy Ranger and Fang, and noticing Prince putting tapes on the machines while Shakey was putting broken reels in a box. Even a newly minted tread could figure out this one. Also, he knew there was a sergeant's slot opening up, and he saw an opportunity to improve his chances for the promotion.

He snitched, and I was caught.

It was now obvious that I would have to admit what I had done. The only thing remaining to resolve was what to do with me.

The headquarters officers and Roadrunner were screaming sabotage and calling for a court-martial. Roadrunner even suggested the possibility of Leavenworth and serious jail time. The headquarters officers thought shooting me as a spy would be a good idea, even though no spy had been shot since World War II. The matter was finally resolved by an unlikely source, the site commander. He had sat quietly, keeping his own counsel throughout the questioning and subsequent debate over what to do.

"Sabotage, my ass! He was drunk. Give him an Article Fifteen," he said.

Roadrunner and the headquarters officers were disappointed, but the Colonel agreed with the site commander.

"Article Fifteen?" I asked Captain Gammon, my company commander. An Article Fifteen was like pleading no contest and getting a reduced sentence. There'd be no court-martial or jail time.

"Article Fifteen," he said. "You get chewed out by the Colonel and he busts you to Spec Four. All in all, you're getting off pretty light."

He was right. The Colonel spent about fifteen minutes raging at me about Valley Forge, Gettysburg, San Juan Hill and the Battle of the Bulge and how if I had been part of the Army then, those battles would have been lost. However, because the modern Army lost its sense of discipline, he couldn't have people like me shot.

"But I can bust your ass and I, by God, am doing that now," he said as he grabbed a pen and scrawled his signature over the paperwork that changed me from a Spec Five to a Spec Four.

"You know you got off pretty light. They really wanted to hang your ass," Hairy Ranger said after I got back to our room.

Jude Patout, now called Jude Patout Iscariot because he sold out a fellow enlisted man, didn't get that promotion he wanted. He was trapped in limbo — none of the EMs would have anything to do with a snitch, and none of the NCOs would have anything to do with him because he wasn't an NCO — and he was a snitch.

When I thought that getting busted was the end of it, I was wrong. I didn't realize that getting busted would end up screwing Berlin Brigade's annual summer war games, but that's how it turned out. After getting busted, I went back on the KP roster and the only way I could get out of that duty was to be a regular trick bus driver. So I took the driving test, got my bus license and got on the drivers roster.

About once a month, I drove the trick bus — one of those regular city transit department buses — from the barracks to the Hill and back to the barracks at the end of the shift.

The only drudge part of the job was having to fill out the trip forms, clean out the bus and make sure the tank was full when it was returned to the motor pool.

On the day that the ASA ruined the war games, C Trick was working days. When the swing shift arrived that afternoon, the drivers of the first two buses told Doc and me that the Aggressors were heading into a trap in the Grünewald.

Doc and I looked at each other.

"Well, why not?" he said.

"Let's do it," I said.

We fired up our buses and headed out, even faster than we normally drove because we wanted to catch up with the Aggressors before they walked into the trap.

When we saw a couple of Aggressor squads, we pulled over and stopped our buses. We opened the doors and told them what was going on and offered them rides.

They jumped at the chance, and we drove through the Good Guy lines without anyone noticing anything different. When we were through the Good Guy lines, the Aggressors got off and attacked the headquarters from the rear, capturing all of the top brass and bringing the war games to a sudden — and completely unscripted — halt.

The Berlin Brigade brass wasn't amused and the next day, Doc and I found ourselves standing at attention in front of the Colonel. Although he chewed us out properly for ruining Berlin Brigade's war game, he did it with a twinkle in his eyes.

Uncle Wally

24 Whoever came up with the "Berlin is eine Reise wert (Berlin is worth a trip)" as a tourism slogan must have been thinking about autumn, my favorite season in the city. The leaves were an explosion of red and gold, the wind was crisp and the air was fresh. The sun gently caressed with its rays as it prepared to go into hibernation during the dreary Berlin winter.

It was a beautiful fall afternoon, C Trick was winding up a set of days, and Uncle Wally decided to go deer hunting.

Uncle Wally was Walter Ulbricht, the president of East Germany. Ulbricht was a native of Leipzig and had joined the German Communist Party in 1919, even serving as a deputy in the Reichstag. When Hitler came to power, Ulbricht went into exile, living in the Soviet Union until the end of the war. After coming back to occupied Germany, he became the head of the SED and was the Soviets' man in Berlin.

I didn't pay much attention when the light began to flash on the console. It mean some bureaucrat in East Germany was making a telephone call. There were 24 channels, so the lights were always flashing. The tapes were running, and I didn't see the point in putting down my coffee to check the new conversation.

After I finished my coffee, I began checking the conversations. There was nothing unusual, just another day in the office for the East German functionaries. Then I pushed the button to see what was happening in the latest conversation, and I heard the district director in Rostock say, "Aber, Genosser Honecker, was soll ich tun? (But, Comrade Honecker, what should I do?)"

Honecker was Erich Honecker, Ulbricht's heir-apparent, the number two man in East Germany and the man who really was running the country.

"Oh, Christ," I said, looking around the room. Everyone was busy, and I was listening to Erich Honecker. We had orders to let the transcribers know whenever Uncle Wally, Honecker or Willi Stoph used the lines, something that had not happened once during the two years I'd been on the Hill.

I thought I'd leave my station, let the tape run and go up to the transcription room, soI was relieved to see Crooner walking down the hallway.

"Hey, Crooner, I got Honecker on the line," I said. "Would you run up and tell the transcribers?"

"No shit? Honecker?" he said.

"Yeah, and he's talking to the head tread in Rostock."

Moments later, Fast Eddie, a pair of headsets dangling around his neck, burst through the door.

"Which one is he on?" Fast Eddie said. I pointed to one of the recorders, and he plugged in his headsets. He frowned as he followed the conversation. Fast Eddie was the chief German transcriber, but I didn't know him very well because he worked straight days. He also was married, had a couple of kids and lived off post, so we rarely saw each other except at the Hill.

"Jesus Christ, have you been listening to this?"

"No, I caught it just a couple of minutes ago."

"Ulbricht wants to go deer hunting."

"Deer hunting?"

"Yeah," he said and grinned. "The old boy wants to kill a deer, so Honecker's shitting bricks."

"Hell, I saw Uncle Wally on the tube the other day, and he looked like a damn corpse. You sure he wants to go deer hunting?"

"Damn right, I'm sure. He wants to go deer hunting, and Honecker wants to make sure he gets a deer. That's why he's on the horn with Rostock. He's got to get things arranged. Don't bother changing the tape. Let it run until it's full," he said and jerked out the plug.

"I'll be back in a few minutes, but give me a holler if

Stoph comes on," he said, referring to the East German premier.

With minutes, everyone on the Hill knew that I was taping Honecker. While the tape spun, I took notes.

"What you taking notes for, Blackie? Fast Eddie's going to transcribe the tape in a few minutes anyway," Prince said.

"They're not for him. They're for the treads to look at so they don't have to look over Fast Eddie's shoulder."

"They're still going to have look over his shoulder. No one can read that shit you've got there," Hairy Ranger said. "Didn't they teach writing in Arkansas, or did you just invent that?"

"Hell, yes, they teach writing in Arkansas. I had to learn to write fast when I was a reporter."

"Good Lord," Crooner said, as he looked over my shoulder. "Somebody get the word to DIRNSA. We don't need any codes. Just let Blackie write all the messages, because the goddam Russians will never be able to decipher that shit."

"Don't you have a song to you need to rehearse, Crooner?" I said.

"I didn't think you'd ask. How about something from Bobby Darin?" he said and grinned. Holding an imaginary microphone in his left hand and snapping his fingers, he began to sing: "Well, the shark bites/with its teeth, dear ..."

"Hey, go get Fast Eddie. I'm going to have to change tapes," I said brusquely.

He nodded and walked briskly from the room. I pulled the tape, dropped it in a manila folder, scribbled the date and time in the log book, and put a new blank tape on the recorder. I handed the tape to Fast Eddie, who had just walked up.

"Honecker still on?" he said and pointed at the recorder with the tape running.

"No, it's just routine garbage now. Want me to let it run or go back on schedule?" I asked. As part of our routine, we pulled tapes every hour.

"Yeah, yeah. Regular schedule, unless Honecker comes back on."

Honecker didn't come back on before the shift ended,

and C Trick went on break

Two days later, C Trick started its swing shift. I nearly collided with Fast Eddie as I came around the corner of the building after checking in at the guardshack.

"Sorry, I didn't see you," Fast Eddie said. He grinned and started walking briskly toward the guardshack.

"Hey, Fast Eddie," I shouted after him. "Got a minute?"

He stopped, looked toward the guardshack and saw the first trick bus pulling away.

"Hey, I'm going to have to wait for the next bus anyway. What do you want?"

"Whatever happened to Uncle Wally's deer hunt?"

Fast Eddie started laughing and motioned me toward the side of the building.

"Man, you should have heard it. Uncle Wally really must have wanted to get a deer, because Honecker was leaning on the head tread in Rostock. Hell, it seemed like he started calling every five minutes, got the army involved and the game wardens. It was a damn madhouse over there," he paused and lit a cigarette.

"Well, let's make a long story short," he said. "They came up with a plan. They got a goddam deer from some preserve near Rostock yesterday. They took it out to where Uncle Wally was and drugged it — not enough to knock it out, but enough to make it move real slow."

"Christ, that's just target shooting," I said.

"Oh, it gets better. Honecker ordered the army to send over a sharpshooter with a scope and a silencer. When they flushed the deer, the sniper was supposed to watch and if Uncle Wally missed, he'd put it down. Uncle Wally got his deer," he dropped his cigarette and ground the butt under his heel. "I got to go catch the bus."

"Well?"

"Well, what?"

"Did Uncle Wally shoot it or did the sniper?"

"Who knows? All that mattered was Uncle Wally got his deer."

Ami Janes

25 I had just left the shower room and had almost reached my room when I heard the ring of the pay phone on the landing between C Trick's rooms on the third floor and A Trick on the second floor. Still dripping and shivering from the cold breeze that always seemed to be blowing through the hallway of the old barracks, I answered the phone.

"Who's this?"

I recognized the caller's voice; it was Rainbow Pete.

"Blackie."

"Great, Blackie, this is Rainbow Pete, and I just saw about forty Ami college Janes. We got visitors."

I didn't believe Rainbow Pete when he said a tour group of college girls from the States had arrived in Berlin. After all, damn few American tourists visit Berlin after the first week of September and it's next to impossible to find any American visitors, except for politicians and Pentagon brass, showing up in Berlin during November.

It's dismal in Berlin during the winter, and no matter what the calendar says, Berlin's winter usually arrives about the first of October. The sun, like some celestial bear, goes into hibernation, not to be seen again until sometime in late March or early April. Most days are soggy, with an almost constant rain that's not quite a rain, and you feel damp for most of the winter.

So when Rainbow Pete called to say about forty American college girls had just landed at Tegel, the big international airport in the French sector, I didn't believe him, and I guess my skepticism hurt his feelings.

"No, goddammit, Blackie, I know what the hell I'm talking about! I'm looking at them now. I swear to God, it looks like forty cheerleaders from UCLA are here. They're collecting their baggage right now."

"Okay, find out where they're staying and get back with me, but make it fast, I'm freezing my ass off here."

"Give me five minutes."

C Trick had started break, and I don't know why Rainbow Pete had gone to Tegel, unless one of his buddies was rotating back to the States, but I decided to wait by the phone for him to call back. I waited because I knew Rainbow Pete, a slight, dark-haired German Mary from Washington or Oregon. A former D Tricker, he had been switched by a clerk who decided D Trick had one too many German linguists. When Pete showed up for his first shift with C Trick, Chief asked where he'd been, and Pete ran down his list of assignments on the Hill: Orange, Blue, Violet, White.

"You're just a goddam rainbow of assignments, aren't you?" Chief said with a sneer. The nickname stuck.

During the summer, when tourists poured into Berlin, most of the C Trickers stopped our pursuit of the German women and chased after the American tourist girls — it seemed most of them were from schools in the East, like Penn State or the University of Maryland. We pursued the college girls, or as we called them "Ami Janes," relentlessly throughout the summer.

We frequented the nightclubs recommended in all the tourist guidebooks, lurked in hotel bars and lobbies, and cruised the outdoor tourist attractions hoping to make a connection. We always had our best luck on break, but days worked out pretty well, once we learned how to live on two-hour naps. Swings never did much good because it seemed like the Ami Janes' chaperones insisted they be in their hotel rooms by midnight, about an hour before we could get cleaned up and get to the tourist clubs. I just didn't bother with mids because even if you managed to connect with an Ami Jane during the day, you'd have to find someone to cover the shift, and because Roadrunner and I didn't get along, he refused to let me off.

Hedgehog came out of his room and glanced toward the landing, his eyes opening when he saw me, dripping wet with a towel wrapped around my waist, leaning against the wall.

"Hey, Blackie, what's going on? You air drying?"

"I'm waiting on a phone call."

"Who from?"

"Rainbow Pete. He said there's about forty Ami Janes at Tegel. He's trying to find out where they're headed and then he'll call me back."

"Want me to call the alert?"

"Not yet. Hell, you know R.P. It could be a group of Belgian nuns, for crying out loud."

Hedgehog walked to the first step of the landing and sat down. He leaned back on his elbows and stretched his short, stubby legs out in front of him. With his round body, dark curly hair and dark eyes, he did look like his namesake, and I guess he'd decided not to take a chance on me skipping out on him if Rainbow Pete did call back.

The phone rang, and I snatched up the receiver.

"Blackie?"

"Yeah, R.P. What'cha got?"

"Ami Janes, my friend, Ami Janes. There's 34 of them, and they want to party. They're going to be staying at a hotel on Savignyplatz — I can't think of the name, but it's the big one right across from where the hookers hang out."

"You sure they want to party?"

"Hell, yes, Blackie. When they found out I'm a GI, they said they wished I could get some buddies to show them around Berlin."

"Bullshit, R.P."

"You don't believe me, asshole, maybe you'll believe one of the Janes. I'm putting one, uh, what's your name?" I heard the muffled sounds of a conversation, but I couldn't make out what anyone said, then I heard a female voice.

"Hi, I'm Cindy. Your friend said you can get some guys to show us around town."

"No problem, we'll meet you at your hotel in about thirty minutes. Will you put Rainbow Pete back on?"

She giggled and I heard her say, "His name's Rainbow Pete," and people start laughing.

"Thanks, asshole. Look, they're taking the tour bus to the hotel now, and I'm going to follow in my car. Meet us in the lobby in about thirty minutes, okay?"

I hung up.

"Hedgehog, call the alert. There're more than thirty Janes heading for Savignyplatz right now. Let's get rolling."

Hedgehog started running back up the steps, but he drew up short when the phone rang.

I grabbed the receiver and heard Rainbow Pete, who sounded almost panicky.

"Don't come to the hotel, Blackie, the Janes want something really different. I told them about the Club House and that's where they want to party," he said, referring to the empty squad room on the fourth floor, just above C Trick's quarters. The room, which had no occupants, had been taken over by C Trick for small trick parties.

"Oh, shit, R.P., how're we going to get thirty Janes into the barracks?"

"I don't know, but you guys can work it out, can't you? I'm telling you, man, the whole goddam bunch wants to party."

"Hold on, let me ask Hedgehog."

Hedgehog looked at me curiously.

"R.P. wants to get the Janes in the Club House. Can we do it?"

Hedgehog grinned.

"Can you get a deuce-and-a-half?" he asked, referring to the popular Army truck.

"Yeah, I think so."

"Then we can do it. I'll get a cleanup crew cracking, and Chief'll get the refreshment squad to collect money and get the beer and chips. I'll tell Chief to get Grumpy John's van to go get the beer and stuff before the commissary closes."

Hedgehog ran back up the stairs and disappeared down the hallway.

"R.P., you still there?"

"Yeah. What's going on?"

"The party's on, but tell the Janes we need about an hour to get things ready. I'm getting a deuce-and-half out of the motor pool. I'll be there in about forty minutes. Ask them if they don't mind riding in the truck?"

"It tickles the shit out of them."

"Okay, give me about forty minutes," I said and hung up the receiver.

I ran up the stairs to go to my room, but when I got to the top of the landing, I stopped. It looked like all of C Trick had been listening in on an extension; I couldn't believe Hedgehog had managed to get the word spread so quickly.

Chief had a paper bag filled enough money collected to buy at least twenty cases of beer. Hedgehog and Hairy Ranger, each carrying a broom and mop, ran past me in the direction of the stairs to the fourth floor.

I threw on my jeans, a dark sweatshirt and started to grab my jacket, but then I changed my mind and grabbed my faded field jacket, the one with the darker green area where the sergeant first class stripes had been. If I were going to be driving a stolen Army deuce-and-a-half through the streets of Berlin at night, I might make it look a little more authorized if I had on a field jacket. I pulled on the field jacket, slapped my baseball cap on my head and rushed from the room, nearly knocking Shakey off his feet.

"Hey, Shakey, get your field jacket and come with me," I said.

"Field jacket? Why?"

"I'm going to steal a deuce-and-a-half, and I need you riding shotgun."

"Bullshit!"

"Rainbow Pete called and he's got about thirty Ami Janes who want to party. All we have to do is get them to the Club House, so I'm going to steal a deuce-and-a-half out of the motor pool."

"You're shitting me."

"I'm not shitting you. Ask Hedgehog, it was his idea. Just get your field jacket and come with me. We need two people in uniform in the cab."

Shakey appeared to mull it over, then grinned and said, "What the hell, I'll meet you downstairs."

A few minutes later, we slipped through a hole in the fence around the motor pool. I knew all of the trucks would have full tanks of gas because drivers couldn't turn in trucks or buses until they'd filled the fuel tanks.

"Wait for me, I'm going after a key," I said, then I slipped across the parking lot to the motor pool office, arriving just in time to see the clerk go to the bathroom. I eased my way in and grabbed a truck key and slipped back outside. If the clerk missed the key, he'd think the last driver forgot to turn in it and he'd get it in the morning.

Within minutes, Shakey and I were roaring through the streets of Berlin, heading for the hotel on Savignyplatz. I could see Shakey had lost his enthusiasm when he realized we were speeding through Berlin at night in a stolen Army truck.

"If we're stopped, our asses are in a sling, so slow down," he shouted over the roar of the engine.

"Don't worry, Shakey, we won't be stopped," I said confidently, but I did ease off on the accelerator.

When I turned off Kantstrasse onto Savignyplatz, I saw Rainbow Pete and a tall, blonde cheerleader-type standing by the hotel entranceway. I slammed on the brakes, skidding to a stop directly in front of a tall wrought-iron fence that opened into a courtyard.

Rainbow Pete waved and about a dozen Ami Janes appeared as if by magic. They came in all shapes and sizes, blondes, brunettes and redheads — all looking ready for an adventure in Europe.

"Oh, my God, I've died and gone to heaven," Shakey murmured. "I bet there's not a hairy armpit in the bunch."

"Jesus, Shakey, is that all you can think about? Hairy armpits?"

Before he could answer, Rainbow Pete banged on the side of the truck, I looked out and he was standing in the street, his arm draped over the shoulder of the tall blonde I had seen in front of the hotel.

"Blackie, this is Cindy. She's a junior at Penn State. She's a music major. Hell, they're all music majors; they're here to study opera or some such shit in Germany."

"Great, now you guys got to climb in the back of the truck and tie the flap down. If we get stopped for any reason, don't make a sound. Will you do that, Cindy?"

She nodded, her eyes wide as if she couldn't believe her luck to become involved in some kind of secret espionage activity in Berlin.

"Forty Ami Janes, my ass, R.P. You're about two dozen short, and that bunch at the Club House'll probably scare them shitless," I grumbled. "Shit, get in the back and, for God's sake, keep them quiet."

Shakey got out to help tie down the flaps; moments later he climbed back in the cab.

"Ready to go," he said, and with a roar of the engine, I pulled away from the curb, turned south onto Kantstrasse and headed back toward Lichterfelde and the U.S. sector. I had driven about a block into the U.S. sector when I saw the blue lights in the mirror; I pulled over to wait for the Berlin police officer to tell me I was detained until the MPs arrived. After World War II, Berlin continued to be occupied by the U.S., British, French and Soviet Union. The Berlin police officers were not allowed to arrest any of the soldiers; however, they could detain them until the military police arrived.

Within minutes, a Jeep carrying two MPs, a tall, thin corporal and a short, stocky sergeant, stopped in front of the truck. One of the German policemen spoke quietly to the sergeant, who nodded seriously and then said, "We'll take care of things from here. Vielen Dank."

The sergeant didn't say anything, just stared blankly at me until the Germans had driven out of sight.

"You played flag football, didn't you?"

"Yeah, 78th ASA. We beat you twice."

"Goddam spooks. That wide receiver you had was one tough son of a bitch. We haven't covered him yet."

He shook his head, remembering the four touchdown passes Hairy Ranger caught behind the MP secondary.

"Well, did you know you're on a restricted street?"

I shook my head.

"What do you mean, restricted?"

"No trucks allowed. What the hell are you doing here at this time of night anyway?"

"I have some supplies I have to get back to Andrews Barracks."

"Blackie, we got a problem," Shakey said.

I turned to see him pointing toward the rear of the truck. I looked in the direction he pointed and saw the MP corporal starting to untie the flaps.

"Goddammit, get the hell away from that truck!"

The MP corporal flushed and unsnapped the flap secur-
ing his .45.

"Sarge, for Christ's sake, I've got classified material back
there," I said pleadingly. "He doesn't have a security clear-
ance to look in there. I'll get my ass in a sling if the colonel
finds out."

The MP sergeant looked at me suspiciously. He motioned
to the corporal to back away from the truck, and I felt a
momentary sense of relief that ended when I heard a dis-

tinctively female giggle.

"Classified material?" the MP sergeant glared at me. "Sounds like classified poontag to me. Corporal, unsecure that truck."

The corporal jumped to untie the flaps. He flipped the tarpaulin back, peered inside, then jumped back, his eyes wide open.

"Goddam, Sarge, the truck's full of women."

"Women?"

The corporal suddenly whirled and rushed to stand beside the cab door.

"Get out of the goddam cab and give me the trip ticket," he shouted, so angry spittle flew in all directions.

I opened the door and stepped down. The corporal's eye's widened when he saw I had civilian clothes on under my field jacket.

"Goddammit! Sarge, he's in goddam civvies."

The sergeant grinned, a slow, malicious grin. He knew he had us.

"Let's see here," he said. "I've got a stolen truck, three goddam ASA assholes without passes, and about a dozen civilian women. I think you three are in some serious shit."

"Well, Sarge, it does look bad, but the girls wanted to go to a real Army party, and we just borrowed the truck to take them to the Club House," I said lamely.

The MP sergeant rubbed his chin and rocked back and forth on his heels.

"Whatcha drinking at the party."

"Beck's, mostly," I said.

"Corporal, secure that classified material."

"Wh-what?" the corporal stammered.

"Secure the classified material so we can escort this truck to the barracks."

"But it's stolen, and there's women back there."

"American women," an irritated female voice could be heard through the canvas cover of the truck, "and some of us have to go to the bathroom."

"Corporal, secure the classified material, and let's get out of here," the sergeant said, then looking directly at me, added softly, "This is going to cost you."

I nodded.

A few minutes later, we followed the MP car, with its blue lights flashing, into the gates of Andrews Barracks and around to the back, where we couldn't be seen unloading the female load.

"This is going to cost you a little extra, Cooper," the MP sergeant said. "You got a problem with the truck."

"What problem? I can get it back in the motor pool, no problem."

"Come back here," he said and walked to the rear of the truck. I followed and saw him pointing at the rear bumper.

"Oh, shit," I said when I saw I had stolen a truck from the 42nd Engineers motor pool.

"I think I can take care of this problem for you, but I think I need a couple of cases of Beck's. Think you can arrange that?"

"No problem, no problem at all. Just give me a couple of minutes."

I went to the back of the truck, untied the flap and leaned into the back.

"R.P., get the girls up to the Club House, and for God's sake, be quiet. We don't need those assholes from A Trick to hear all these women going upstairs. Shakey, when you get up there, get a couple of cases of Beck's from Hedgehog. Tell him we really need it down here."

Within minutes, the group disappeared into the barracks. I leaned against the truck until I saw Shakey, carrying two cases of Beck's, walking across the parking lot. I took one of the cases and handed it to the MP sergeant; Shakey turned over the other case to the MP corporal.

"We'll take care of things from here, Cooper. It won't be any problem to adjust the mileage. Besides the motor pool clerk owes me a couple of favors. Thanks for the beer, and next time, steal one of your own trucks."

I didn't say anything, just watched as the MP car, followed closely by the deuce-and-a-half, rolled across the parking lot, turned left onto the street and headed in the direction of the motor pool.

I took a deep breath.

"You're a lucky son of a bitch, Blackie," Shakey said.

"Me? Hell, I think all three of us were pretty goddam lucky."

"Let's go to the party," Shakey said, and chuckled softly. "Think that corporal would have shot you?"

"Probably."

When I reached the fourth floor, I knew the party had started rolling: loud music, raucous laughter, clatter of bottles, giggles and thumps of bodies bumping against the walls meant Big Ed and Big George were demonstrating the fine art of belly-busting. I pushed open the door just in time to see Big Ed, his face flushed and sweaty, slam his belly against Big George, who lost his balance and fell into the pile of empty Beck's bottles near the wall.

Raising his hands above his head like he'd just won the world's heavyweight title, Big Ed acknowledged the applause of the young women. When he saw me standing by the door, he grinned, walked over and slapped me on the shoulder.

"Hey, Blackie! We never thought you'd be here. Shakey said the MPs were going to shoot you!," he said.

"They took a bribe, Big Ed."

"Yeah, Big Ed, they took two cases of our Beck's," Prince said. "Blackie, your sorry ass isn't worth two cases of Beck's."

"Would you rather the girls be with the MPs or up here?"

"Good goddam point," Prince said seriously, then handled me a bottle of Beck's, which I took gladly. I turned it up and took a deep drink, the beer soothing my nerves.

Prince draped his arm around my shoulders; I probably looked surprised, so he said in a conspiratorial tone, "See that good-looking Jane over there looking at the records?"

I saw two young women standing by the record player. "Which one?"

"Which one? Hell, there's only one. The one with the hat — I call her Miss Hat."

I noticed one of the girls, tall and slender with fiery red hair that seemed to explode around her face, wore a dark blue Greek fisherman's hat.

"Jesus, Prince, she's gorgeous."

"Yeah, we call her Miss Hat. You know I'm going to get

some of that tonight."

"Bullshit, Prince. She looks like she's got too damn much class for you."

"Blackie, I have to tell you; she wants me."

"Good luck, but it'll never happen. Besides she looks like she's interested in Hairy Ranger. Look how she leans toward him."

"She's telling him to haul ass."

Apparently Miss Hat told Hairy Ranger to haul ass because he grinned, an embarrassed "How the hell do I get out of here and still manage to look cool" grin, and slowly walked across the room and got another beer. However, he didn't go back near Miss Hat.

During the next two or three hours, Miss Hat remained aloof, coolly rebuffing all approaches.

"Hell, she's probably a lesbian," Chief said.

"No, she's not a lesbian; she just doesn't think her shit stinks," Hairy Ranger said.

"Both of you are just pissed because she's not interested in you," I said.

"No, she's got to be a lesbo," Chief said and nodded as if he were agreeing with himself.

The other girls didn't seem to be as particular as Miss Hat. They tried to match the C Trickers beer for beer and danced with everyone who approached. Cindy, the Ami Jane who had been with Rainbow Pete outside the hotel, even danced twice with Grumpy John, ignoring his hand which kept sliding down and rubbing her ass.

About two in the morning, Rainbow Pete staggered over to where I had taken a seat by the wall, supporting a sodden Cindy who had suddenly passed out.

"How're we going to get the girls back to the hotel? You don't still have the deuce, do you?"

"No, MPs took it back to the motor pool. Who all's got vans?"

"Hedgehog's got one, and I think Buffalo Head does."

"Hell, if we can get their vans we can slip the girls back to the hotel. We're going to have to do it pretty damn soon before the Phantom gets here. He might overlook the beer, but he'll shit if he finds a dozen women in the barracks."

"I'll round up the Janes," Rainbow Pete said and weaved over to where Hedgehog stood, looking up at a tall blonde who looked vaguely like Big Monica, only not quite so puffy. After a few minutes, Hedgehog and Buffalo Head had rounded up all the girls — except Miss Hat.

"Jesus, where's Miss Hat? We can't leave anyone behind," Hedgehog said nervously.

I looked around.

"Where's Prince? Oh, my God, don't tell me ...," my voice trailed off because just at that moment the door opened and Prince, grinning broadly and wearing a dark blue Greek fisherman's hat, ushered Miss Hat back into the room.

"It happened," he said proudly.

The party had ended.

Within minutes, the Ami Janes were in the two Volkswagen vans, on their way back to the hotel. When Rainbow Pete when by the hotel the next evening, the American college students had already checked out and left Berlin.

Duck and the Baby Jesus

26 Nicknames don't just happen. There has to be some thought given to a nickname. Probably as much thought goes into coming up with a good nickname as was given to a person's real name. They're usually based on something about the person or something that person's done.

Often the nickname says the opposite of what the person really is. For example, a big guy might be called Tiny. The female mess sergeant was called Ma because she had no maternal instinct and was unable to come up with anything resembling Mom's home cooking.

Some nicknames were given after an incident. Chief, for example, got his new name one night at the Berliner Hofbräuhaus. He had been drinking beer from liter mugs and chasing it with shots of vodka. After a few rounds, he was soused and decided to dance to the German drinking songs the band was playing. Chief didn't really dance — he stumbled, he staggered, he jumped and he fell, but mostly he whooped and hollered.

Doc, who joined me in helping our friend out of the Hofbräuhaus and away from the disapproving glares of the annoyed Berliners, looked at our buddy.

"He's like an Indian who's had too much firewater," Doc said.

"Have you ever seen a drunk Indian, Doc?" I said.

"No, but if an Indian did get this drunk, this is what he'd be like," Doc said. "Come on, Chief, let's go home."

Chief just giggled.

Sometimes a nickname is so obvious that you're almost embarrassed to give it.

Duck earned his nickname because of physical characteristics. He just looked like a duck. He had tiny feet, a large rear end, narrow shoulders and peculiar gait — he leaned forward and took short, quick steps as he walked. His big rear end would move from side to side, giving him the appearance of a duck waddling toward a pond.

Duck was good-natured about his insulting nickname, but he didn't really have a choice. He wasn't a fighter and couldn't scare people into not calling him Duck — and he probably realized that he did look like a duck.

Because he was such a nice guy, we all began to feel sorry that he was having to live with his nickname, but once a nickname's given, it's almost impossible to lose it. Duck remained Duck, like it or not, and probably would have done his time in Berlin quietly and gone home to where people didn't call him Duck, but he met the Baby Jesus.

Duck met the Baby Jesus early one Sunday a few days before my second Christmas in Berlin. The meeting wasn't one of those miraculous religious events. Duck wasn't born again, but he still met the Baby Jesus.

C Trick had just ended its shift of days. The guys were ready to go out, drink more than was good for them, and just act crazy. Although no one would say it, most of us secretly wished Rainbow Pete would find another group of Ami Janes who wanted to party throughout our break. But it was December and the chance of a group of college girls from the States being in Berlin so close to Christmas was slim, so we would just have to party on our own.

Duck normally was one of the saner members of C Trick. He didn't smoke, he didn't drink to excess, and he budgeted his pay so that he always had money left on payday. He was the picture of moderation, maturity, and responsibility.

On most occasions when the guys would leave the barracks to go bar-hopping, someone would stop in Duck's room and ask him to join them. Nearly every time, Duck would politely decline the invitation and go about his business, usually doing his laundry, cleaning up his room, or wandering over to the PX snackbar.

But on this cold, snowy Saturday night when Grumpy John and I stopped by his room and asked him if he wanted to go have a few beers, Duck put down his book and left with us.

He chose the wrong night to change his pattern.

When we left the barracks compound, we were leaving an area that was made as festive as possible by the American occupiers. There were Christmas decorations in all of the PX windows. The mail clerks were working extra hours to make sure that those Christmas packages and cards from home were in our mail boxes in time for Christmas. The little chapel, which was set back in a grove of trees to the northwest of the PX , was a mass of decorations as the Catholic and Protestant chaplains tried to outdo each other in heralding the Baby Jesus' birth.

Just to the right of the front door of the chapel was an elaborate Nativity, complete with life-size figures of Mary, Joseph, the shepherds, and the wise men all gathered around the straw-filled manger in which lay the Baby Jesus.

Duck, Grumpy John, and I made our first stop at the Scum.

From the Scum, it was a walk of less than a block to Linda's Lounge for the second or third beer of the night. After leaving Linda's, we were a relaxed threesome, and we walked few more blocks, where we stopped in at the Blue Moon for more beers, to listen to the jazz on the bar's juke box, and to let Grumpy John argue with young Germans about why the U.S. was in Vietnam.

Grumpy John actually had no real opinion about Vietnam, but he enjoyed arguing about it with the young Germans, most of whom opposed the U.S. involvement in Southeast Asia.

After a while, everyone became bored with the debate over the war, and Grumpy John, Duck and I caught the bus and went to the International Bar, where we drank more beer and talked with the streetwalkers who came in during the night to get off their feet.

It was nearly three in the morning when we got back to the Scum. Grumpy John and I decided to stay at the bar until six, when the mess hall would begin serving breakfast. Duck, however, finished his beer and tried to stand up, but he fell out of the booth. He giggled and stood up, swaying from side to side, and grinned drunkenly.

"It's been great, guys, but I'm going to the old room," Duck said.

"Don't you want to stick around and get some breakfast?" Grumpy John said.

"Nope. I'm going to take a leak and hit it to the old room. I'm too shitfaced for breakfast," he said.

Duck, unfortunately, didn't make it back to his room.

He staggered across the street, but in his drunken fog all he could think of was a warm place to sleep and sober up. Then he spotted an ideal place to rest until the world stopped spinning. There was plenty of room and plenty of straw to keep him warm. He settled in and soon was sound asleep.

A few hours later, the first families arrived for chapel, and the first thing they saw was Duck, sleeping soundly in the manger with the Baby Jesus clasped tightly to his chest.

A horrified Protestant chaplain called the MPs, who started laughing when they arrived. After shaking Duck awake, they took him to the MP station and called Phantom, who decided a week of KP would be just what Duck needed.

Duck never went out bar-hopping again.

On Leave

27 After two years in Berlin, the Wall was beginning to close in on me. I grew up in southwest Arkansas and was used to being able to get in a car and drive for miles and miles around the state, so the knowledge I was behind a concrete barrier I couldn't pass through whenever I wanted made the huge city seem smaller and smaller with each passing month.

Although I had taken several passes for short trips into West Germany on the U.S. or British duty trains, a three-day pass just didn't give me the sense of freedom from the Army I wanted. So when I got my chance to go on leave, I decided to go to Spain, whose travel brochures promised would be warm and sunny — a welcome break from February's cold, gray and dreary Berlin.

I was in high spirits as I walked into the station to catch the U.S. military train to Frankfurt am Main. I was traveling light, with everything stuffed in a small backpack I'd borrowed from Red Larry.

Red Larry was a gregarious South Carolinian who picked up his nickname because he considered himself a Communist and refused to acknowledge the concept of private property.

"Private property is theft," I overheard him telling Hairy Ranger during one of their frequent arguments. Hairy Ranger was very open-minded about political philosophies, but he did draw a line when it came to his possessions. He might loan a sweater or a shirt, but he fully expected to it to be returned. On the other hand, Red Larry might just pass a borrowed item along to someone else, so I didn't really know whose backpack I was carrying to Spain.

Maybe because it was February, there were few passengers. Looking around the depot, I saw a Russian Mary from D Trick who had drawn courier duty for the month. I didn't really know him, but I'd heard he'd just re-enlisted and I didn't want to have anything to do with him, so, I just nodded when he spoke. There also were three or four 'Gators, who I supposed were being transferred to the Zone because they had their duffel bags and big manila envelopes from their personnel office.

Because there were so few passengers, I had the compartment to myself for the trip through East Germany and on to Frankfurt. After giving the train commander my flag orders and ID, I read a few poems in the Charles Bukowski book I'd borrowed from Crooner, turned out the lights and went to sleep.

Except for having to get up when my orders and ID were returned, I slept soundly almost all the way to Frankfurt. When the train pulled to a stop at the main station, I went straight to the ticket office for the German Railway and bought a round-trip ticket, coach class, to Barcelona, Spain. My train wouldn't be leaving until the next morning, so I had nearly 24 hours to spend in Frankfurt.

It was the first time I'd been in the city since I flew in two years earlier on a chartered a chartered Pan Am 707 that flew from McGuire Air Force Base near Trenton, New Jersey, to Rhein-Main Air Base. I spent about three days in a transient barracks near the old I.G. Farber building, which had been converted into the ASA's European headquarters. I had to go through some security briefings at the headquarters, but mostly I sat in the day room, playing pinochle or hearts with some Russian and German Marys who were being shipped to a detachment at Augsburg, and waiting to go to Berlin.

It was a surprisingly warm day for February in Germany. The sun was shining and there was not much wind, so it was comfortable as I walked around the city. It was so pleasant that I stopped at a small restaurant and ordered a cup of coffee, which I drank at one of the tables on the sidewalk. A couple of blocks away from the restaurant was a tobacco store. I went in and bought a Cuban cigar, which

I puffed on as I walked up one street and down the other, absorbing the sights and sounds of Frankfurt.

About one o'clock in the afternoon, I realized that I had not eaten since the day before, so I stopped at a sidewalk vendor and ordered a bratwurst, potato salad and a hard roll, which I washed down with a cold beer. At a news kiosk across the street from a small park, I bought a copy of Herald-Tribune and walked to the park, where I found a small bench in the sunshine. The front page of the newspaper was filled with reports about heavy fighting in the Mekong Delta, and I was glad I was in Germany, not South Vietnam.

After finishing the paper, I walked to trash receptacle and stuffed it inside. Then I started walking aimlessly, stopping now and then to peer into a store window. When I came to a book store, I thought I might want something to read on the train, so I went inside. When I found it had an extensive English-language section, I bought a couple of spy novels, which I stuffed the books in my backpack and resumed my walk. But because it was twilight, I decided to go back to the area near the train station, get something to eat and then find a pension for the night. I hadn't gone more than three or four blocks when I saw the narrow entranceway to an alley. It was too narrow for a car, so the only way you could get in was to walk or ride on a bicycle. The entranceway had an old metal sign, one of those with the old script that went out of style during the Thirties. When city officials changed all of the street signs, they probably overlooked the little sign for this obscure alley.

I was a little nervous as I stood there, peering into the darkness and seeing only a dim flicker of a blue neon light at the far end. There was no light except for the streetlight behind me and the flickering blue light in the distance.

But I was curious, so I took a deep breath before plunging into the darkness. This was the type of alley I'd heard about, one of those dangerous little passageways between buildings where pickpockets, muggers and other criminals lurk about and wait to pounce on the unwary or the unfortunate.

I walked swiftly, the sound of my footsteps on the cobblestones echoing off the buildings on both sides of the alley.

I know it wasn't that loud, but I thought it sounded like gunshots.

I could see more clearly now; a blue neon light shining brightly, and I could hear music. I could hear the thud of the bass drum, the clash of the high hat, the deep drone of a baritone saxophone and the thumpa-thumpa-thumpa of an upright bass — not an electric bass, but the old-fashioned upright kind..

"Oh, my God," I said aloud, even though no one was with me to hear. It was a jazz club, one of those little bars with a house band, packed with young people wanting to listen tomusic and argue about politics, art, music or movies.

When I entered, I found it as crowded with young Germans, most about my age. Thejazz combo I had heard was on a small raised stand at one end of the long, narrow room. A bar about half the length of the room was to my left. A crowd of people were standing in front of the bar, smoking, drinking and laughing heartily. I pushed my way to the end of the bar, where I was surprised to see an empty stool. I slid onto the stool and waved at the plump, rosy-cheeked young woman working behind the bar. She had curly red hair sticking out from under a black beret and was wearing a baggy black sweater with the sleeves pushed up above her elbows and she smiled cheerfully when she walked toward me.

I ordered a cognac and a beer. While she was pouring the cognac, I shifted the backpack, which had slipped and was uncomfortable. She looked up in time to see me trying to get the backpack to sit comfortably and when she placed my drinks in front of me, she said in a melodious voice, "If you want to take it off, you can put it behind the bar. I'll watch it for you."

"That's be great," I said and gratefully shrugged out of the pack and handed it to her. She slid it into a cubbyhole under the bar.

"Thanks, I was getting tired of lugging it around," I said.

She nodded, grinned at me and then waved, acknowledging of a customer at the other end of the bar. I slowly sipped on my beer and watched her as she kept things running smoothly, filling orders rapidly and managing to avoid collisions with an older man who was also working behind the bar.

About an hour after I entered the club, she wiped her hands with a small towel, poured some cognac into a small snifter, walked over toward me and collapsed onto a stool in the corner. She took a sip of the cognac and grinned at me.

"I'm Franziska — Franzi," she said and extended her hand to me. "You're American, aren't you?"

"I'm Don," I said, shaking her hand, "and, yes, I'm American. Am I that obvious?"

"Yes."

"How is it so obvious? I haven't spoken English in here and the people in Berlin say I have a French accent."

"It's how you walk. You Americans don't walk like Europeans. You swagger, real cocky like you own the world."

"Some of us think we do," I said and laughed.

"Do you?"

I shook my head.

"What are you doing here?"

"I'm on leave and I'm going to Spain, but my train doesn't leave until tomorrow morning."

"On leave? You're in the Army?"

"Yeah, I'm stationed in Berlin."

We chatted idly for several minutes until her break was over, but I stayed where I was at the end of the bar. Every so often, she look my way and smile. Whenever she got another break, she'd come back to sit on a stool across from me and talk, peppering me with questions about everything from what music I liked to if I had been to California and seen any movie stars.

I learned she was from Rudesheim and her father worked for a vintner. She was studying art, liked rock 'n'roll better than jazz, and wanted to move to London.

I was enjoying myself so much that I didn't pay any attention to the time, and when I looked at my watch I was surprised to see it was nearly one o'clock.

"Oh, my God," I said and leaned over the bar to grab my backpack. "It's nearly one. It looks like I'm going to have to spend the night in the train station. I'll never find a pension now."

She patted my arm.

"Stay there. I get off in a half hour. My apartment's right upstairs. You can stay there tonight."

"Are you sure?" I asked.

"Of course," she said. "In this job, I get to know people, and you're all right."

Thirty minutes later, she finished washing glasses, folded the hand towel and draped it over the faucet. I followed her outside and up a stairway on the side of building. She pushed open the door and we entered a small, but very cozy apartment. An easel, covered with a paint-splattered dropcloth, was on the left side of the room, almost touching the wall. Several canvasses of varying sizes leaned against the wall; paintings and sketches, some framed but most not, seemed to fill all of the wall space. A table covered with brushes, tubes of oil paint, sketchbooks and pencils and charcoal sticks, was close by the easel.

A towering chifferobe was in the far right corner of the room, directly across from a small bed. A ornate lamp with a globe on a nightstand beside the bed was the only light in the room, and a small cookstove and apartment refrigerator were near the center of the wall to my right. A big, over-stuffed sofa was directly in the center of the room.

Franzi rushed to the sofa and pushed books and maga-zines on the floor, making room for us to sit. I dropped my backpack on the floor and, suddenly feeling exhausted, collapsed onto the sofa, throwing my arm across the back. Franzi settled beside me, patted me on the leg and then curled inside the crook of my arm, which she pulled down around her shoulders, my hand resting lightly on her left breast.

The little apartment felt so warm and I was so comfort-able that I dozed off. A few minutes later, I was awakened by the sound of a door closing. I looked around and saw Franzi, nude and damp, walking across the room, rubbing her hair.

She grinned at me.

"I needed a shower," she said. "Now I'm ready for bed."

She reached down, took my hands in hers and tugged gently. I stood and followed her to the little bed. I took off my clothes and dropped them in a pile beside the bed and slid beneath the covers with her. She reached behind her and turned off the light.

It seemed like just minutes later when I heard a church bell ringing. I pulled my arm out from under the covers and looked at my watch. It was six o'clock, two hours until I needed to catch the train to Spain. I looked at Franzi, sleeping soundly, her red hair tousled, framing her round face. She sensed me looking at her, opened her eyes slowly and smiled.

"Good morning, lover," she said drowsily. "Are you leaving?"

I nodded.

She sat up and kissed me, then lay back down, pulled the covers up and quickly was snoring softly.

I dressed quickly and eased out of the apartment.

A few minutes later, I was sitting on a bench in the train station, eating a Danish and drinking a cup of coffee. I was ready to catch the train to Spain. My granduncle in Oklahoma, an oilman who had traveled all around the world, once told me to take the chance to learn something on every trip you take.

On the trip to Spain, I did learn one thing — never take coach class in Spain. I'd saved a few dollars by taking coach from Germany, through Switzerland and southern France. The accommodations were comfortable, but if I wanted to take a nap, I had to make do because coach class didn't have sleeping compartment. However, when I crossed the French-Spain border, I found out that "coach" doesn't have quite the same meaning in Spanish.

When I found my seat, I swear it was in a poorly converted cattle car with what looked like church pews bolted to a wooden floor. The luggage rack was lattice and was secured to the wall dangerously close to passengers' heads.

It wasn't too bad when I first boarded at the customs point just south of Portbou, France, but when the train stopped in La Jonquera, Spain, people began crowding into the compartment.

The last person to enter the compartment was a tiny, wizened, white-haired woman, dressed entirely in black and carrying a crate of chickens. She looked around, spotted an empty place on the luggage rack. With the help of a middle-age man, she stowed the crate of chickens directly above my head.

I felt as if the sword of Damocles was hanging over my head. The car was full, and I had no place to go. I tried to stand outside in the passageway, but the conductor spoke sharply and motioned toward the compartment. I didn't speak Spanish, but I could understand he was insisting that I take my assigned seat.

I believe I held my breath for the next half hour or so as the train moved slowly through the Spanish mountains toward its next stop. When the train pulled into the station, the little old lady stood up. I jumped up to help her get the crate of chickens, which mercifully hadn't done anything.

She took the crate of squawking chickens and backed out of the compartment. Just before she turned to move down the passageway, she looked right at me and grinned, a big, wide, toothless grin.

The rest of the trip was uneventful, but I was glad when the train pulled to a stop in Barcelona's main train station. I brushed past youngsters who were trying to get passengers to go to pensions or hotels. Thanks to Grumpy John, who had given me the address of a cheap, clean pension at the head of the Ramblas de Catalunas, I knew where I wanted to go, so I hailed a cab.

The pension was on the third floor of the building, above a restaurant and some apartments. It turned out I was lucky to get a room because a group of Canadian students had checked a few days earlier and were occupying all but one room.

When I entered the room, I blinked at the sunlight streaming through the tall, curtainless windows. The room was tiny, with a small iron bed against the wall beneath the windows, which overlooked a small courtyard. There was a small table and chair at one end of the room and a sink at the other. Two towels and washcloth hung on a bar next to the sink, and small mirror was mounted in the wall above it.

I tossed the backpack on the bed, removed my jacket

and hung it over the back of the chair. Then I rummaged through the backpack and pulled out my toiletries. After nearly twenty-four hours on the train, my mouth tasted like cotton, so I went to the sink and began to brush my teeth vigorously.

A few minutes later, I was strolling down the Ramblas, a broad, tree-lined avenue. In the wide media between the two traffic lanes, merchants had set up colorful kiosks, selling a wide variety of wares. I walked around for hours, stopping at a bakery where I bought a small loaf of bread and a small shop that sold cheese. Back at the pension, I ate part of the bread and cheese, read a couple of chapters in one of the books I had bought in Frankfurt. Later I heard voices speaking in French, laughter and doors slamming.

The next day, I walked around the city again, enjoying the warm sunshine, the smells of the flowers and fruits. Soon I was at the harbor, where I was surprised to see a replica of Christopher Columbus' flagship, the Santa Maria. I decided to take the tour.

When I stepped aboard the ship, I heard a familiar accent, a high-volume Texas drawl.

Oh, Christ, another Texan, I thought and remembered my first European encounter with residents of Arkansas' big neighbor to the west.

I don't know if Texans were the inspiration for Graham Greene's book "The Ugly American," but it they were, they probably were from Fort Worth. Before arriving in Germany, all of my travel had been confined to the United States, so I'd never seen American tourists overseas.

The first time I came across the Ugly Texan was during my first summer in Berlin. I stopped in a small shop on the Kurfürstendamm. While I was browsing through sweaters, I overheard someone shouting in a Texas drawl. I turned and saw a heavyset man, his face red and the veins bulging out on his forehead as he tried to talk to the sales clerk, a nervous young woman wearing a button showing she was a trainee. Her customer apparently believed knowledge of English could be transferred through sheer volume.

"How much is that in dollars?" he shouted. It might have been my imagination, but I believe the clerk actually was moved backward by the force of his shouting.

"Little girl, I asked you — how much is that in dollars?"

I walked over and offered to try to bridge the language gap, and within a couple of minutes he had made his purchase and paid — in U.S. currency — and the sales clerk wasn't being forced to stand in the wind tunnel.

While his purchase was being wrapped, he grabbed my hand and shook it vigorously, so vigorously that I was afraid my arm would be dislocated.

"Name's Dawson — Tom R. Dawson, from Fort Worth, Texas," he shouted. "Who're you and whatcha doing here?"

"Don Cooper," I said. "I'm in the Army."

"Pleased to meet you, son. I was in Korea myself. Got winged during the In'chon landing," he said and grinned broadly. "Where you from, boy?"

"Arkansas," I said.

"Well, how about them Hawgs?" he bellowed, slapping me on the back and nearly knocking the breath out of me. The Razorbacks had beaten their archrival, the University of Texas Longhorns, in an exciting football game the past season, and he let me know he'd been in the stands at the University of Arkansas stadium.

We chatted a few more minutes before I was able to get away from the gregarious Texan, and now I could hear another Tom R. Dawson.

Probably from Fort Worth, I thought.

I joined several other people, obviously tourists with all the packages and cameras, on the wooden deck where we gathered around the guide. Speaking in English, a short, lean and wiry Spaniard with dark, close-cropped hair explained the design of the ship, its weight and capacity, as well as shedding light on ocean navigation in the late 15th century.

As the guide finished, a bulky man bellowed:

"You call this a ship? Son, my bass boat's bigger than this."

I cringed.

I couldn't help myself. I walked over to loud tourist.

"Where are you from in the States?" I asked.

"Fort Worth, Texas. Where you from, boy?"

"Canada," I said quickly and walked to the other side of the ship.

I noticed a young man, about my age and wearing an Army fatigue look at me sharply when I ended the exchange with the Ugly Texan. He followed me as I walked down the gangway to the dock and hailed me.

"You're not Canadian, eh?" he asked.

"No, I'm from the States," I said.

"Why did you say you're Canadian?"

"I thought that asshole would leave me alone if he thought I weren't from the States."

"Good idea," he said and chuckled. Then he extended his hand and introduced himself. "I'm Gerard Chaillot and I'm really Canadian."

"Don Cooper, and I'm really not Canadian," I said.

As we walked back toward the Ramblas, he told me he was an art student from Quebec and was traveling with a group of other Quebecois art students. They had visited museums and galleries in Italy and France before arriving a few days earlier in Barcelona to see the Picasso collection in one of the city's main museums. I was pleasantly surprised to learn his group and I were in the same pension.

The lodging included an evening meal, so I accepted his invitation to join the group, which included three young women and another young man. I was glad Gerard was there because the students spoke only French and he cheerfully provided a running translation of the conversation. When the meal was over, I followed along as the students wandered along the Ramblas, stopping in at a small bar, where they drank wine and argued loudly about post-Impressionism, avant-garde and other schools of art.

During one heated exchange between a diminutive girl named Jolie and Bernard, a dark-complexioned young man with a wispy mustache, Gerard leaned toward me.

"Do you smoke?" he asked and grinned.

I nodded.

He reached inside his fatigue jacket and pulled out a small plastic bag holding several tightly rolled marijuana cigarettes. He took out one, lit it and took a deep drag, holding the smoke deep inside his lungs. Then he passed the cigarette to me, and I also took a hit on it.

We sat quietly, passing the joint back and forth and listening to the argument across the table, which seemed to become less heated even though Jolie and Bernard appeared to be just as passionate.

Gerard waved to catch the waiter's attention. Then he held up the empty wine bottle and gestured to bring two more bottles. When the waiter brought the bottles to the table, he raised his eyebrows when he saw the smoldering remains of the cigarette Gerard was holding.

"It's on me," I said and handed several bills to the waiter. "Keep the change."

He smiled and nodded before going to take the order from a couple at a nearby table.

"You tipped him more than the wine cost, you know," Gerard said.

"I didn't have a clue," I said. "But, what the hell? I'm having a good time."

An hour or so later, when we walked back toward the pension, the students sang loudly in French, drawing some annoyed looks from the Catalans we passed. I was floating as we climbed the stairs to the pension, and when I went my inside my room, I collapsed on the bed and was almost immediately sound asleep.

It didn't seem like I had been asleep more than a few minutes when I heard an insistent knocking on the door. I opened my eyes and blinked at the sunlight streaming in the window. I rubbed my eyes, yawned and stretched, then slowly walked to the door. When I pulled it open, I saw Gerard, grinning broadly.

"Good morning," he said cheerfully. "I just wanted to say good bye. We're heading out to Madrid. I heard the cops in Madrid aren't as understanding as they are here, so I wondered if you'd like to buy my supply."

"How much are we talking about?" I asked.

"Six."

We haggled briefly. Within a couple of minutes, he was folding the mixture of U.S., German and Spanish currency in his pocket and I was putting a plastic bag with a half-dozen joints in my backpack.

After the Canadians left, I spent the next two days alone, just wandering about the city, drinking coffee or wine on the Ramblas, and sitting in the sun at the harbor. When it was time to catch the train back to a cold Berlin, I thought briefly about sending a postcard to Roadrunner telling that I had decided to quit the Army. But I only thought about it briefly.

The trip back to Frankfurt was uneventful, even pleasant, because I had switched my tickets for a first-class compartment. I relaxed, read and enjoyed the scenery as the train rumbled through France, Switzerland and Germany. When I arrived in Frankfurt, I decided to go see Franzi. But when I was almost within sight of the little alleyway, I decided I'd rather hold onto a good memory, so I turned around and went back to the train station.

A few hours later, I was sitting alone in a compartment, listening to the clickity-clack of wheels rolling along the rails. After the train commander took my flag hours and ID, I dug the plastic bag out of my backpack and smoked one of the joints.

I was completely relaxed and mellow when I arrived back in Berlin. I didn't even care that it was cold and overcast.

Zulu Worship

28 My initiation into Zulu worship came on my first night back on the Hill after my trip to Spain. Except for the night I spent in Frankfurt with Franzi, I spent my leave wandering around Barcelona. I walked from one end of the Ramblas de Catalunas to the other, exploring the harbor, prowling through museums and art galleries, and just sitting on a park bench, letting the sun's rays take the Berlin chill out of my bones. When I got back to Berlin, I had a dark tan and three joints left from the half dozen I bought from Gerard.

I also had a note from the first sergeant letting me know I would be driving the trick bus for the next month, a duty I didn't mind because it meant I wouldn't have to pull KP.

C Trick had started its rotation on mids when I came off leave. I didn't look forward to the night because my body's clock and the shift weren't synchronized. I had gotten accustomed to daylight hours, but C Trick started mids.

A light snow fell as I left the barracks and trudged across the parking lot toward the motor pool. I lit one of the carefully stashed joints and smoked it as I walked through the darkness to the motor pool at the far side of the sprawling Andrews Barracks compound. A sleepy corporal looked curiously at me while I signed out a bus.

"Do you smell something funny?" he said, his nose twitching.

"Must be this cigarette. It's a weird French brand I picked up on leave," I said.

"Oh."

While the bus warmed up, I finished the joint, feeling a mellowness and warmth flow through my system. I opened

the big window beside the driver's seat before pulling out of the motor pool. I still felt warm a few minutes later when I turned into the parking lot, where I could see several C Trickers huddled in a small group, stamping their feet in the cold.

"Goddam, Blackie, why's that window open? Close the son of a bitch, it's colder than a well-digger's ass out here," Grumpy John said when he climbed aboard the bus. He turned up his collar, pulled the flaps of his pile cap down over his ears and slid into a seat near the rear of the bus.

"Yeah, asshole, close the goddam window," Prince said, his voice muffled by the thick scarf around his neck.

Hairy Ranger stopped a moment, craned his neck and sniffed the air, like a bloodhound on a scent. He grinned and leaned over from behind me and closed the window.

"Where'd you get the devil weed?" he said in a whisper.

"Spain."

"You have to share, you know."

I nodded.

"You got some with you now?"

"No. I only have two left and they're stashed in a safe place. With any kind of luck, they'll get me through part of mids."

"Where's the safe place?"

"Christ, Ranger, if I tell you, I might as well just kiss them good bye. You'll have them both smoked by the time I can get my bus turned in. Just wait, and I'll split them with you."

He grinned and sprawled on the seat behind me.

The drive to the Hill went smoothly, although the lights seemed brighter than any other time I'd driven the trick bus on mids and the snowflakes seemed to fall in slow motion, twisting and turning like gymnasts on their way to the ground.

I more or less drifted through the guard shack, even greeting Roadrunner who sat on the counter checking to see if everyone on his duty roster actually arrived.

"You okay, Blackie?" Prince asked when we arrived in Violet to replace B Trick at the banks of radio receivers and tape recorders.

I shrugged, took the headsets from a yawning newk, settled onto the chair, put my feet on the small desk and lit a cigarette.

"Not as good as those roll-your-own, is it?" Hairy Ranger said and chuckled.

"Certainly not as mild," I said.

"What were they? Menthol?" Rock Weed said as he slipped out of his field jacket.

"No, just a non-filter brand I got in Spain — French, I

think," I said.

"French? What kind?"

"Christ, Weed, I don't know. Just French."

"If you remember the name, let me know because I'd like to get something really mild. I was thinking about going up to check out the French PX on break and I can get us both some."

"I doubt if you'll get this brand at the French PX," I said.

"Then again, you might," Hairy Ranger said and giggled.

Rock Weed looked curiously at Hairy Ranger. He spun on his heel and walked back to his chair, right under the big digital clock which read 23:27.17. It was 27 minutes, 17 seconds after eleven o'clock. On the Hill, the clocks were set on Zulu, or Greenwich Mean Time, an hour behind Berlin. Everything on the Hill, and at all ASA sites around the world, was logged in Zulu time, so the analysts back in the Pentagon or the National Security Agency knew exactly when a conversation was recorded without having to figure out the time zone differences.

Because those of us assigned to Violet monitored the East German political communications, the bureaucrats all were home, sleeping or whatever, so we spent most of a mid shift drinking one cup of coffee after another, chain-smoking cigarettes or taking naps. I had just dozed off when I got my introduction to Zulu worship.

"ZU-LU, ZU-LU, ZU-LU."

The chanting from the Pit startled me and I nearly fell from my chair. I looked around the room. I was alone, just the flickering lights from the electronic gear and me. I jumped from my chair and rushed to the Pit, nearly colliding with Hairy Ranger, who stood in the corridor, munching on a peanut butter sandwich and sipping a cup of coffee.

I looked in the Pit and saw Doc, with the cover of a ten-inch tape reel on his head. The cover had been painted white and had a garish red "Z" logo on the front. He held a patch cord, like those used by operators of the old telephone switchboards, which he used to gesture toward the Russian and German Marys, several of whom had dropped to their knees. The entire group chanted at the top of their lungs: "ZU-LU, ZU-LU, ZU-LU!"

"Jesus Christ, Ranger, what the hell's going on? Have they lost their goddam minds?" I said.

"It's prayer meeting," he said.

"Prayer meeting?"

"It's time to pray to the Great God Zulu."

"Jesus Christ."

"No, Great God Zulu, DIRNSA is his prophet, and the Hill is his temple," Ranger said, grinning broadly. DIRNSA is an acronym for Director, National Security Agency.

"When did this shit start?"

"I'm not sure, but I know Doc first sprang it on us while you were in Spain."

"What brought it on?"

"Hell if I know. He just looked up at the clock on swings and started that goddam chant, and it took off from there. Scared the hell out of Roadrunner. The silly shit was certain everybody was nuts and probably going to start decapitating treads. It's not a bad idea, but we just make noise."

The chanting stopped, and the worshippers began to move back to their work stations. I waited until the Pit cleared out, then I walked over and took a seat next to Doc, the lanky New Yorker who monitored the Russian military.

"Doc, what's this Zulu worship shit?"

"Oh, very sacred, very sacred," he said, his blue eyes twinkling. "It came to me in a whirling of propellers, and a voice from DIRNSA telling me to spread his gospel."

"You're full of shit."

"Most likely, but do you want to know about the sacred rituals?"

"Yeah, go on."

"Well, as I was saying, I had an epiphany on swings. I don't know why, maybe it was a message from DIRNSA, but I looked at the clock and it read all twos. I got to thinking about that clock, how we have to use it for everything — logging in tapes, logging out tapes, going to the shitter, taking a break — and it's always Zulu. At every goddam site in the world, it doesn't matter where you are — Herzo, Sinop, Phu Bai, Asmara or Meade — it's the same damn time everywhere. I mean, if you're on mids here and you log in a tape, you use the same damn time as that Vietnamese Mary in Phu Bai or a diddy-bopper on Shemya. So, I thought there's got to be something sacred in the worship of Zulu."

"Zulu worship?"

"Obviously, there're some times that are more sacred to Zulu than other times. The most sacred time of all is midnight when the clock's all zeroes. The other major times are when it's all ones and all twos. There're also two minor worship times, oh-one-two-three-four-five and one-two-three-four-five-six."

"So, when did the chanting start?"

"I just started, you know, ZU-LU, ZU-LU, ZU-LU, and everyone in the Pit just picked up. There, you have it."

"What about the treads?"

"Scares the hell out of them. They don't really know what's going on, but they're afraid to say anything. I think the Colonel said it's okay if it's a morale booster. Shit, you can do almost anything if you can make it a morale booster."

"I want to get out of the Army early."

"I said almost anything."

At twenty-three minutes, forty-five seconds after one o'clock, we had another session of Zulu worship. I guess the treads had become used to it because I saw Roadrunner and Dirty Joe lurking in the background.

The next night, Hairy Ranger joined me on the walk through the snow to the motor pool. I had retrieved the two joints barracks and we smoked them as we made our way to pick up the bus, finishing the last draws about the time I turned the bus into the parking lot.

The aroma of marijuana could be detected as C Trick began climbing aboard the bus. Prince turned his head, sniffing like a bird dog, and he looked at Hairy Ranger, sprawled on the front seat.

"Ranger, where's the weed?"

"All gone."

"Gone? You asshole, you could've saved some for me."

"Tough shit. Anyway, I only had one joint and you'd bogart the hell out of it."

"You're a royal asshole, Ranger. Just see if I share any with you."

"You never share anything now."

"I might have sometime."

Grumpy John bumped Prince from behind.

"Move on, asshole. The rest of us'd like to get a seat sometime tonight. Jesus, what's that smell?" Grumpy John said, and he shook his head.

"French cigarettes, Grumpy," Hairy Ranger said. "Cooper had them."

"French? No shit. I had some, but they didn't smell like flower farts."

Jesus Christ, I should have deserted and stayed in Spain, I thought.

Like the night before, I enjoyed the drive to the Hill; the lights twinkled on the snow, and danced across the cobblestones. I glanced back at Hairy Ranger; he smiled at nothing in particular.

I settled in before the banks of receivers and tape recorders, and I got a surprise: East German communication. I pushed one of the buttons to listen in, and heard an assistant director in the SED district headquarters in Leipzig complaining to his wife about having to work late. Some NSA analyst reading this transcript will probably lose a lot of sleep trying to figure out what the East Germans are up to if this party hack's working so late, I thought and grinned to myself.

I had forgotten about Zulu worship, but I received a sudden reminder when the clock clicked to all zeroes and the ritual began in the Pit with Doc, the self-proclaimed Great High Priest of Zulu, leading the chant.

"ZU-LU, ZU-LU, ZU-LU!"

We had reached an almost feverish pitch when Doc turned and saw Roadrunner had joined in, chanting "ZU-LU, ZU-LU," his prominent Adam's apple rising and falling like a roller coaster at a carnival.

Doc stopped chanting and fixed a fierce stare on Roadrunner. Within moments, we all fell silent and stood staring at Roadrunner, who looked nervously at the group of Zulu worshippers. As we walked back to our work stations, he grinned self-consciously, rubbed the stubble on the top of his head and rushed away from the Pit.

"Jesus Christ, Doc, did you see how jumpy Roadrunner got? You'd thought his hair started growing and he couldn't cut it," Big Ed said.

"Shit, it's pathetic," Doc said as he tossed the High Priest of Zulu's crown on top of a file cabinet.

"What's pathetic?" Big Ed said, idly opening and closing the cap of his Zippo lighter with a casual flick.

"Goddam tread trying to join in and be one of the guys."

C Trick held sessions of Zulu worship for another week or two before losing interest, but Roadrunner didn't try to participate.

A Faded Field Jacket

29 To the annoyance of all but a few treads, the 78th seldom had to play soldier. It wasn't as if we didn't know we were in the Army, we just didn't have to go through the regular military training that the 'Gators had to endure.

But twice a year, we received a solid reminder we were still in the Army; we had to dig our gas masks out of the bottom of our wall lockers and go to the Berlin Brigade training center for a refresher, and later we would go to the firing range to stay reasonably familiar with the Army .45 and a machine gun.

C Trick had just finished a set of eves, and I was sleeping soundly after closing down the Blue Moon, a hole in the wall about five or six blocks from the barracks, when I was suddenly jerked from dreams.

"Cooper! Up and at 'em!"

I sat bolt upright in my bunk. I fumbled on the table beside my bunk, grabbed my glasses and slid them into place. When my eyes came into focus, I saw the Phantom standing at the end of my bunk.

"What's up, Sarge?"

"Get over to the motor pool and check out a bus. C Trick's got gas training."

I pulled a set of fatigues from the bottom of my wall locker, hoping Phantom wouldn't look too closely at the wrinkles. When I sat on the bunk and started pulling on my boots, Phantom spun around on his heel and walked briskly to the door, pausing to look back at me.

"Don't forget your gas mask. You're going to need it," the Phantom said and slammed the door, waking Hairy Ranger.

"What the hell's going on? Can't anyone get any sleep around here?" he said groggily.

"Get your gas mask; we're going to play soldier."

"What the hell for? Everybody knows we're not soldiers."

"Phantom thinks we are. Get your gas mask; it's training day."

"Shit," Hairy Ranger said as he swung his legs out from under the covers and sat on the edge of his bunk.

"Damn! It's cold. Why don't they let this shit wait until summer."

"Inconvenience, it's the Army way. Shit, where's my damn gas mask? I know I had it around somewhere," I said as I rummaged around the bottom of the wall locker before finding the mask under a pile of clothes. "Here it is," I said as I brushed dust off the case.

I grabbed my toilet kit and went to the latrine. While brushing my teeth, I decided to skip shaving and hope the treads wouldn't be paying to much attention.

When I got back to the room, Hairy Ranger was pulling on his fatigue shirt.

"I got to go pick up a bus," I said. "You want to be the assistant?"

"Yeah, yeah," he said absently. "You seen my field jacket?"

"It's hanging right there," I said and pointed at the dark green, crisply starched jacket in his wall locker.

"No, no, not that one. I can't wear that one, it makes me look like a goddam newk."

When he was in his uniform, Hairy Ranger always wore an old, worn field jacket without any insignia and which had faded almost completely white, with dark patches where bullet holes had been repaired. He got the field jacket several months earlier while we were standing in line at the PX snackbar. A 'Gator, wearing the worn field jacket and a shoulder patch showing he was an Army Ranger, was just ahead of us in line.

"Hey, were those bullet holes?" he said, tapping the 'Gator on the shoulder.

"Yeah."

"How'd you get them?"

"Well, I wasn't wearing it at the time, if that's what you mean," the 'Gator said.

"What happened?"

"I had washed it and laid it out on top of some bushes to dry. It was still on the bushes, when the VC opened up on us. When it was all over, there were three bullet holes in the jacket. I'm just damn glad I wasn't in it."

"You want trade it?" Hairy Ranger said. "We're about the same size; you can have my field jacket. Hell, it's pretty new and doesn't have any holes in it."

The 'Gator rubbed the bristles on the top of his closely cropped head.

"It's kind of a lucky jacket. I hate to just trade for another one," he said hesitantly.

"Look, I really would like to have it. How about I throw in a Russian belt, too," Hairy Ranger said, pulling open his field jacket to display a brown leather belt with a brass Red Army buckle. "It's the real thing. I had to give a Russian border guard at Marienborn a carton of Marlboros and a 'Playboy' for it."

The 'Gator looked closely at the belt and buckle, and rubbed his chin as he mulled over the offer.

"Okay, deal," he said, and shrugged off the old, faded field jacket as Hairy Ranger removed his belt. Within seconds, the exchange was completed.

Hairy Ranger was smiling like he'd just closed a major real estate deal.

"That damn thing's worthless, Ranger," I said. "It's liable to fall apart before we get out of here. What the hell did you want it for?"

"I have a theory," he said. "You're judged by your field jacket."

"You're full of shit."

"No, no, I mean it. Look at that old piece of shit you wear. No one thinks you're a new when you're wearing it. It's worn; it's faded; it says that you've been here a long time, and you're not someone who gives a shit. On the other hand, when you're wearing a new field jacket, it means you're either a newk or a goddam tread, because only a tread would want a brand-new field jacket."

"I guess you could be right," I said.

"Besides it's still got a Vietnam patch on it. I might be too chickenshit to actually go over there, but that doesn't mean I don't respect the guys who do."

The old field jacket — minus the name tag and patches — became Hairy Ranger's most prized possession, and now it was missing.

"Goddammit, I can't go out there with that newk jacket," he said, and slammed the wall locker door.

"Maybe Red Larry appropriated it for the good of the people," I said.

"That miserable piece of shit," Hairy Ranger said. "I ought to kick his ass."

"Well, you're going to have to do that later," I said. "Just grab that jacket and let's go."

"Let me borrow yours," he said plaintively.

"No."

"Why not?"

"I don't want to look like a newk. Why don't you just go down to his room and reappropriate it?"

"Hell, B Trick's on days; the miserable turd's on the Hill."

I shrugged, picked up my gas mask and walked to the door, where I paused.

"Look, Ranger, I'd love to help you, but I got to go get the bus before the Phantom has a stroke. You coming or what?"

"Go ahead, I'm going to see if Red Larry forgot and left my jacket in his room."

"Okay, catch you in the parking lot."

A few minutes later, I turned into the parking lot behind the barracks where a sullen group of C Trickers, bundled up against the cold, were waiting. I didn't see Hairy Ranger among them.

"Where's the Ranger?" I asked Grumpy John when he collapsed into the seat directly behind me.

"Who gives a shit?" he said and shivered. "It's colder than a welldigger's ass. You got the heater on?"

I nodded.

Hairy Ranger still hadn't arrived when the last stragglers settled into their seats.

"Close the goddam door! What're we waiting on?" Rock

Weed said and pulled his pile cap down tighter over his ears.

"I'm waiting on the Ranger. He's supposed to be here."

"Shit, leave him. Let's get this show on the road," Fang shouted from the rear of the bus.

I slammed the door, shifted the bus into gear and began to press the accelerator when I heard the knocking on the side of the bus.

"It's the Ranger," Rock Weed said.

I slammed on the brakes and opened the door to let the panting Hairy Ranger swing aboard and collapse in the front seat next to Rock Weed.

I glanced at him. Despite the cold, he didn't have on a field jacket, although he had his scarf wrapped tightly around his neck and over the lower part of his face.

"Damn, Ranger, where's your jacket?" Rock Weed said.

"Red Larry stole it."

"Why didn't you wear your other one?"

"I'd rather be cold than look like a goddam newk."

As I drove through the gate at the gas training range, the heater began to work and Hairy Ranger had loosened the scarf.

I parked the bus, and walked over to the low, square, gray concrete building beneath tall, frost-covered trees. I opened the door and saw a master sergeant, holding a clipboard, a staff sergeant and a corporal standing near the center of the room. Boxes of tear gas canisters were stacked neatly behind them. Directly opposite the door I had entered was another door, which led to the outside.

"Sergeant, I've got the 78th ASA out here," I said.

The master sergeant glanced at the clipboard, and appeared to be looking at my faded field jacket.

"Okay, Corporal, get them to line up by the door, and we'll bring them in one at a time," he said, and the corporal, now wearing a gas mask, walked to the door, where he shouted for everyone to get in single file and put on their masks. I was standing near the center of the room, wondering what to do next and watching as the two NCOs put on their masks. The staff sergeant looked at me, slid his mask back on his head and said, "You get over there by the exit and help them out."

"Yes, Sergeant," I said loudly and took up my post beside the door, just outside the gas chamber.

In the gas training, the soldiers, wearing their gas masks, walked to the center of a room where tear gas canisters were spewing a fog of the gas into the air. After a few seconds, the soldier was ordered to remove his gas mask and shout his name, rank and serial number. When the mask was removed, the first instinct was to take a breath, drawing in the choking fumes.

The master sergeant stood at the center of the room, giving the orders, while the staff sergeant would propel the choking, wheezing, near-blind C Trickers to the exit door, where I'd guide them away from the building and into fresh air. Within a couple of minutes, the effects of the tear gas would be gone. After I helped Fang to fresh air, the staff sergeant stepped out of the exit and looked at me.

"That was the last one," he said. "Are you the driver?"

"Yes, Sarge," I said and tried to sound as respectful as possible.

"Get outta here, you don't need to mess up your eyes," he said with a grin.

"Thanks, Sarge," I said gratefully.

Before he could change his mind, I rushed to the bus, slid in behind the steering wheel and hit the ignition. Within minutes, I was driving through the gates, leaving the gas chamber behind.

Hairy Ranger was sitting on the top seat, closest to the heater. He looked up at me and said, "You didn't have to go through that shit, did you?"

"No, they told me I didn't have to."

"How come?"

"The staff sergeant said it was because I wasn't wearing a newk field jacket."

"Screw you."

Doc and the Archgrommet

30

After losing interest in being the high priest of Zulu, Doc decided he wanted to become an archgrommet.

Doc was a disappointment to his family, or so he said.

His future was planned from the day he was born. He was the grandson of Irish immigrants. The tall, sandy-haired New Yorker would be the first in his family to earn a college degree, and then he would go on to medical school, becoming the family's first doctor — or so his family planned.

But the family's hopes to have its first doctor were put on a four-year hold because Doc entered the ASA, not medical school.

"My mother got hysterical when I didn't go to medical school. The only thing my old man's said to me in the last three years is, `You're breaking your mother's heart,'" Doc said over a beer in the El Oso. "They just couldn't get it through their heads, I was just sick and tired of school. I just wanted to get away from it all — the grades, the study, being the family's first doctor. Christ! I was going out of my mind with it all."

"Think you'll ever be a doctor, Doc?" I said.

"Probably not. I never really was all that hot on the idea anyway. It was all my folks' idea. They think the family won't be poor Irish anymore if there's a doctor in the family. They aren't poor Irish. The old man makes damn good money and they live in the suburbs. Hell, the old man makes more money than a lot of my friends' fathers, but you don't see them still thinking they're poor Italians, or Greeks or whatever. But, my folks still think they're shanty Irish, for

Christ's sake!"

We finished our beers and I was getting my money out to order another round, but Doc pushed his chair back and got up.

"Save your money, Blackie," he said. "Let's go over to the Märkische Hof and have some of their goulash."

I was glad to go, because the Märkische Hof was one of those little neighborhood bars that are so common in German cities. Nearly every neighborhood has a lokal, or bar where families congregate, swapping stories and enjoying the company of their neighbors.

The Märkische Hof was a couple of blocks from the barracks, but it wasn't one of the bars that was frequented much by the GIs, like the Scum, which was just two or three doors down the street. The Märkische Hof was spared the rowdiness that was typical of GI bars because its regular patrons were the families of the neighborhood. A GI would often stop in at the Märkische Hof, look around and see the families. He'd gulp down his beer and dart out, unlikely to stop in again.

There were a few of us who liked the Märkische Hof simply because there seldom were any GIs in the place. It was a place where we could sit quietly, nurse our beers, and listen to German marching music on the antiquated jukebox that stood against the wall.

When Doc and I walked in the Märkische Hof, it was almost empty, something that was unusual for a Sunday evening in February. There were a couple of the regulars at the bar and a couple with a young child sitting at a table near the door leading to the back room. I went to the bar and ordered two bowls of goulash and two Bock beers and went to join Doc at an oval table in the corner of the front room. Martina, the barmaid, looked at us curiously when she brought over our food and drink, but she didn't say anything.

"I wonder what her problem is," Doc said as he tore away a piece of his hard roll.

"Probably trying to figure out what two Americans are doing in a quiet little place like this and not over at the Scum making asses of themselves," I said.

Our attention was focused on our goulash and beer, so we didn't notice the four old men who came in the Märkische Hof. If we hadn't been so wrapped up in our meal, we would have seen them head toward our table, then suddenly stop and stare at us in amazement. They muttered to each other before shrugging and taking seats at another table on the other side of the room, from where they glared ferociously at us.

Doc and I finished our meal, then we ordered another round of beer. When the barmaid brought us our two mugs of dark, frothy Bock beer, she asked if we would rather sit at another table.

"No, we're okay here," I said.

"Are you sure you really wouldn't like the table by the window better? It has a good view of the outside," she said.

"But it's dark outside, for crying out loud," Doc said. "Why should we move over there anyway?"

"Well, the men over there," she said, pausing and nodding toward the old men on the other side of the room, "they always sit at this table. It's their table."

"Their table?" I said.

"Their table?" Doc echoed. "What do you mean, 'their table'? There's no reserved sign on it."

"Yes, but they always have sat here," she said. "This is the table where they always sit. So, it's their table."

As Doc and Martina were talking, I looked at the group of old men. They were glaring at us. I was about to tell Doc that maybe we ought to let them have their table, when the old men suddenly stood up as if they were soldiers snapping to attention when an officer entered the room. An incredibly old man, leaning on a highly polished cane, came into the room. He stopped when he saw Doc and I, glared at us, and moved slowly to the table where he was welcomed warmly by the other old men. After exchanging handshakes with his table companions, he settled uncomfortably into his chair, which had been surrendered to him by one of his younger companions.

"Jesus Christ, he looks like the Kaiser," I said.

"Hell, it probably is the Kaiser," Doc said. "Hell, let's get out of here. Fuck them if they can't take a joke."

We drained our beers, shoved our chairs back and headed for the door. As I was pushing the door open to go outside, Doc suddenly whirled around and loped to the bar. He motioned to Martina and handed her some money.

"What was that all about?" I said.

"Hell, I just bought the old buzzards a round of beer," he said.

"Why?"

"Shit, I don't know. It just seemed like the thing to do."

"I wonder who those old guys were. As old as they were, they probably were in the Kaiser's Army. Who knows, maybe they were even stationed at our barracks," I said.

"Grommets," Doc said.

"Grommets? What the hell's a grommet?" I said.

"They were grommets," he said. "When I was a kid, that's what we got to calling the old guys who always were hanging out in the bar down the street from my house. They always sat in the same place, and always ordered the same thing. I think there's an international grommet brotherhood and those old guys are members."

"Grommets? Why grommets?" I said.

"I don't know. Maybe they just looked like grommets. You know, back there in the Hof, I bet the youngest guys are grommets. The older guys were master grommets. But that old guy, the one who looked like the Kaiser, he was the head honcho. He was the archgrommet. He was the pope of grommets."

"Archgrommet, my ass," I said. "You've lost it, Doc. I thought you'd lost it with Zulu, but this time you've really lost it."

"Maybe so, Blackie. Maybe so."

I didn't see Doc for several days. I drew a special assignment, driving a busload of golfers to the course every day for the ASA's European tournament. On the last day of the tournament, after I had deposited the last of the golfers at their hotel and turned in my bus, I decided to drop in at the Märkische Hof for a quiet night, a few beers, and a heaping bowl of their goulash.

The sound of German marching music was floating through the air when I pushed open the door and went inside. As I headed for the bar, I glanced toward the table at the end of the bar. There was a group of old men seated at the table, but I suddenly came to a screeching halt when I looked more closely. Sitting directly across from the old man who looked like the Kaiser was Doc.

Spotting me, Doc excused himself and got up and walked over to the bar where I was ordering a beer.

"What's going on, Doc? What are doing there with all those grommets?" I asked.

"Getting my wings, Blackie. I'm getting my wings. I've got a goal. I want to be an archgrommet someday."

"I guess you got to start somewhere. What are you, an apprentice grommet?"

"Hey, I like that. Yeah, I'm an apprentice grommet," Doc chuckled.

"What do you have to do to become an archgrommet?" I said.

"It's hard to say. But from what I can make out, you just have to drink a lot of beer and live a long time," he said.

Doc got out of the Army a few months later, taking a European discharge. After hiking through "the mysterious Balkans," as he liked to say, Doc finally went back to the States. Although I haven't talked to him in years, I heard that he moved down South and became a graduate assistant at some small college until his GI Bill benefits ran out. Then he bought part interest in a bar -- still working on becoming an archgrommet.

Street Fighting Men

31 In April 1968, angry students battled police across Berlin after Rudi Dutschke was seriously wounded in an assassination attempt. Although the main targets of the student protesters were Axel Springer's media empire and police brutality, the demonstrators also protested the war in Vietnam, so the Berlin Brigade commander restricted all U.S. service personnel to their barracks and work.

Crooner and I decided to check out the protests, so we slipped out of the barracks and went to the fence. We pushed the fence open, slipped through, I put it back in place, and we walked quickly to the cab stand at the corner. A driver who was sitting on the fender of his cab saw us, flipped his cigarette into the street and slid into the driver's seat.

"Europa Center," I said as Crooner and I got into the cab. The driver pulled away from the curb and we were on our way to the Europa Center, which was in the British sector and safely away from the U.S. military police.

"You know, that's the first time I've ever gone through the fence before it's completely dark," Crooner said and grinned broadly.

"Me, too," I said.

A few minutes later, we were at the Europa Center. There were hundreds of police officers lining the street. Milling around were groups of students, many holding placards protesting Springerpress, police brutality and the Vietnam War. Some of the protesters were chanting slogans; others are milling around aimlessly; others are clustered in small groups, talking. The helmeted police were nervous, waiting to see what would happen.

Crooner and I crossed the street and stood near a small group of students at the fringe of the protest area. The demonstrators began to move along the street, and the smaller groups converged, making a large mass. As the police moved parallel with the protesters, Crooner and I trailed along. I saw a young woman a placard that read: Ami, bleiben hier und trink Schultheiß Bier (American, stay here and drink Schultheiß Beer). I grasped Crooner's elbow and pointed at the sign. He laughed, and we waved at the young woman, who wagged the sign and waved back.

"Ami, 'raus! Ami, 'raus Vietnam!"

The chants grew louder, and the crowd surged forward. From the back of the group, Crooner and I exchanged looks when we saw bottles flying out of the mass in front of us, but we continued to follow the demonstrators. Suddenly, the ranks broke, and students began running up side streets. We stopped and looked as a group of protesters ran past us, back the way we had come. Then we saw a large group of police officers moving into place behind the demonstration. The students scattered, but a water cannon that had been wheeled into place unleashed a torrent of water.

Crooner and I walked quickly across the street toward. When we saw police wielding truncheons, we decided to get out of their way.

"Let's get outta here," I shouted.

"That way," Crooner said and pointed toward a narrow street.

We ran toward the street, but when we got near the mouth of it, we were confronted by a group of angry policemen. Crooner stopped in his tracks, but I decided to run around them, but two large officers grabbed me and swung me around so I was facing a third officer who was drawing his truncheon. He raised it and was getting ready to whack me with it, but he stopped when he heard a shout.

Crooner, the officers and I looked and saw Tommy Ackermann, the drummer for the combo that Crooner sings with, running toward us.

"Halt, das sind meine Freunden! " he shouted.

The officers relaxed their grips, and I moved away to stand next to Crooner and Tommy.

The Brandenburg Gate, 1968

"Thank God, you're here," I said.

"What the hell are you two doing here? Have you lost your minds?" an agitated Tommy said. "You're just damn lucky I was here. Get the devil out of here. You might be so lucky next time."

"Okay, we're outta here," Crooner said. "Thanks, Tommy."

"Hey, I owe you one," I said.

"Don't worry about it, just get out of here. Go that way," Tommy said and pointed toward the narrow street where we had been going.

As we walked quickly away from the protest, our eyes began to sting.

"Damn, that's teargas," Crooner said.

"That was close," I said.

"I thought you were going to be worked over."

"Thank God for Tommy."

"I wonder if Siggy was here. You know, Tommy soaked him with a water cannon at a big protest, and they played a gig that night, like nothing had happened," Crooner said.

"All in a day's work."

We walked aimlessly for several blocks, stopping once to buy a bottle of vodka, and ended up at the Brandenburg Gate, which seemed to sparkle in the spotlights that shined on it. We sat on the observation platform where nearly five years earlier President Kennedy had stood and looked across the Wall into East Berlin. I took a drink from the bottle and handed it to Crooner, who also took a drink and then passed it.

"It sure is quiet now," I said.

"I'm not complaining," Crooner said.

"Wonder what they're doing now, on the other side?"

"Probably wondering how they can get over here."

"Ever want to go over there — just walk around and see what it's really like?"

Crooner took a sip from the bottle and looked across at the East.

"Sure."

"Think we ever will?"

"Probably not in our lifetimes," Crooner said.

"What the hell," I said, and we continued to drink from the bottle, passing it back and forth.

A Good Idea at the Time

32 It must have seemed like a good idea at the time.

Some light bird, or lieutenant colonel, at Berlin Brigade headquarters probably was looking at the organizational chart and discovered that the 78th ASA hadn't been going out into the field with the Brigade during its regular training alerts. The officer, who had little idea of what the 78th ASA was doing at its installation on top of Teufelsberg, knew that all elements of Berlin Brigade should participate. After all, when the 82nd Airborne roared into the Dominican Republic in 1965, an ASA unit went along to gather intelligence.

It had to be a lieutenant colonel, because Berlin Brigade had more lieutenant colonels than there were jobs for them to do. The man must have thought that when the Brigade moved out on alert, there should be a unit from the ASA moving out with it.

The 78th ASA Contingency Team was born. I "volunteered," although I operated under the ASA adage, "Never volunteer for anything." I just shrugged and said okay when Roadrunner came by, rubbed his chin and pulled at the crotch of his pants a couple of times before telling me that he had volunteered my service for a German linguist spot on the team.

I never would have volunteered for the team because I thought it would probably be a major pain in the ass. However, I didn't mind it so much when I found out that members of the contingency team didn't have to pull KP. After all, sitting out under the trees in the Grunewald for a couple hours now and then wasn't nearly so bad as spending sixteen hours scrubbing pots and pans at the mess hall.

Our team had two German and two Russian linguists,
one a radio operator and the other a transcriber; a diddy-
bopper, or Morse code transcriber; a cryptographer; a technician for the electronic gear; and a mechanic to keep the
vehicles running. The team was commanded by a bored
warrant officer who volunteered for the job because he had
nothing better to do.

We had a jeep, a pickup and a couple of one-ton trucks
with what looked like oversized campers mounted behind
the cabs. The German linguist team, Prince and I, and the
cryptographer, Buffalo Head, used one truck. The Russian
linguists, Doc and Fat Kenny, and the diddy-bopper, Rock
Weed, were crowded into the other. Casteel, the technician,
and Grease Monkey, a wizened little mechanic from the motor pool, shared the pickup, which also pulled the generator
that would power our electronic eavesdropping gear.

Shortly after the contingency team was set up, the members got together at the motor pool, where our vehicles and
equipment were stored. We sat around for several minutes,
smoking and wondering exactly what a contingency team
was supposed to do and waiting for our team commander,
Chief Warrant Officer Bob Semanski. We were pleased that
our commander was going to be a warrant officer and not
a commissioned officer. We called warrant officers "Mister,"
and we wouldn't have to say "sir" all the time like we would
if he were a lieutenant or captain.

When he arrived, Semanski pulled out a big stainless
steel ring loaded with keys and opened the two communications trucks, giving us our first look. Inside the campers
were mounted radio receivers, transmitters and tape recorders.

"My God, it's the Hill on wheels!" Doc said.

"Yeah, but without nearly as much room," Buffalo Head
said. "I tell you assholes one thing. You better take a goddam shower before you get in there with me."

"And don't eat any beans or sauerkraut, either," Rock
Weed said.

"Well, I'm damn glad Casteel and me are by ourselves in
that pickup," Grease Monkey said.

"What the hell difference does it make, Grease Monkey?

We can still smell you even if you're wandering around on the other side of the goddam Grunewald," I said.

"Bite me, asshole. You just be thankful Cigarette got shipped out. Can you imagine being locked inside that tin can with him?" Grease Monkey said.

"Okay, knock it off. We got to get our shit together on this thing. Okay?" Semanski said.

"What the hell do we do, Mr. Semanski?" Rock Weed said. "Phantom just came by and told me I was on a contingency team, but he didn't say what the hell it is."

"Do any of you guys know what this is all about?" Semanski said.

"Shit, no," we all said in unison.

"Well, that figures," said Semanski, a short, stocky New Yorker who sported a neatly trimmed black mustache. He rubbed his index finger along his mustache, and sighed.

"Someone at Berlin Brigade thought the 78th's getting off light because we don't go out and play soldier in the woods every time they have an alert," Semanski said. "So, the Colonel gets called in and is told that his unit's going to start participating in all the alerts. The ol' man raised holy hell, so they backed off a bit and just told him to send out a small unit. And that's you, gentlemen. When the 'Gators go out to the woods, we go out to the woods."

"What the hell do we do when we're out there?" Casteel said.

"The same thing you do on the Hill. Only instead of the Russkies and East Germans, you listen to our guys. You especially try to see if they're doing something that could blow a code," Semanski said.

"We don't have enough tape to record all the 'Gator fuckups," Prince said. "Every time they get on the radio, they blow some code. Jesus Christ, the last time they were on alert, one of the stupid shits gave the coordinates and then gave directions when they got lost."

"You know that and I know that," Semanski said, "but Berlin Brigade thinks we don't. So, we listen. It'll make Berlin Brigade happy and that'll make the Colonel happy, and if he's happy ...."

"Yeah, yeah, you'll be happy, and if you're happy, we'll be

happy. Right, Mr. Semanski?" I said.

"You got it."

"What do we do when there's an alert?" Buffalo Head said.

"You get your gear and haul ass right here to the motor pool. We'll assemble here and move out to the field from here. I don't know where we're supposed to set up, but I'm supposed to be told when I get a call about the alert. When we move out, you can just follow my jeep," Semanski said.

"Who's supposed to drive the trucks?" I said.

"Anyone but you, Cooper," Semanski said. "When the ol' man found out you were on the team, he specifically said you don't get behind the wheel. He really does think you tried to run him down with that deuce-and-a-half."

"The hell I did. If I'd been trying to hit him, I would've hit him. I just came around the corner a little too fast," I said, grinning as I had the pleasant memory of seeing the bird colonel diving for the ditch as the deuce-and-a-half bore down on him. It cost me my driver's license for a month and I had to endure a tongue-lashing by the colonel. I also had to attend a safety course, but somehow it was worth it.

"Well, that doesn't matter. You don't drive. Whoever else does is no matter. Whoever gets here first and has a license can drive. Just work it out among yourselves," Semanski said.

We stayed ready. We knew it was getting about time for the brigade to have an alert, and we wanted to be in the field as swiftly as possible. We knew the 'Gators had a pretty low opinion of our ability to do soldiering, and we wanted to show them that we could do whatever they did.

Our preparations were complete four or five days later when the alert was called — to the surprise of no one. We always knew a day or so in advance that an alert was going to be called, because the commanders of all of the units in Berlin would be called to Berlin Brigade headquarters to get their marching orders. The Berlin Brigade brass always wanted things to move smoothly in their alerts, so they made sure that no one would be surprised when one was called. After all, people who were surprised often did things that weren't part of the script — and the brass didn't like things not going as planned.

So when the alert was called at ten o'clock one cool September night, the ASA Contingency Team was already sitting in its vehicles, waiting to move out, when Semanski arrived. He and his driver, Rock Weed, climbed into his jeep, and we all roared off to our designated area in the Grunewald.

We were to set up our generator and trucks in a clearing, not too far from the main road through the Grunewald and adjacent to Teufelsee, a small lake in the forest.

Semanski nervously paced around, chain-smoking his Pall Malls, as we hooked up the generator that would provide the power for our communications gear. It took just a few minutes to get all of the cables connected, then Grease Monkey gave a fierce tug on the starter cable and the generator sputtered, coughed, and roared to life, sending the electrical current racing through the lines and powering up our receivers and recorders.

"Okay, gather around and listen up!" Semanski said. "Because we're just monitoring Berlin Brigade, we don't need two of you Marys in the vans. So whoever's not monitoring signals will man a guard post." He then picked Doc and Prince to man the listening posts. Rock Weed, Fat Kenny, Casteel, and I were told to set up a perimeter guard.

"No one gets inside our perimeter unchallenged. I don't care if it's the commandant of Berlin himself, every swinging Richard is challenged. You got that?" Semanski said.

"Goddam fucking Army," Fat Kenny said. "Who gives a shit about what we're doing out here? I can't believe they take this toy soldier shit so seriously."

"Oh, come on, Kenny," Casteel said. "It's no big deal. Hell, if you weren't out here in the middle of the Grunewald in the middle of the night, what'd you be doing anyway? Probably lying in your rack and whacking your meat."

"Fuck you, Casteel," Fat Kenny said. "If I wasn't out here, I'd be in bed with your wife making her scream."

"You'd probably make her scream all right, Fat Kenny, but it sure as hell wouldn't be for pleasure. She'd be screaming because she'd be afraid she would be catching 27 kinds of VD," Casteel said.

"Cut the bullshit," Rock Weed said. "Let's set up our posts. No need to piss off Semanski. Hell, he's already scared shitless that something'll go wrong."

"I'm with you, Rock Weed," I said, "but let's set up our guard posts our own way, okay?"

"What you mean, 'our own way'?" Rock Weed said.

"Hell, you've seen enough of these alerts. The guards are always standing out in the open. Shit, everyone knows where they are. Why don't we hide our guard posts, so the treads won't know where we are? You know, climb up in a tree or lie behind a log, shit like that."

"Goddammit, Blackie, that's a damn good idea. Can you imagine a tread's reaction if someone drops out of a tree behind him? He'll shit bricks," a laughing Rock Weed said. "I got that tree right there. Here, hold my rifle and hand it up to me when I get up in the tree."

Rock Weed leaped up, grabbed one of the lowest branches and pulled himself up into the tree. I handed him his rifle and he climbed up higher to a perch where he was hidden by the foliage.

Fat Kenny looked up at the tree, looked down at his waistline, and shrugged.

"I think I'll hide behind a log," he said, as he shuffled off into the darkness.

"I'll hide out somewhere over there," Casteel said, pointing to an area on the other side of the communications trucks.

"Okay, I'll take the other corner," I said. Like Rock Weed, I found a tree with sturdy branches and climbed it. I settled into a perch against the trunk, hidden from sight by the thick leaves.

I relaxed against the tree's trunk, now and then taking a sip of the vodka and ginger ale that I had substituted for water in my canteen, and waited for the first Berlin Brigade tread to venture inside the ASA Contingency Team's perimeter. Even though I knew the other guards were going through the same routine that I was, I still was surprised when I heard a banshee scream, followed by the rustling of leaves, snapping of branches and a surprised, "What the fuck's going on here?"

I dropped down from my tree, slapped my helmet on my head and ran as swiftly as I could toward the commotion.

When I got there, I saw Fat Kenny with his rifle pointed at an indignant man wearing khaki pants, a sweatshirt, and a dark blue windbreaker who apparently was accompanied by a bemused sergeant major. I ignored the two and walked up to Fat Kenny.

"What you got, Fat Man?" I said.

"These two came inside our perimeter, Blackie," he said, struggling to appear serious.

"Who are they?"

"I don't know. They didn't identify themselves."

"I'm the vice commandant of Berlin Brigade," the man wearing civilian clothes said pompously.

"Got any ID?" I said.

"Yeah, how do we know you're not a Russian spy?" Fat Kenny said.

"I've told you who I am. Ask the sergeant major."

"We're talking to you, asshole, not him. Besides, anyone can get a uniform," I said.

"I am the vice commandant of Berlin Brigade," he said.

"We're the ASA Contingency Team guards and you're not supposed to be inside our perimeter," I said.

"Let's take them to Mr. Semanski," Fat Kenny said. He pointed his rifle at his two prisoners and, motioning toward the clearing, said, "March!"

"You two might think this is funny now, but your C.O. will have your asses," the civilian-clad man said as he stomped toward the clearing where our equipment was set up. The sergeant major said nothing, just strolled along behind his comrade.

As our little group approached the communications vans, Semanski was hanging up his field phone.

"What do we have here — oh, sweet Jesus!" he said and snapped a salute, which he had to hold for a few seconds longer than usual because the angry colonel was glaring at Fat Kenny and me.

"What the hell do you think you're doing out here, Mr. Semanski? This screaming hooligan dropped out of a tree, almost on top of me," the furious prisoner said, pointing at

Fat Kenny. "And this one," he said, pointing at me, "is inso-lent and insubordinate. He's just like a goddam civilian."

"Thanks," I said and grinned at Semanski, who rolled his eyes and sighed.

"I'm terribly sorry, sir," Semanski said. "They just took their orders about guard duty to heart. I'm sure they weren't intentionally insolent."

"Bullshit! They're two of the most insubordinate soldiers I've ever seen. They're a goddam disgrace to the uniform, and I intend to make that very clear to your C.O. I expect him to make an example of these two, and especially this hooligan (he pointed at me) who called me an asshole," he said. Then, motioning to the sergeant major, he stomped back through the woods.

"Jesus Christ! What did you two think you were doing? That was the goddam vice commandant of Berlin Brigade. He can have your balls!" the highly agitated Semanski shouted. "Jesus H. Christ, what a goddam mess this is! How the hell am I going to explain this to the colonel? Jesus Christ, Cooper, don't tell me you called him an asshole."

"Don't worry about anything, Mr. Semanski. That ass-hole's not pissed at you, it's our asses he wants," I said. "Big deal. We get an Article Fifteen and everybody's happy as pigs in sunshine. So what? That guy's an asshole."

The angry lieutenant colonel had carried out his promise to notify our unit commander. When I got back to my room, there was a note on my bunk from the first sergeant. The Colonel had extended an invitation for me to visit with him in just a few hours.

At exactly nine o'clock, Semanski, Fat Kenny, and I were standing at attention in front of our Colonel. He sat silently, looking through the stack of papers as he delayed, trying to make us nervous. It was working, because despite our bra-vado, Fat Kenny and I really didn't know what the Colonel would do.

Finally, the Colonel looked up. His clear blue eyes were icy as he glared at Semanski. The little warrant officer's prominent Adam's apple bobbed up and down as he swal-lowed. He didn't move, staying rigidly at attention as he braced himself for the expected explosion.

"Mr. Semanski, did these two men drop out of trees and confront the vice commandant of Berlin Brigade when he entered the Contingency Team's perimeter?" the Colonel said softly.

"Yes, sir. I mean, not exactly, sir," Semanski replied.

"Not exactly?" the Colonel said.

"Well, Fat Kenny, excuse me, Specialist Loeffler, actually had been behind a log. Cooper was in a tree, sir, and responded to the, uh, activity."

"They actually detained the vice commandant?" the Colonel said.

"Yes, sir."

"Good. You all have done exactly what you're supposed to do in a combat situation," the Colonel said, a broad grin spreading across his face. "I'm not sure that I approve of how you set up a guard position, but you men did what any good soldier should do. I know what the vice commandant said occurred, but I believe I have to support my men, even when they get a bit more enthusiastic in carrying out their orders than they should be. But you two are damn fortunate he was out of uniform."

"Thank you, sir," we said in unison.

"You're dismissed," he said, "but one thing — another stunt like this one and you'll find yourselves up to your asses in alligators. Cooper, no more calling any officer an asshole, even when he's out of uniform. Do you understand me?"

"Yes, sir!"

We saluted, spun on our heels and marched smartly out of the office.

"Jesus Christ, Fat Kenny, I can't believe we got off," I said. "I was pretty damn sure we were going to get our asses fried. Hell, last time I saw the Colonel he threatened to ship me to Herzo or another shithole in the Zone."

"Only reason I was worried was because I was having to go in there with you. Shit, the ol' man still thinks you tried to run over him with that deuce-and-a-half. I was afraid he'd nail me just because I was with you."

"Maybe he didn't nail me because I was with you."

Fat Kenny pursed his lips.

"Could be. You heard him call me a good soldier, didn't you?"

"Shit, I'd rather be called a civilian."

A few days later, Fat Kenny and I were replaced on the contingency team.

Catfish

33 Catfish never really fit in with C Trick. He tried hard enough, but he just never could fit in with the group of malcontents that made up most of C Trick. Catfish was a redneck in a group where even the Southerners didn't like rednecks. He had joined the Army because of his sense of duty and patriotism, not because he was about to be drafted and knew that by enlisting he could improve his chances of not being sent to Vietnam.

While most of C Trick had serious problems with authority, Catfish loved the authoritarian lifestyle of the Army. He enjoyed having someone tell him when to get up, when to go to work, where to be, and when to be there. While most of us in C Trick thrived on chaos, Catfish loved order.

Catfish loved the Army and wanted to make it his career. He even volunteered for a spot on the contingency team after Fat Kenny and I were given the boot. That he wasn't a German Mary never seemed to sink through to Catfish, he just wanted to be part of something in the Army he considered to be special. Unfortunately for him, he not only didn't fit in with C Trick, he also didn't fit in with the Army. Try as hard as he could, Catfish just wasn't a good soldier. He was a short, fat, near-sighted South Alabama boy who just couldn't be what the Army wanted in its career people.

He was one of those people who knew where the Army wanted him to be and what time the Army wanted him to be there, but he either would get lost on the way or his watch would stop and he'd get there late. He lived his life on a treadmill, running as hard as he could but not getting anywhere.

He fell into a limbo. He didn't fit in with most of us on C Trick, and he didn't fit in with the treads.

With the Vietnam War expanding and the Pentagon shipping thousands more of America's poor and minorities to the jungles of Southeast Asia every week, the Army was ready to lower its standards for its career people. Catfish, as dense as he was, knew that his chance for a military career was being helped out by the war.

He decided he would be a soldier and turn back the Communist hordes that were threatening the world in general and South Alabama in particular.

With the idea that he would save the nation, Catfish headed to town one hot, humid afternoon intending to join the Marines, a proud outfit that he was certain had only true, red-blooded American patriots in it. But on the way to the recruiting station, he decided to stop in Sutton's Drug Store for a strawberry milk shake. He lingered over his milk shake, relishing each swallow of the thick, creamy shake and gazing longingly at the heavy breasts of Angela Sutton, the pharmacist's well-developed sixteen-year-old daughter.

Finally sucking the last few drops of the shake through the straw and taking a last longing look at Angela's breasts, he walked down the street to the recruiting station, only to find that the Marine gunnery sergeant who was the recruiter had closed up for the day.

Determined to join a military outfit, Catfish spotted the Army recruiting sergeant across the street. Although he also was ready to shut down and go home, the sergeant, who needed another body to meet his monthly quota, decided to stay open a few more minutes and get Catfish properly signed up for the U.S. Army Security Agency. The ASA was a four-year enlistment, a year longer than other Army enlistments, but he thought if the enlistment were longer, then the outfit probably would be tougher and the duty more dangerous.

After taking several batteries of tests, Catfish ended up in Fort Devens, Massachusetts, where he learned how to take apart radio receivers and tape recorders and put them back together. Then he was shipped to Berlin.

In Berlin, Catfish tried to be as good a soldier as his

great-grandfather, who had served in the Civil War. But he never achieved that goal. He would spitshine his boots, but on the way to the inspection, he'd stumble and scuff them. His fatigues, no matter how crisply starched they were when he got them back from the laundry, would become rumpled immediately when they touched his body. No matter how straight he stood and how hard he sucked up his gut, his belly still sagged over his belt.

Catfish's biggest obstacle to being a good soldier, however, had to be his flatulence. No matter how he tried to squeeze his asshole shut, no matter how he avoided eating gaseous food, he couldn't control his farting. When he stood in line for inspection, he never failed to fart — loud and odoriferous — at the precise moment the inspecting officer stopped in front of him.

"Soldier, are you trying to be funny?" the Colonel shouted when Catfish let loose with a particularly foul and loud fart during one of C Trick's infrequent command inspections. After his first inspection of C Trick, the Colonel decided its members just weren't good soldiers, and he didn't want to risk elevating his blood pressure by looking at all the improperly shined shoes, unpressed uniforms and non-regulation haircuts.

"Sir! No, sir!" Catfish sounded off in his best military fashion, only to be undermined by a second fart. The second fart managed to be even more foul and loud than the first, a cacophony of sounds that caused Chief to snicker. A quiet giggle spread to Tiny, then to Buffalo Head, then to me before everyone in C Trick burst out laughing. I glanced to see if Phantom was laughing. The first sergeant had managed to keep a straight face, although I could swear I could see his lips twitching.

The Colonel whirled on Captain Gammon, the unfortunate company commander.

"Goddammit, Captain, this is the most pathetic group of soldiers I've ever come across. I don't care how you do it, but don't you ever have this bunch out here for an inspection. If I had my way, they'd all be drummed right out of the Army right now," he said furiously, then stormed across the parking lot toward the unit headquarters, leaving a crestfallen company commander standing in front of Catfish, who managed to break wind one more time.

Catfish truly wanted to be a good soldier, wanted to make the Army his career, but the treads couldn't stand him. Because he wanted to be a career soldier and was such a redneck, almost no one on C Trick would have anything to do with him, leaving him trapped between two worlds and suited for neither.

Summer had begun to give way to autumn when Catfish's chances for an Army career went down the drain. The days were shorter and the nights longer and cooler, but even with the cooler weather, now and then a warm day would come along.

Catfish and I had been put on Doob guard for the month. I'm not sure why Catfish had been picked for Doob guard, but I had a good idea the Colonel had "volunteered" me after he kicked me off the contingency team.

Everywhere the German construction workers went on the Hill, a Doob guard went with them. When they took a smoke break, the Doob guard took a smoke break. When they took their morning and afternoon beer breaks, the Doob guard would sneak behind a building or truck and have a beer break, too.

Well, I did, but Catfish didn't. He wouldn't take a beer break because it wasn't authorized by the Army. He even discussed turning me in for taking the beer break with the workers, but I think he really believed me when I patted the .45 I had strapped to my hip and said I'd kill him first.

During the beer breaks, Catfish, with his M-14 rifle slung over his shoulder and glaring fiercely at me, would march back and forth in front of the Germans, making sure that he had each one in sight at every moment.

He dropped his guard only one time.

The Germans were breaking up the slab where one of the first buildings on the Hill had stood. The building became too small for the ASA's needs and was demolished after it had been abandoned. Now, a bigger and newer building was going up on that site, so the Germans were having to use a jackhammer to break up the concrete before the ground could be prepared for the new building.

Catfish was watching intently as Herbert Baugatz, one of the older German workers, manned the jackhammer.

He flipped the switch, and the hammer fell quiet. He looked a moment at Catfish, now standing uneasily with his M-14 slung over shoulder and rocking from one foot to the other.

"Would you like to try my hammer?" Herbert said.

"You bet I would," Catfish said, and a big grin spread across his round face.

"Oh shit," I said softly, and I slipped around to the other side of the building, where several other Germans were working. I had just gotten out of sight when trouble arrived for Catfish.

The Colonel, paying one of his rare visits to the Hill, came around the corner of the building and spotted Catfish manning the jackhammer, cheerfully breaking up the con-crete while Herbert the German construction worker, enjoying a smoke break, stood nearby, watching — with Catfish's M-14 slung over his shoulder.

I knew Catfish's faint hope of a military career had vanished when I heard the Colonel shout at me.

"You, Specialist! Get over here and relieve this pitiful piece of crap," the Colonel said.

I eased around the corner of the building, leaving my group of German workers standing with gaping mouths as they peeked and saw a red-faced bird colonel towering over a quivering enlisted man.

A pale, trembling Catfish, his eyes bulging behind his the thick lenses of his glasses like his namesake, handed the M-14 to me.

"You come with me," the Colonel said, almost barking at Catfish, then spun on his heel and marched toward the site commander's office.

By the time the shift ended, Catfish's gear had been packed and orders cut shipping him to the ASA unit in Asmara, Ethiopia. The Colonel wanted Catfish as far away from Berlin as possible, but he didn't want to hurt the war effort by shipping him to Vietnam.

Roadrunner and the Memo

34 One of the bad things about mids was it gave you time to think, especially when all you had was about eight hours of time on your hands. In the Army, thinking is something that's discouraged by the brass, who believe enlisted personnel's thoughts naturally would be subversive.

C Trick was on mids and I had too much time on my hands when I had my last in a series of run-ins with Roadrunner.

Roadrunner and I had our first confrontation more than two years earlier. It was my first night on the Hill, when I wore a field jacket with its previous owner's name still stitched above the right front pocket. I'm not sure Roadrunner ever fully accepted my explanation. He seemed to think I was an East German spy.

Our second run-in came a couple of months later when C Trick went on mids, and I had nothing to do but drink coffee, smoke cigarettes, and try to avoid him.

At my little desk in front of the equipment, I fidgeted, squirmed and stretched, hitting the clipboard that held the papers on which we logged all the tapes and knocking it to the floor. I picked up the clipboard and slowly an idea began to take shape. I took the tape log from the clipboard and replaced it with a legal pad. Then I got a ballpoint pen, stood up and walked out of the room.

I walked around the site, stopping to chat with other drowsy linguists and Morse code operators. As I was walking down the hallway toward the break room, I nearly bumped into Roadrunner.

"Hmm, Cooper, what are you doing?" Roadrunner said,

his Adam's apple bobbing up and down furiously and he jingled the coins in his pocket.

"Doing an inventory of door facings, Sarge," I said, holding up the clipboard and trying to sound like I was on an important mission.

"Hmmm, counting scene? Carry on," he said and rushed on down the hallway.

I had learned the secret power of the clipboard. Carry one and no one, not even your boss, will question that you're doing something very important.

I pulled it off, at Roadrunner's expense, and I managed to while away the rest of that shift by wielding my clipboard and taking phantom inventories.

Of course, someone (I still think it was Prince, although he swears he never said a word) let Roadrunner know what had happened, and he spent several minutes when C Trick came off break letting me know how he figured out my game and that he would be keeping an eye on me until I finally left Berlin.

Roadrunner kept his word. He watched me like a hawk until I left the Hill, especially when C Trick went on mids.

On this particular night, Roadrunner was off, giving me the freedom to roam the site. I had been outside looking at the stars and the lights of Berlin, when my bladder sent me a message. As I left the latrine, I noticed that the door to the site commander's office was ajar. Obviously, someone had forgotten to lock the door. I started to lock the door and pull it shut, when I glanced inside. A file cabinet drawer was partially open — another security violation that could get someone into serious trouble the next morning — so I went in the office to close the file cabinet and then lock up the office.

I don't know why I did it, but I looked in the file cabinet and saw the drawer contained forms, carbon paper, and typing paper. On whim, I took several blank forms, carbon paper, and typing paper.

When the shift ended, I gathered up the forms, typing paper, and carbon paper and put them inside an old copy of BZ, a Berlin tabloid newspaper, and went outside to catch the trick bus back to the barracks. At the same time, I was thinking about how to explain to the guard what I was doing with the forms.

Fortunately, the guardshack was manned with Elephant Ass, whose size was matched only by his laziness. Although the guards were supposed to check everything, including newspapers and magazines, that were being carried out of the site, Elephant Ass was too lazy to get out of his chair by the window to actually check anything. That was how I managed to get by for nearly three months with having a picture of Nikita Khruschev pasted over my photo on my security badge. All I had to do was walk through, flash the badge and Elephant Ass would wave me on through — never looking at whose picture was on the badge.

As I moved through, Elephant Ass looked up and spotted the newspaper.

"What you got there, Blackie?"

"All kinds of secrets, Albert," I said. "I took lots of secrets and I'm going to defect with them as soon as I get back to the barracks."

"Yeah, yeah, wiseass," he said.

I took my seat by the window near the rear of the bus. Hairy Ranger slouched down the aisle and plopped down next to me.

"Goddam, I hate mids," he said. "I'm too goddam tired to go do anything, and if I go to bed now, I'll be too goddam tired to work tonight."

"Yeah, mids really suck," I said. "But at least you've got something going on all the time over there on low-level. On SED, there's nothing going on. It's a struggle to stay awake. Christ, I must've had thirty cups of coffee and I still got sleepy."

"Why don't you just take a few winks?" he said.

"Hell, I would, but every time I doze off, goddam Roadrunner shows up and throws a fit."

"You and Roadrunner don't get along too good, do you?"

"Shit, no," I said. "I can't stand the bastard. Hell, I wouldn't piss on him if his face was on fire."

Hairy Ranger chuckled and slid down in his seat, bracing his knees against the back of the seat in front of us.

"God, I'm tired. Look at Grumpy John, the lucky bastard," Hairy Ranger said, jerking his thumb toward the rumpled Arkansan who was already snoring in the seat across the aisle. "He's so short I don't think he's got to work any more mids. Say, can I look at your BZ? Don't they run pictures of chicks with their tits hanging out?"

"No, that's one of the Brit papers," I said as I opened the newspaper and pulled out the materials I had stuffed inside.

"What's that you got there?" Hairy Ranger said.

"Oh, just some forms and things I helped myself to.".

"What are you going to do with them?"

"I don't know yet. I might write my own memos and see what happens," I said.

"Hell, why don't you write one sending me home early?"

"Ranger, if I could do that, I'd write one for me. I thought you loved this shit. Why would you need to get out any earlier?" I said.

"Eat shit."

When I got back to my room, I put the forms, typing paper, and carbon sheets in the top of my wall locker and forgot about them.

A few days later, one of those warm fronts whipped across northern Europe, giving us notice that summer soon would arrive. Although it certainly wasn't as hot as a May day in southwest Arkansas, it was still warm enough that our long-sleeved fatigue shirts were uncomfortable, and we couldn't wait to get inside to our work stations on the Hill. Inside, we'd strip off the fatigue shirts and work in the relative comfort of T-shirts.

Listening to the griping about the heat and how long sleeves made things worse gave me an idea. We were now on swing shift, so when I got up about mid-morning, I gathered up the forms, typing paper, and carbon sheets and went to the barracks day room, where there was a battered old Royal typewriter that the company clerk had managed to trade in for a new, electric model.

It wasn't a pretty typewriter, but it worked very well, if you didn't mind having a e that would stick. If you knew about that stubborn key, it was easy to adjust.

I put together a form, a sheet of carbon paper, and a

sheet of typing paper, rolled them into the carriage, and went to work.

"What are you doing, Blackie? Writing a book?" Rapid Roger asked me as he was racking up the balls for a solitary game of eight ball.

"Naw, I'm just writing a poem," I said.

"A poem? How's it go?"

I thought for a moment, trying to remember something I could recite. All I could remember was a bit of doggerel I had heard back in high school.

"The wind blew; the leaves flew; the villain he pursued her; down her leg ran the white of an egg; the dirty bastard screwed her."

"Shit! You're not typing that, are you?"

"No, I'm just fooling around with some forms."

Rapid Roger stopped chalking his cue stick, walked around the pool table, and stood where he could look over my shoulder.

"That's a memo form. You're writing a memo," he said.

"No shit, Sherlock. I'm writing a memo."

"You helping the company clerk?"

"In my own way, Ro-jay, in my own way," I said.

Rapid Roger watched intently as I continued to bang away on the typewriter. When I typed in a combination of letters and numbers for an Army regulation.

"Goddam, Blackie, how did you know that reg?"

"I don't. I just make them up as I go. Hell, no one knows all those goddam regs anyway. All you have to do is make them look right and people'll believe they're real," I said.

"Well, it sure looks official to me."

"That's the idea, Ro-jay. Who do you think ought to sign this memo?" I said.

"I don't know, but it ought to be someone whose name looks real. Not like I.P. Freely or Seymour Butts or one of those joke names."

We both thought a minute, then Rapid Roger snapped his fingers.

"Blackie, how about this? Only a fathead will look at a memo like this and do whatever it says do without question. Why don't you have it signed by Dick Schaedel?"

"Perfect, perfect," I said. "'Dick Schaedel.' I like it."

In German, dick schädel meant thick skull, or fathead.

"It's perfect," I said. "Only we need to make it more official. After all, he's going to be a light colonel."

"Well, if you want formality, how about Richard Schaedel?"

"Lt. Colonel Richard Schaedel. It has a nice ring to it," I said.

I scanned the memo that I had written. It looked real. I had filled in all the blanks and I had put in the correct sequence of letters and numbers for the Army regulations, even if they were the military equivalent of gibberish.

"How do you like it, Ro-jay?" I said.

"I like it, Blackie. I like it. Hell, it'd be a good idea to have short-sleeved fatigue shirts for wearing during the summer anyway. If it's not a real memo, it should be. Jesus Christ, I get hot up on the Hill during the summer. It's a great memo, especially that bit there," he said, then began to read from the memo: "'The bottom of the sleeve is to be one and three-eighth inches above the mid-point of the elbow when flexed.' That's a great touch, Blackie."

"Well, it's ready for the signature," I said, and took care of it.

Then I rolled the papers out of the typewriter carriage and signed the name with a flourish.

It was nearly noon and I heard the first sergeant leave his office, locking the door behind him. Rapid Roger followed me out into the hallway. The first sergeant's office was locked and the company commander was on leave, so there was no one around. We dashed to the bulletin board and found a vacant spot and put up our memo, right next to the real ones.

I had just about forgotten about the memos until two days later when C Trick went on days. I had drawn the clean-up detail for the site break room, so I was emptying ash trays and cleaning out the coffee pot, preparing to brew the first pot of the day, when the site commander walked into the room.

"How long's it going to be?" he asked.

"Couple of minutes," I said.

Captain Weldon moved to the side, watching as I put the coffee and water in the pot. Just as I flipped on the switch to brew the coffee, I saw Captain Weldon's eyes widen, then narrow and he frowned as Roadrunner, carrying a mug, entered.

Roadrunner was wearing a fatigue shirt with short sleeves.

"Sergeant, what the hell are you wearing?
" he said.

"Sir?" Roadrunner said, sounding confused.

"Are you trying to be stylish with that uniform?"

"No, sir. I'm just following the memo on short-sleeve fatigue shirts."

Captain Weldon glared at Roadrunner.

"Exactly where is that memo?"

"On the bulletin board in the company."

"Who signed it?" Captain Weldon said.

"A Lt. Col. Richard Schaedel — he's with the Quartermasters."

"Schaedel? Richard Schaedel? Hmmm, Dick Schaedel," Captain Weldon said and grinned. "Dick Schaedel. Sergeant,do you know what 'Dick Schaedel' means?"

"N-no, no, sir," Roadrunner stammered in confusion.

"It means "fathead." You've been hoodwinked," he said and laughed.

Roadrunner's face turned red, and he glared at me because I was grinning.

"Wipe that smile off your face, Cooper," Roadrunner snapped, then he looked at Captain Weldon. "You mean it's not real?"

"Nope, phony as a three-dollar bill."

"Well, what should I do? I've got two other pairs," Roadrunner said plaintively.

"Do whatever you want with them, just don't wear them to the site," Captain Weldon said and started to leave the room, then stopped and looked sternly at Roadrunner.

"Sergeant, get your ass back to your quarters and get a proper uniform."

"Yes, sir," Roadrunner said and rushed from the room.

Captain Weldon waited, then began to laugh. He looked

at me.

"I don't suppose you know anything about this, do you?"

"Not a thing, sir," I said, as innocently as possible.

"I didn't think you would. But that 'Dick Schaedel' bit was good. Yep, it was really a nice touch.," Captain Weldon said and chuckled. He looked at me and grinned conspiratorially. "It was truly a nice touch."

I could hear him laughing to himself as he walked down the hallway toward his office.

"Yes, sir, it was," I said to myself.

A Business Transaction

35 After more than two years, I knew Roadrunner had decided I wasn't an East German spy, but he still didn't want me on C Trick. So when an opportunity came along to get rid of me, even if it were for only a few days, he took advantage of it.

Roadrunner had picked me as C Trick's member of a special detail that was supposed to build a fence around the site. It was supposed to take us less than a week to finish the job, but we managed to stretch the spring detail into more than a month. After we finally finished the fence, Roadrunner had me shifted to straight days for a special project in Violet, another month-long stretch that kept me away from him.

When the project was finished, I was ready to join C Trick on eves, but Roadrunner had other ideas. The regular supply driver was on a 30-day leave, and Roadrunner had recommended me as the substitute driver. I didn't mind the detail because all I had to do was check a deuce-and-a-half out of the motor pool and carry supplies or equipment between the Hill and Site 1, which was at Rudow in extreme southern Berlin, or back and forth to headquarters. It was an easy detail, with little or no supervision, and I would have volunteered for it without Roadrunner's encouragement.

It was summer in Berlin. I had loaded the deuce-and-a-half with office supplies, boxes of recording tape, toilet paper and cleaning materials at Rudow, and stopped at Teufelssee, a small lake in the Grünewald, to eat a sandwich and ogle the bikini-clad girls sunbathing on the shore.

After finishing my little picnic, I drove on up to the Hill, and carried the supplies into the storage room.

After I finished unloading the truck, I went to the break room to get a cup of coffee. While I sipped on my coffee, I looked through the door into the room where the diddy-boppers were transcribing Soviet and East German Morse code messages that had been recorded earlier in the day.

Hammerhead, his headsets firmly in place, was sitting beside a bank of tape recorders, pounding away at the typewriter with its continuous feed paper, and slamming the carriage return with such force that I thought it would sail right out and through a wall.

While I was watching, Hammerhead reached over and stopped the tape. Then he removed his headsets and carefully hung then on a hook mounted to one of the tape recorders. He unrolled the paper and placed it carefully on top of its book.

I heard someone come into the break room behind me. I looked over my shoulder and saw Buffalo Head and Rock Weed.

"Hammerhead's pissed off again," I said.

"Oh shit," Buffalo Head said. "I wonder what he's going to do this time?"

"What's he pissed off about," Rock Weed asked.

"It could be anything," I said.

"It's got to be the goddam Morse Code. I know I'd go crazy if I had to sit there all day and listen to that shit," Buffalo Head said.

No one said anything as Hammerhead stood up and stretched, rolling his head from side to side to release tension. Then he picked up the typewriter and slammed it as hard as he could onto the concrete floor, sending keys, springs and screws in all directions.

Using his toe, he pushed the shattered remains of the typewriter against a trash can and walked over to a four-shelf rack in the corner of the room. He examined the typewriters on the rack, pressing the keys, checking the carriage return. When he found one that suited him, he picked it up and took it back to his work station, rolled in the paper onto the platen, sat down and put on his headsets, turned on the tape recorder and resumed typing fiercely.

"Lord, I wish I had the typewriter contract," Buffalo Head said. "Those diddy-boppers really run through them."

"What's gonna happen to him?" Rock Weed asked.

"Nothing. The diddy-boppers do that all the time," Buffalo Head said.

"You're shitting me. The treads don't do anything?"

"Shit, Weed, you sit there eight hours a day listening to that goddam Morse code, you'll go apeshit, too," I said. "If the treads cracked down the diddy-boppers over a typewriter now and then, there wouldn't been any left to transcribe that shit."

"I sure would like to have the typewriter contract," Buffalo Head said and shook his head.

"Well, you don't have it, Buff, so get over it," I said.

"Yeah, I don't have it, but I can have a peanut butter sandwich," he said, and opened a cabinet shelf where the peanut butter and bread were kept. He layered the peanut butter thickly on a slice of bread, folded it over and took a big bite. "Damn good, even if it is green."

I was about to pour another cup of coffee when Roadrunner rushed into the room. He peered into the diddy-bopper room, where Hammerhead was calmly transcribing a tape.

"He bust another one?" Roadrunner said.

We nodded.

"Shit, now I'll have to fill out another report," Roadrunner said and glared in Mad Dog's direction. Then he whirled and pointed at me.

"Cooper, you come with me, the Old Man wants to see you."

"What about, Sarge?"

"He'll tell you," Roadrunner said brusquely.

You don't know what he wants, I thought.

We walked quickly around the Pit and down the hallway to the site commander's office. Roadrunner knocked on the door before entering.

"Here's Cooper, Sir," he said and gestured for me to follow him into the office. I stepped inside just as Captain Weldon, the site commander, a lanky Southerner with dark, close-cropped hair, pushed his chair back and stood up. He came out from behind his desk and said brusquely, "Come on with me, Cooper."

We walked to the supply shack, where all of the spare parts and equipment was stored. Captain Weldon pointed to the reels of antenna cable stacked neatly at one end of the building.

"We've got too many reels of cable in here," he said.

"Sir?"

"The IG's coming in next week and we've got too many reels of antenna cable. I need to get rid of 157 reels."

"Do you want me to haul them out to Rudow?"

"No, no. The IG's going to check out there, too. We've got to rid of them. Get someone to help you, and you two haul them down to the dump. Let me know when you're done, understood?"

"Yes, sir. I'll go get the truck."

A few minutes later, I had backed the truck down the narrow driveway to the storage building. I took off my fatigue shirt and tossed it into the cab of the truck. Before doing anything else, I decided I would go find someone to give me a hand loading and unloading 157 reels of antenna cable.

As I walked into the Pit, I saw Doc logging in a tape.

"Doc, you want to give me a hand?"

"Doing what?"

"The IG's coming to town, and the Old Man wants me to get rid of 157 reels of antenna cable. I'm hauling them down to the dump."

"Those reels are kinda heavy, aren't they?"

"Not especially. You going help?"

"Shit, no."

I shrugged and said, "No big deal, I'll go get the Ranger or Prince."

But before I could leave the Pit, I heard a soft, modulated voice, with a trace of a Boston accent.

"Hey, Blackie, I'll give you a hand. It's got to be better than sitting in the Pit listening to this low-level shit."

Crooner stood up, dropped his headsets on the table in front of the radio receiver and tape recorder where he had been listening to the Soviet military. We went to the break room where Roadrunner was pouring another cup of coffee. He just nodded when I said Crooner was helping me with Captain Weldon's detail.

"Why the hell do we have to dump this cable," Crooner said, as we counted out 157 reels.

"There were a couple of shipments of cable that didn't have any paperwork," I said. "No one ever said anything about it. Now the IG's coming to town, and the Old Man doesn't want the extra stuff lying around without any papers on them. So he just wants us to dump them."

"Jesus Christ, this stuff's expensive, and we're just dumping it?"

"That's what the man wants," I said.

Crooner climbed into the bed of the truck and slid the reels to the back as I lugged them out of the warehouse. About 40 minutes later, I stopped and wiped the sweat from my forehead.

"How many have we loaded?" I asked.

"Eighty-one."

"That's enough for this run. Let's get rid of this and come back for the rest," I said.

Crooner nodded and we climbed into the cab to make the drive down and around the Hill to the dump. When we drove up, I saw several German workers unloading their trucks near a giant pit. When I stopped, Crooner jumped out and ran around to the back to lower the tailgate.

He climbed into the bed and pulled several reels to the back. I got one and carried to the edge of the pit and tossed it over the edge. It rolled several times and came to stop against a large block of concrete.

I saw a heavyset German tramp down to the cable. He reached in his pocket and pulled out a knife and quickly sliced the insulation from the cable.

"Copper," he said in heavily accented English. "Do you have more?"

"Ja," I said.

"Wie viel?" he said, as he bent over and picked up the reel.

"Blackie, come here a sec," Crooner shouted.

"Moment mal, bitte," I said and went back to the truck.

"Blackie, you know we're two lucky bastards," Crooner said. "These guys will pay to take this stuff off our hands. What do you think?"

"You're singing my tune, Crooner. I'm with you," I said.

Crooner jumped down from the truck, pursed his lips and whistled, a sharp, piercing sound that got the attention of the German workers. He waved his arms, motioning for them to come to the truck. Slowly, the curious ones, made their way to the truck, gathering near the back.

Moving methodically, Crooner pulled a Swiss Army knife from his pocket and sliced away the insulation on one of the reels.

"Copper, my friends," he said. "This is real, guaranteed, prime U.S. Army copper, and we are willing to let go of it for a fair price."

While I leaned against the end of the truck, I watched as Crooner, who had become fairly fluent in German after a few months in Berlin, negotiated with the Germans. Within minutes, the truck was empty, and Crooner was counting the proceeds. When he finished, we had made more than $100 in both German and U.S. currencies, as well as two liters of vodka and eight bottles of beer.

"Let's take our time," Crooner said. "The word will get out and maybe we can score even better with the next load."

I agreed, and we sat in the cab, drinking the warm beer and chasing it with vodka.

"Jesus, I can't believe the Old Man didn't think of this himself," Crooner said, his words slurring slightly.

"He's a tread. He's not allowed to think for himself," I said and giggled. I knew it was a giggle, not a laugh, but suddenly I was lightheaded.

As we loaded the final 76 reels, Crooner and I stumbled frequently as the mixture of vodka and beer began to take its effect. Whenever one of us stumbled, we both would burst into laughter.

At the dump, the negotiations with the German workers went smoothly, and when the last reel was pulled off the truck, Crooner and I had another $83 in U.S. and German currency, another liter of vodka, four more beers and one Cuban cigar that had been purchased in a tobacco shop in

the British sector.

"It's not coming out even, Blackie," Crooner said as he counted the currency.

"Shit, it's only three bucks. You take that, and I'll take the cigar. Okay?"

While I bit the end off the cigar and lit it, Crooner shoved the extra three dollars into his pocket, and then we sat on the ground beside the truck and drank the beer and vodka.

I looked at my wrist, then remembered I had forgotten to put on my watch when I got up.

"What time is?"

Crooner looked at his watch and laughed before starting to sing, "It's a quarter to three, and no one's in the place ..."

"We gotta go," I said. I stood, nearly losing my balance and bumping into Crooner who staggered when he stood.

Crooner and I were lightheaded and giddy when I drove up to the guardshack. I slammed on the brakes, throwing a shower of gravel when the truck stopped with the front bumper nudging the gate. I saw Elephant Ass look out of the window and glare at us. Then he picked up the phone.

"Crooner, I think we might be in some trouble," I said. "Elephant Ass probably called Roadrunner."

"What for?"

"He probably thinks I'm drunk because I nearly ran into the gate."

"That's no reason, you always drive like you're drunk. Besides you've hit the gate, the guardshack and the Colonel's car at one time or another."

"Shit, that sorry bastard did make a call. Here comes the Old Man and Roadrunner," I said, and both of us tried to sit up straight while Captain Weldon and Roadrunner walked toward the guardshack.

"Get out of the truck," Elephant Ass said as he waddled around from the back of the truck. I dropped down out of the cab. I heard the door slam on the other side as Crooner jumped out.

"Your ass has had it this time, jerkoff," Elephant Ass said with a snarl.

He's still pissed about the Khrushchev picture, I thought.

"Fuck off, Elephant Ass," I said.

Elephant Ass didn't answer, just snapped to attention.

"What's going on here?"

I stood straight, but weaved slightly, when Captain Weldon stood in front of me.

"Nothing, sir. I just came a little close to the gate, and the corporal took exception," I said.

"Goddammit, son, you're drunk," Captain Weldon said.

"Well, not exactly. I'm just a little lightheaded, sir. I think it's the sun and working in the heat."

"Oh, bullshit, you're shitfaced and you know it," he said. "How the hell did this happen?"

"Well, sir, the Germans down at the dump offered to buy the cable, but some of them only had beer and vodka. So we didn't want to carry all the stuff around, so we decided to drink some of it."

"Is that all you got?"

"Not quite, sir," Crooner said. "We got about 90 bucks apiece in cash."

He shook his head, and I thought I saw a flicker of a smile.

"Are we going to arrest them?" Elephant Ass asked.

"No, no. Not this time," Captain Weldon said. "But you damn sure can't drive the truck back to the barracks. Sergeant, get someone out here to drive these two back to the barracks."

"Sir?" Roadrunner said.

"Just get someone to take these two drunks back to the barracks," Captain Weldon said. "You two are lucky I'm in a good mood because that cable's gone. But don't pull anything like this again or I've have your balls, you understand me?"

"Yes, sir," Crooner and I said in unison.

As Shakey drove us back to the barracks, Crooner softly sang Sinatra tunes and I puffed contentedly on the Cuban cigar. Shakey let us out at the mess hall, but neither Crooner nor I wanted anything to eat. We went inside the barracks at the end farthest from the first sergeant's office and made our way to the third floor.

"What's on your schedule tonight, Blackie?" Crooner said as we reached my room.

"Nothing. I'll probably hang out at the El Oso."

"Why don't you come along with me. I'm singing with the guys at the Blue Note. As drunk as I am, it ought to be fun or a goddam disaster."

We cleaned up and were walking out the front gate when

the first trick bus roared by. I saw Roadrunner sitting near the driver. He glared at me as I waved.

The night was memorable for Crooner. He ran through most of the old Sinatra standards without missing a note, switched to classic rock and finished up the night by doing some country numbers.

"Man, I was on tonight. I was really cooking," he said while we helped the band pack the equipment.

"I've never heard you do so many different things so damn good."

"Yeah, but I sure as hell don't want to do it that way again."

Rapid Roger and John Wayne

36 Things were beginning to change on C Trick during my last summer in Berlin. As the war in Vietnam expanded, so did the military in other parts of the world. The 78th, which had been a small unit of about 300 men when I arrived in Berlin, had swollen to nearly 1,500 in a little over two years and had gone through two name changes. From the 78th Special Operations Unit, it had grown into the 54th Special Operations Command, then it ballooned into the ASA Field Station-Berlin.

However, the real change wasn't in the name, it was in the people who made up the unit. As the unit grew, the type of soldier changed. There were more and more good soldiers, those guys who never questioned an order, who always had crisply starched uniforms and spitshined boots, and who actually seemed to take the military life seriously. These soldiers most certainly wouldn't wear a field jacket with the wrong name on it, or steal a general's stars, or piss on a group of NCOs or write phony memos. These guys were horrified by the tales of how C Trick had been.

At the same time, the guys whose distaste for the military and sense of rebellion had made the 78th and C Trick special, were nearing the end of their enlistments and were beginning to go home.

One by one, they started leaving. At first, it would be one or two guys at a time. But like an avalanche, it seemed to pick up speed and people started leaving in bunches, five and six at a time.

It seemed that I was being Abandoned, because all of the people that I was closest to, the old 78th crowd, were "dying," and I felt like I was the only survivor.

No one actually died, but it started when Big Ed left.

"Where's Big Ed?" Rock Weed said to Fang.

"He died."

"Died? What of?" Rock Weed said, dumbfounded. "He wasn't sick or anything, was he? Was it an accident or something?"

"No, dumbass." Fang laughed. "He's getting out. He's gone back to the States. He died — like he don't live here anymore."

Most of the time when it was your time to die, your friends would take you out on the town for your last night in Berlin. It was pretty much like an Irish wake, only the corpse was still very much alive and enjoying himself.

But Grumpy John, Fang, Rapid Roger, Chief, and Buffalo Head were all due to rotate back to the States on the same day, so they changed things a bit. They decided to go out with a real flair. They decided they would pool their money and throw a party to end all parties.

In the Grunewald, a sprawling forest in western Berlin, was a small lake, Teufelsee. Nearby was the road that the trick buses took on the way to the Hill, so the five decided to have a never-ending lake party. It was late spring, a pleasant time in Berlin. The days were warm enough that you could enjoy a swim in the lake, but the nights were still cool enough for a light jacket or a sweater.

The five short-timers borrowed Tiny's VW van and roared off to the PX commissary, where they bought twenty cases of Beck's beer in returnable bottles. When the beer was finished, they'd gather up the empties, return them for the deposit and use the money to buy more cases of beer. This way, they could repeat the process for as long as anyone wanted to keep on partying at the lake.

It was a party that took on a life of its own.

At the start, there were the five short-timers and most of C Trick, which was on break. They gathered around wash tubs, "borrowed" from the company, and ice chests, drinking Beck's and playing in the water. The carousing coming from the clearing by the lake aroused the curiosity of Berliners, who came over to see what was happening. Several of these on-lookers stayed to join in the festivities.

The party had slowed by late afternoon, as the Berliners went home and many of the C Trickers headed back to the barracks to clean up and go to the mess hall.

"The party's not breaking up, is it?" Grumpy John said. "Hell, look at all the beer we still got."

"Naw, Grumpy, the party lives!" Fang said. He had spent a good portion of his afternoon demonstrating his famous moon technique and now was sitting on a blanket amid a pile of empty beer bottles. "Don't worry, the trick bus just went by a couple of minutes ago. D Trick knows about the party. They'll be out here tonight."

He reached into an ice chest and pulled out a Beck's, and walked over to the edge of the lake to stand with the other four short-timers. They were standing by the water, each wrapped up in his own thoughts, when suddenly a horn blared.

They whirled around and saw the trick bus roaring down the narrow road that led from the main roadway through the forest to the lake. The bus slid to a stop, throwing gravel in all directions. The door flew open, and nearly 30 D Trickers, still in their fatigues, hurried off the bus and rushed to grab a cold beer.

"Leave some for me. I'll be back as soon as I get rid of this goddam bus," Clifford Jefferson said. After spending most of his first week with the 78th on KP, Jefferson rushed to the Berlin Brigade Transportation detachment to get his bus license and avoid finding his name on the KP roster again.

"Man, I had to get that bus license. Motherfucking Phantom would keep me on KP the whole time I'm here. Hell, driving the bus for a week at a time every three or four months is no big deal. Shit, I'd rather drive a bus every day of the week that spend one day on KP," Jefferson said.

"How'd Phantom take it? You know, not having you to take up that permanent slot on the KP roster?" Fang said.

"I don't know and I don't care. Let him stick some other poor bastard on it. I've had enough KP to last a lifetime. Hell, I wasn't sent here to stand in water and scrub greasy trays every goddam day."

The party continued through the night, with revelers sacking out on blankets under the trees or in cars and VW vans. The drowsy group was awakened the next morning by the blaring of the trick bus horns as another shift headed up the Hill. A few minutes later, a bunch of A Trickers, who had been on mids, piled off the trick bus to join the party and spend most of the day, still in their fatigues, splashing around in the lake and drinking beer.

The routine continued for three days. A couple of Berlin police officers, who had been keeping a wary eye on the partying and wondering if they were going to have to call the military police, decided to join in the festivities.

After a few beers, the two officers, ties undone and hats askew, started showing how to do wheelies in their VW patrol car, much to the delight of the appreciative Americans.

The party was a major success, with no fighting or even much bickering. People came and went, and empty bottles were gathered up and returned to the commissary for the deposit. More beer was purchased and brought out to the lake, where the whole process began again.

The only sour note was sounded on the party's final night.

Rapid Roger, with a beer in hand, tripped as he was running toward the lake. When he fell, the bottle smashed and he received a long, shallow gash on his forearm. Standing up, he looked at his arm and saw the blood.

"Oh, shit! Ro-Jay's going to pass out," Grumpy John said.

"That's just a scratch, for Christ's sake," Fang said. "Hell, it's already about stopped bleeding."

"The hell it has, I'm bleeding to death," Rapid Roger said.

"Ro-jay, you say that when you nick yourself shaving. Look at it, for God's sake. It's barely bleeding," Fang said. "Shakey, take a look at this. Is Ro-jay bleeding to death or not?"

"Fuck him, it'll just mean more beer for us if he does," Shakey said drunkenly.

"You're a miserable little shit, Shakey. I'm bleeding to death and all you think about is who gets more beer," Rapid Roger said. He looked at his arm, which really had stopped bleeding, and started swaying. He sat down quickly.

"Oh, God! I'm going to die. I'm going to get gangrene and lose my arm. I'd rather die than lose my arm."

"Fuck you, Ro-jay," I said. "You never were going to pitch for the Dodgers anyway. All you got is a little scratch."

"Yeah, Blackie, but what if his arm does get infected or something?" Fang said.

"Do what John Wayne does when he gets shot."

"What do you mean, Blackie?" Rapid Roger asked.

"Don't you ever watch the movies, asshole? Every time John Wayne gets shot in one of his movies, he pours whiskey on it to stop infection."

"We don't have any whiskey," Fang said.

"I know that. But we got lots of beer," I said.

"Sure, Blackie, but does it work with beer?" Fang said.

"Why not? Beer, whiskey. What the hell, they both got alcohol. Ro-jay, give me your arm," I said.

Rapid Roger extended his arm, and I poured the remaining contents of my beer bottle over the gashed arm.

"Okay, you're done, Ro-jay. John Wayne couldn't have done better himself, if I do say so," I said proudly.

"No, he couldn't. Thanks, Blackie, you're a real John Wayne," Rapid Roger said as he wrapped his arm with a strip of torn T-shirt.

The party continued through its final night. The next morning, when the rays of the sun filtered through the trees and glistened on the lake's surface, the few remaining revelers were awakened by Rapid Roger's screams.

"Omigod! Omigod! My arm's falling off! My arm's falling off!"

"What the shit?" Buffalo Head said as he jumped up, slamming his head against the top of the VW van. He jumped out of the van and rushed across the clearing, arriving at Rapid Roger's sleeping bag at the same time as Grumpy John, Fang and I.

"Ro-jay! Ro-jay! What's the matter?" Buffalo Head said.

"My arm! My arm!"

"What's wrong with it?" Buffalo Head said.

"My God, what is wrong with it?" I said as Rapid Roger pushed back the cover of his sleeping bag to expose his grotesquely swollen, purplish arm.

"Jesus Christ! What the hell's wrong with that arm. It looks like a goddam purple bockwurst," Grumpy John said. "Shit, it was just a little scratch last night. What the fuck's happened?"

"Omigod, it hurts. Omigod, I'm going to lose my arm! I got gangrene," Rapid Roger said.

"Shut the hell up, Ro-jay," Buffalo Head said. "Let me look at it."

Rapid Roger moaned while Buffalo Head held the arm, turning it first this way and then that way.

"Well, it's infected, that's one thing for sure," he said. "Look at that, there's even some puss where your arm was cut. You've got a Class-A infection. Why the hell didn't you ask me for the first aid kit in my van?"

"I didn't know you had a first aid kit, and besides, Blackie helped take care of it."

"What exactly did Blackie do?" Buffalo Head said quietly.

"Well, it seems that he told Ro-jay that when John Wayne got shot in the movies, he always poured whiskey in the wound to keep it from getting infected," Fang said.

Buffalo Head looked at me.

"You poured whiskey on that arm?" Buffalo Head said.

"Not exactly," I said.

"Exactly what is not exactly? What'd you pour on it?" he said.

"Beer."

"Beer! Jesus Christ, don't any of you shitheads know that beer only makes it worse. Jesus H. Christ, what a bunch of assholes. You didn't have whiskey so you used beer instead. Hell, why didn't you piss on his arm if you didn't have any whiskey?" Buffalo Head said.

"I wasn't going to let anyone piss on my arm," Rapid Roger said.

"Jesus Christ, what a dipshit," Buffalo Head said in exasperation. "Well, get your ass in gear, Ro-jay. I guess someone's got to get his head out of his ass around here. I'll get you to the infirmary and get that thing taken care of."

"Well, Blackie said it worked for John Wayne," Rapid Roger said as he shuffled toward Buffalo Head's van.

"John fucking Wayne, my ass. God, what an asshole," Buffalo Head said. He and the sheepish Rapid Roger got in the VW van and Buffalo Head hit the ignition, threw it in gear, and began to turn the van around. He stopped, leaned out of the window and shouted at the small group of us standing near the ice chests. "You guys get this area policed up while I take care of Ro-jay. I'll see you at the Scum later."

"Buff seemed a bit pissed," I said to Grumpy John as we picked up empty beer bottles and put them in the empty cardboard cartons.

"Yeah, well, Ro-jay's a jerkoff who could piss off the pope."

"Wonder what's going to happen at the infirmary?" I said.

"Hell, he'll probably lose his arm and get a goddam Purple Heart or something," Grumpy John muttered.

Rapid Roger didn't get his Purple Heart and he didn't lose his arm. What he did get, however, was a stay in the brigade hospital while the doctors pumped him full of antibiotics to kill the infection and inserted a tube in his arm to drain off the puss.

The stay in the hospital didn't bother him much because Rapid Roger didn't mind just lying in bed all day, dozing and having people bring him his meals. What did bother him, however, was what happened while he was in the hospital — the orders for his rotation were canceled and he was extended until his arm healed.

Four days after the big party ended, Grumpy John, Fang, Buffalo Head and Chief walked across the tarmac at Tegel Airport and boarded the Pan Am jetliner that took them back to the States and their discharges. While the plane carrying his four fellow short-timers roared down the runway, a morose Rapid Roger was lying in the hospital bed looking at his arm, which was slowly returning to its normal size.

Rapid Roger, who could now be called Surly Roger, was released from the hospital two days later — the same day that Grumpy John, Fang, Buffalo Head and Chief were being returned to civilian life. He had to wait for the Army to cut new orders to let him rotate back to the States.

While Rapid Roger waited for the new orders, the Phantom, who thought a busy soldier would always be a happy soldier, found numerous little chores to keep his unhappy soldier busy. Rapid Roger was busy, but he certainly wasn't happy — especially when he shuffled back to his room at the end of a day spent picking up cigarette butts or painting rocks to find a picture of John Wayne taped neatly to his door.

His orders came through, and Shakey and I drove Rapid Roger on a final trip through the streets of Berlin to Tegel — three weeks late — for his flight back to the States.

As the plane carrying him home was winging its way across northern Germany toward Amsterdam, where it would make its last stop before the flight across the Atlantic, Shakey and I were heading back toward Lichterfelde and Andrews Barracks — and its dwindling numbers of old-timers, as we now called those of us who had been around when the unit was still the 78th.

"Ro-jay wasn't exactly the happiest person I've ever seen," I said.

"No, and he's going to be even less happy when he opens his duffel bag," Shakey said with a grin.

"Okay, what'd you do? What'd you put in his duffel bag?" I said.

"Let's just say that when he opens it, the first thing he'll see will be John Wayne."

Short-timer

37

Fang once said being a short-timer is a state of mind. That may be so, and for most of the people on C Trick, it was. We became short-timers and had the short-timer attitude when we were still counting the years and months, not the days, until getting out of the Army.

On C Trick, you became an official short-timer when you had 69days left until boarding the plane that would take you back to Fort Hamilton, New York, and your return to civilian life. I don't know who decided 69 was the magic number for achieving short-timer status, but I do know there was a sexual connotation in the selection.

I went short officially a few days after Rapid Roger, packing his John Wayne poster, flew back to the States. Being short gives you a certain status in the unit. For one thing, the treads know you're leaving their Army, so they stop leaning on you, but the rest of the world isn't quite so impressed with your status. That's why I got a scare shortly after I went short.

In Czechoslovakia, young people and some enlightened politicians, like the new Communist Party boss, Alexander Dubcek, came together in the spring of 1968 to open up the society, to make the system more democratic. The movement even became known as the Prague Spring.

But just like the seasons, the Prague Spring didn't last because in 1968 the Soviet Union was still intact and powerful. The Soviet leadership, as well as the puppet regimes in East Germany, Hungary and Poland, were afraid that the democracy movement in neighboring Czechoslovakia might give their citizens some unwelcome ideas. In August, just a few short months after democracy bloomed in the Prague Spring, troops from the Soviet Union, East Germany, Hungary and Poland poured across the Czech borders, crushing the democratic movement. Dubcek was kicked out of the Communist party and put to work for the forestry administration.

On the Hill, we knew something was up. Suddenly there was a surge in coded communications between Moscow and its Warsaw Pact allies in East Berlin, Budapest, and Warsaw. In early August, there was absolute silence. There was no military communication, just an eerie silence, like the calm in the summer just before the first clap of thunder.

The Soviets and their allies were moving in place and then they poured across the borders into Czechoslovakia and there was a downpour of military communication.

In Berlin, the brass of the new ASA Field Station canceled all leaves and passes and froze the tricks. When the tricks were frozen, it meant three tricks that were working stayed on their shifts with no days off until the freeze was lifted. If your trick was on mids, it stayed on mids indefinitely, rather than rotating to days. The members of the trick on break were divided among the other three and went back to work.

When the invasion started and the tricks were frozen, I had about sixty days left before rotating back to the States. Having C Trick frozen on days didn't bother me, but I was scared the Army would exercise its option and extend my enlistment. This extension, which had happened to a couple of guys during the Middle East war of 1967, usually was for sixty days, which would mean I wouldn't be going back to the States until January.

Rock Weed was philosophical, but then he could afford to be. He wasn't going to be getting out until January anyway.

"Look at this way, Blackie. If you're extended, you'll still get your three squares and the pleasure of our company. Why would you want to go back to the States in October anyway? Hell, that was just a goal. Don't you ever look at your records? You know, where it gives the ETA? That means 'estimated time of arrival.' The Army's just estimating you might get back to the States in October. Hell, it's like calling in a plumber, he only 'estimates' what it's going to cost, then he slams you with a big bill. It don't matter what the ETA is, the Army still owns your ass," he said.

"Fuck you," I said. "I signed up for four years — not four years, two months. They expect me to stay in for the full four years, so I expect them to let me out after four full."

When I had arrived in Berlin nearly three years earlier, being a short-timer carried a prestige that was missing by the time I had gone short. Back then, the 78th was a small unit, with less than 300 officers, NCOs and EMs. We had a camaraderie, a rebellious, don't-give-a-shit attitude that was lacking now that the unit had swelled to more than 1,000.

If the Army had planned to put all of its military misfits, rebels, malcontents and cynics in one unit, it couldn't have done nearly so well as it did randomly with the old 78th. With the exception of the officers and the top NCOs, the unit was made up of people for whom the military, its traditions and its rules were something to be challenged unceasingly, and authority was to be questioned without fail.

But as the months went by, the old guys began going back to the States and the unit began to expand rapidly. The new arrivals were less likely to question orders. They also were more ambitious, more willing to play the game to get promotions.

As the old guys — Grumpy John, Doc, Big Clyde, Buffalo Head, Chief, Shakey and Fang — rotated back to the States, I began to feel isolated, like an anachronism. Hairy Ranger, Prince and Fat Kenny were still around, but they had been shifted to other tricks and we only saw each other in passing.

I hated the Army and I was now surrounded by people who enjoyed military life — and even talked about making it a career. They were fresh-faced, enthusiastic, and their uniforms were always crisply starched and sharply creased. They all looked like they just stepped out of recruitment posters. With my seldom-starched, faded, and rumpled fatigues, my lackadaisical attitude, and general air of resentment about the military, I felt — at 22 — like a grizzled veteran, the old bull who wandered alone across a prairie where, just a few years earlier, millions of bison had roamed.

I really didn't like most of the weeds and what had happened to the unit. I still said I was in the 78th, two years and two name changes after the 78th had disappeared. So, I spent most of my off-duty hours to myself, wandering around Berlin, going to the museums, haunting the jazz clubs, and always drinking as much beer as possible. I didn't have much to do with the weeds because I didn't have that much in common with them. They seemed to think — an idea encouraged by the treads — that I would be a bad influence on them, possibly even hurting their chances at promotions.

The biggest difference, I guess, was how the weeds all seemed to enjoy following the rules. That difference between the attitude of the old 78th toward rules and regulations really became evident about a month before I was due to rotate.

There had been some student disturbances and anti-war protests going on, so the brass decided we should keep a low profile for a few days. All passes were canceled and we were restricted to the barracks and where we worked. I decided I wanted to see what was going on — and drop in on a few pubs while I was at it. To be safe from the MPs, I planned to go to the British sector, where the Brits didn't care one way or the other what I did. All I had to do was get out of the barracks compound and grab a bus to the British sector and everything would be fine.

For as long as I had been in Berlin, there was a way to get out of the compound without having to get by the gate guards or try to climb over the fence, maneuvering your way through the strands of barbed wire at the top. Several years before, Big Clyde had managed to lift a set of bolt cutters from a tool shed on the Hill.

One rainy night, Big Clyde slipped the bolt cutters under his raincoat and found a section of the fence next to the street and out of the sight of anyone looking out the first sergeant's office window. Next to a pole, he cut down the side of the fence. Then he cut about three feet across, top and bottom. When he was through, he had made a gate that was big enough for a large man, like Big Clyde, to slide through. All he had to do was push the fencing back into place and no one could see that it had been disturbed.

Big Clyde kept quiet about what he had done, telling only a few trusted friends. The gate to freedom, which remained open long after Big Clyde rotated back to the States, was a closely guarded secret, shared only by the more rebellious members of C Trick.

While my weed roommate was lounging on his bunk, I gathered up my soap, towel, and shaving gear and walked down to the shower room. After showering and shaving, I went back to my room and started going through my clothes until I found a shirt and pair of pants I had bought at the British PX. I hoped the British look would give me an edge if I should be spotted by any U.S. MPs.

While I was changing clothes and collecting my money, including dumping a jar of pennies on the bunk and going through the coins to pick out any German coins that might have gotten in there by mistake, my weed roommate, an earnest-looking Iowan named Douglas, peered over the top of his copy of Stars & Stripes.

Douglas had joined the Army and volunteered for the language school in hopes he would be sent to Monterey to study Vietnamese. He was terribly disappointed when the Army decided he should go to Fort Devens and become a diddy-bopper. Not only did he miss what he thought was a wonderful opportunity to serve his country by going into the Southeast Asian jungle to interrogate Viet Cong prisoners, he missed Vietnam by about 10,000 miles, winding up in Berlin. Desperate to prove his prowess as a soldier, and to impress his Marine veteran father, he had applied for helicopter school, which he saw as his ticket to Vietnam and battlefield glory.

"Where you going, Blackie? PX?" Douglas asked.

"Naw, I'm going to go have a couple of beers," I said.

"At the EM Club?"

"No, no. I'm going to a place I know in the Brit sector, off Kantstrasse," I said.

"But we're restricted to barracks. You're not supposed to leave the barracks."

"So?" I said.

"So, you'll be violating an order of the commandant," Douglas said.

"Fuck him if he can't take a joke. You want to go?"

"Absolutely not. We've been restricted to barracks and I'm going to stay right here where I'm supposed to be, and where you should be," Douglas said.

"Stay, for Christ's sake, but I'm out of here," I said and stomped out of the room, making sure to give the door a good slam behind me.

What I didn't know was that Douglas was curious about how I planned to get past the MP guards who were pacing back and forth behind the huge locked iron gates.

His curiosity must have been really aroused when I didn't head toward the front gate and attempt to bluff my way past the guards. Instead, I went out the back of the old barracks building and darted across the narrow lawn on the side. When I reached the fence, I loosened the clips that Big Clyde had fashioned several years before to hold the fencing onto the post, pushed the gate open, crawled out, and reattached it.

After spending a peaceful night wandering around the British sector, where I found no violent demonstrations or confrontations between the students and the Berlin police, I went back into the barracks through Big Clyde's gate. When I got back to my room, I was cheered to see that Douglas was sleeping soundly, so I read a couple of articles in Der Spiegel, a German news magazine, before dozing off.

I slept contentedly that night, and awoke a few minutes before Douglas' alarm clock sounded. I hated his alarm clock, it was a double-bell affair that didn't just wake you, it blasted you out of sleep.

While we getting ready for work, Douglas seemed to be in a hurry.

"You sure are in a hurry to get to the Hill and start listening to all that diddy-bobbing, Dougie," I said.

"I've got to see the first sergeant before the trick bus leaves," he said as he lifted first one foot, then the other on to the top of his foot locker and gave the already-high gloss a final buffing.

"Yeah, well, if you're bucking for a promotion, it doesn't hurt to kiss a little ass now and then, Dougie," I said.

"What?"

"Hey, it was just a suggestion. You don't have to kiss ass if you don't want to."

Glaring at me, Douglas checked himself over one more time to make sure that every button was buttoned and every speck of lint was gone from his sharply creased fatigues, then he darted out of the room.

Later at the Hill, I decided it was time for a coffee break. I turned over my headsets to Casteel and walked through the Pit and down the long hallway to the break room. I was pouring myself a cup of coffee when Rock Weed peered around the corner.

"Did you hear about the fence?" he said.

"What fence?" I said.

"The fence, clown. The fence behind the barracks."

"Where our gate is?"

"Yeah, that one."

"Well, what about it?"

"Your asshole roommate told the first shirt there's a big goddam hole in it and maintenance's already patched it up. We can't use it anymore," he said.

"Goddammit! That miserable, goddam weed shithead!" I said. "I ought to go kick his motherfucking ass up around his ears. What the hell did he think he was doing? Jesus Christ, what a worthless goddam toad."

"I know one thing. If you want go kick his goddam ass, you're going to have to take a number. He's not too damn popular around here anymore. Even the people who didn't know about the fence are pissed off at him for being such as goddam suckass," Rock Weed said, shaking his head.

"Christ, Rock, I'm short. The fence is no big deal to me, but there's a bunch of you that still could have used it," I said.

"Don't worry. I've got a set of bolt cutters. If you want to help me tonight, I'll make us a new gate in the fence. All we have to do is move down a couple of sections. Hell, the first shirt won't look anywhere else," he said.

"Yeah, I'll give you a hand," I said, taking a sip on the

hot, steaming coffee. "We can do it after dark. But before we cut the fence, I'm going to make life miserable for little Dougie."

When I got back to the barracks, I stormed into our room, raging at Douglas.

"You miserable, sniveling little shit. You ass-licking, cocksucking weed!" I yelled as I flung the door open, causing it to crash against the wall. "You're a real piece of shit, Dougie. I can't believe you're such a suckass that you got the fence fixed. You just had to go to the first shirt, didn't you? You just couldn't leave well enough alone, you miserable fuckwad!"

Douglas was taken aback by my tirade. He didn't say anything, just looked helplessly toward the door, where other barracks residents were gathered.

Halopowski, showing more and more spunk the longer he was away from his wife, grabbed my arm. "What the hell's the matter with you, Blackie? What the hell's going on?"

"That miserable piece of shit weed roommate of mine told the first shirt about the fence. It's been fixed," I said.

"Why you shithead," Halopowski said, glaring at Douglas. "I hope Blackie does kick your ass."

"I know one thing, asshole, you're not staying in this room," I said. I grabbed the end of his bunk, dragged it out of the room, and left it in the hallway. Then I stomped over to his wall lockers and started grabbing his clothes, which I took to the door and tossed into the hall.

"What the hell are you doing?" Douglas said.

"Moving your miserable ass out of my room, weed," I said. "Now you can do it your way or you can let me do it, but I'm going to the EM club and I want you the hell out of here by the time I get back."

"I can't just move into another room. I was assigned to this one."

"You're unassigned. Get your ass out," I said as I stomped out of the room.

Other George, who had been leaning against the hallway wall and watching the show with a look of amusement, fell into step beside me.

"Damn fine show, Blackie," he said. "I think you had Dougie convinced you were going to kill him."

"It was pretty good, wasn't it?" I said and chuckled. "I do wonder where Dougie's going to end up?"

"Probably with Fat Kenny. The way he snores, there's always an empty bunk in his room."

Other George was right. While I was gone, Douglas went to the trick sergeant and begged for another room assignment. He was assigned to the only room that had an empty bunk — Fat Kenny's.

A few days after Douglas got the fence fixed, the brass lifted the restriction, allowing everyone to come and go as usual. Even though we didn't need to, Rock Weed and I took the bolt cutters and, finding another location, made another gate in the fence.

One good thing about the fence episode was getting rid of the weed roommate and having the room all to myself for the final month I had in Berlin. I didn't have to worry about waking anyone up when I came in after my nocturnal wanderings around the city. I could lie in bed and read as long as I wanted and not wonder if my light was keeping a roommate awake. It was a wonderfully peaceful conclusion to my 33 months in Berlin.

On my last day in Berlin, I was getting ready to go downstairs and catch the shuttle bus to Tempelhof for my flight. Everything was in order. I had all my paperwork, all my gear had been turned in, the linen and blankets had been returned to the supply room, books and records had been crated up and shipped back to Arkansas, my duffel bag was packed.

I was looking around one last time when Hairy Ranger, Prince, and Fat Kenny came in.

"Let's go, Blackie, we're taking you to catch the plane," Hairy Ranger said cheerfully.

"Yeah, we're the official farewell committee," Fat Kenny said.

I looked at all the familiar sights as we roared through the streets of Berlin in Prince's battered old VW van. It was like seeing an old friend for the last time and I hated to leave. As much as I hated the Army and wanted to return to civilian life, I hated leaving Berlin, a city where I had learned so much about the world and where I had been able to enjoy life — even the seamiest parts of life — to the fullest.

We waited awkwardly at the airport. Although we swore we would keep in touch, we knew that it was unlikely, and I was relieved when my flight was announced. I shook hands with Hairy Ranger, Prince and Fat Kenny, said my last fare-wells, and headed out across the tarmac to the plane.

The flight back to New York was uneventful. I slept most of the way.

When the plane landed at JFK International, I was met by a surly Spec Four, who waited impatiently until my duffel bag finally arrived at the baggage claim carousel.

"The bus's out this way," he said, heading toward an exit.

"Just a sec. I want to get a magazine," I said, pointing to the newsstand off to the side of the terminal.

"Yeah, yeah. Hurry up, I ain't got all night."

I walked over to the newsstand. My duffel bag was hanging from one shoulder; my 35-mm Agfa camera was hanging from the other shoulder. I reached up and got a copy of *TIME*. Fumbling for my wallet, I slid the camera off my shoulder and put it down on top of a stack of newspapers. I took about three steps to my left, paid for the magazine and turned around to pick up my camera.

It was gone.

Welcome back to the States.

Epilogue

For nearly 30 years, West Berliners spraypainted the slogan *"Die Mauer muß weg!"* ("The Wall must go!") on their side of the concrete block wall that slashed from north to south through the heart of the city, splitting it and dividing families. On November 9, 1989, after widespread demonstrations erupted in Leipzig and the flight of East Germans to Hungary, the East German rulers relented and the winds of change blew holes in the Wall.

For the people of both sides of Berlin, the Wall was the focal point of their lives since the first sections of the Wall were erected in August 1961.

None of the principals, both East and West, involved in the erection of the Berlin Wall remain. Both President John F. Kennedy, who stirred the world in June 1963 with his declaration that as a free man "ich bin ein Berliner," and Soviet leader Nikita Krushchev are dead, as are West German Chancellor Konrad Adenauer and East German leader Walter Ulbricht.

Presidents and prime ministers came and went, but the Wall remained.

For those of us who have lived in Berlin, the Wall was always there, often unseen but never forgotten. Not only did that concrete barrier trap 1.5 million East Berliners inside the city, it also held 2.5 million people hostage in West Berlin.

We could not escape it. It was always there, creating a sense of claustrophobia. Get in a car and drive just a few kilometers, and you would have to stop because of the Wall. Get on the subway under the city's streets and you would notice the U-bahn did not stop at Friedrichstrasse — that was in East Berlin and the exit was blocked.

Teufelsberg offered a beautiful panorama of the city lights, both in West Berlin and East Berlin. But nearly every night, the beauty of the city was marred by the flashes of machine-gun tracer bullets. Rabbits or other small animals would venture into the no-man's land behind the Wall, setting off alarms and triggering the machine-gun fire.

For one who was used to being able to come and go freely, the knowledge that I was behind a concrete barrier that I could not go through whenever I wanted made the huge city seem smaller and smaller with each passing month.

That sense of claustrophobia remained with me after leaving Berlin. I became a gypsy journalist, shifting jobs and moving on when the town and job became too confining. That may be why I fell in love with the vastness of West Texas and open skies of New Mexico, and why I felt the sense of joy that surged through Berliners when the Wall was opened on November 9, 1989, and people could move freely around the city, making Berlin truly *"eine Reise wert."*

Appendix A: U.S. Army Security Agency in Berlin

(This summary of the U.S. Army Security Agency's presence in Berlin was compiled by Jeff Gammon, a German linguist assigned to C Trick between April 1967 and April 1970.)

The U.S. Army Security Agency began conducting operations in Berlin as early as 1951. Detachments would be moved into Berlin on a temporary, or TDY, basis to conduct operations out of a variety of makeshift sites within the city.

January 1951: USASFS 8606 (Herzo Base) relocated to Berlin to carry operations, staying in the city until June when it was returned to its home base in Herzogenaurach, West Germany.

April 1952: Detachment E, also from Herzo Base deployed to Berlin, but it had a different mission than Detachment F. In June, its status was changed when Berlin became a permanent duty station. The detachment moved from vans and tents into permanent housing. In 1953, Detachment E was designated Detachment F.

July 1, 1953: Detachment C deployed from Herzo Base to Berlin to join Detachment E. In 1954, the number of ASA personnel in the city increased when Detachment B, Headquarters, USASA Europe arrived. To streamline administrative control and logistics, Detachment B assumed control of the two Herzo Base detachments.

Also in 1954, tactical ASA units began operating in Berlin. Detachment A, 302nd Communications Reconnaissance Battalion arrived to conduct tactical operations in and around the city. The following year, two small ASA teams, Team 6 and Team 620J1, arrived requiring the expansion of the Headquarters ASA Europe detachment to a provisional company.

October 1957: Provisional company redesignated 280th ASA Company. Separate from this activity, the 9539th Technical Service Unit, organized in 1954 at Fort Myers, Virginia, was redeployed to Berlin soon after activation and was subordinate to the Chief Signal Officer, U.S. Army.

November 1955: The 9539th Technical Service Unit was reassigned to the Commander, ASA and redesignated 22nd ASA Detachment. In 1957, the detachment again was redesignated as the 260th ASA Detachment.

Command, control and support of all these companies, detachments and teams required further changes. Detachment B (ASA Europe), Detachment C (Herzo Base), Detachment F (Herzo Base) and Detachment A (302nd Battalion) were discontinued. Detachment A's personnel were redeployed to their battalion in West Germany while the remaining personnel were consolidated within the 260th ASA Detachment.

October 15, 1957: The 260th ASA Detachment redesignated as 280th ASA Company. The company had an assigned strength of seven officers, two warrant officers, and 136 enlisted men. Company headquarters were located at Andrews Barracks, occupying space formerly occupied by Detachment B and the 260th ASA Detachment.

June 15, 1961: The 280th ASA Company redesignated as 78th ASA Special Operations Unit. Operations in the city also began to be conducted at Teufelsberg. In July, the 78th ASA first used Teufelsberg to monitor East German and Soviet communications from mobile vans. By November 1963, a semi-permanent structure was in place to house those operations.

June 1966: Additional structural changes were implemented when the 78th ASA SOU was redesignated the 54th USASA Special Operations Command. The 54th ASA SOC was restructured with a Headquarters & Headquarters Company, and Companies A and B.

December 15, 1967: The 54th ASA SOC was redesignated USASA Field Station Berlin.

April 1969-September 1972: The site at Teufelsberg underwent additional renovation and construction, making it a more durable and permanent.

ASA Europe was discontinued in 1972 and the USASAFS Berlin was reassigned to Headquarters, ASA.

January 1977: The ASA deactivated, and the station was designated U.S. Army Field Station Berlin and was assigned to Headquarters, INSCOM, which replaced the ASA.

The end of the Cold War in 1989 made the station unessential, and it was closed in the early 1990s.

Appendix B: GI Reading Materials

Reading materials were readily available to GIs stationed in Berlin. There were plenty of paperbacks and magazines at the PX newsstand, and every base had a library. The Army also had a couple of publications that it distributed throughout the world. There were *Stars and Stripes*, a daily newspaper that the Army published in Darmstadt, Germany, for the European forces, and *Army Times*, a weekly tabloid that really was a giant Army newsletter.

But one of the most popular newspapers among the GIs was *Overseas Weekly*, a tabloid that was geared toward the EMs and which regularly gigged the Army and the lifers. These satirical pieces were published in a 1967 edition of OW:

The Army Ten Commandments

I. Thou shalt not think.

II. Thou shalt not place thy hands in thy pockets.

III. Thou shalt know the chain of command and all other missing links.

IV. Thou shalt not laugh at second lieutenants.

V. Thou shalt not use words beyond the comprehension of NCOs.

VI. Thou shalt not do things in a reasonable manner.

VII. Thou shalt fear those of higher rank and scorn those of lower rank.

VIII. Thou shalt not laugh at re-up posters.

IX. Thou shalt not speak without using profanity.

X. Thou shalt believe in non-existing Army bennies.

Then for all future civilians, there's another one:

The Short-timer's Code of Conduct

1. I am an American short-timer. I serve in the forces into

which I was so carelessly taken. I am prepared to leave it at the time so designated by the Department of the Army, or sooner if possible.

2. I will never extend or re-up of my own free will. If I am in command, I will never permit my fellow short-timers to fraternize with lifers.

3. If I am called before the CO, I will continue to resist his re-up talks by all means available. I will make every effort to escape.

4. If I should become victim of an involuntary extension, I will keep faith with my fellow short-timers. If I am the shortest, I will take command. If not, I will obey the lawful orders of those shorter than I.

5. When questioned, should I become the object of a re-enlistment interview, I am bound to give only name, rank, service number, date of birth and ETS.

6. I will never forget that I am an American short-timer, responsible for my actions and dedicated to the principles which have made carefree, happy civilians of thousands of short-timers before me.

About the Author

Don Cooper was a German linguist for the U.S. Army Security Agency in Berlin during the Cold War. After his military service, he earned a degree in history and sociology from Henderson State University in Arkadelphia, Arkansas, and began his journalism career, working as an editor-columnist-cartoonist at small newspapers in six states. He won numerous professional awards for feature and editorial writing, political columns and editorial cartooning.

In addition to "C Trick," Cooper has written "Chasing Teddy Ballgame," a semi-autobiographical novel; and "Slap Happy, Arkansas," a novel; and three screenplays — "C Trick" and "Chasing Teddy Ballgame" and "Lozen" He also is the creator of the syndicated comic strip "The Mild West."

Cooper and his wife, artist-poet Annette, and their twelve dogs, eleven cats and two potbellied pigs live on a small farm in the Texas Panhandle.

10328157R0

Made in the USA
Lexington, KY
14 July 2011